ROUTE 66

TURBOCHARGED FOURTH EDITION

ADVENTURE HANDBOOK

SANTA
MONICA
PRESS

Published by: Santa Monica Press LLC
P.O. Box 850
Solana Beach, CA 92075
1-800-784-9553
www.santamonicapress.com
books@santamonicapress.com

Printed in the United States

Santa Monica Press books are available at special quantity discounts when purchased in bulk by corporations, organizations, or groups.
Please call our Special Sales department at 1-800-784-9553.

ISBN-13 978-1-59580-059-6

Library of Congress Cataloging-in-Publication Data

Knowles, Drew, 1956-
 Route 66 adventure handbook / by Drew Knowles ; foreword by David Knudson. —
Turbocharged 4th ed.
    p. cm.
 Includes bibliographical references and index.
 ISBN 978-1-59580-059-6
 1. United States Highway 66—Description and travel. 2. United States Highway 66—Guidebooks.
3. West (U.S.)—Description and travel. 4. West (U.S.)—Tours.
5. Automobile travel—West (U.S.)—Guidebooks. 6. West (U.S.)—History, Local.
7. United States—Description and travel. I. Title. II. Title: Route sixty-six adventure handbook.
 F595.3.K67 2011
 388.10973—dc22
                       2011003280

Cover and interior design and production by Future Studio

All photos are by the author, with the exception of p. 80, p. 137, p. 184 (lower left), p. 231, and p. 251, all of which are by Lauren Knowles.

Mixed Sources
Product group from well-managed forests and other controlled sources
www.fsc.org Cert no. SW-COC-002283
© 1996 Forest Stewardship Council
FSC

CONTENTS

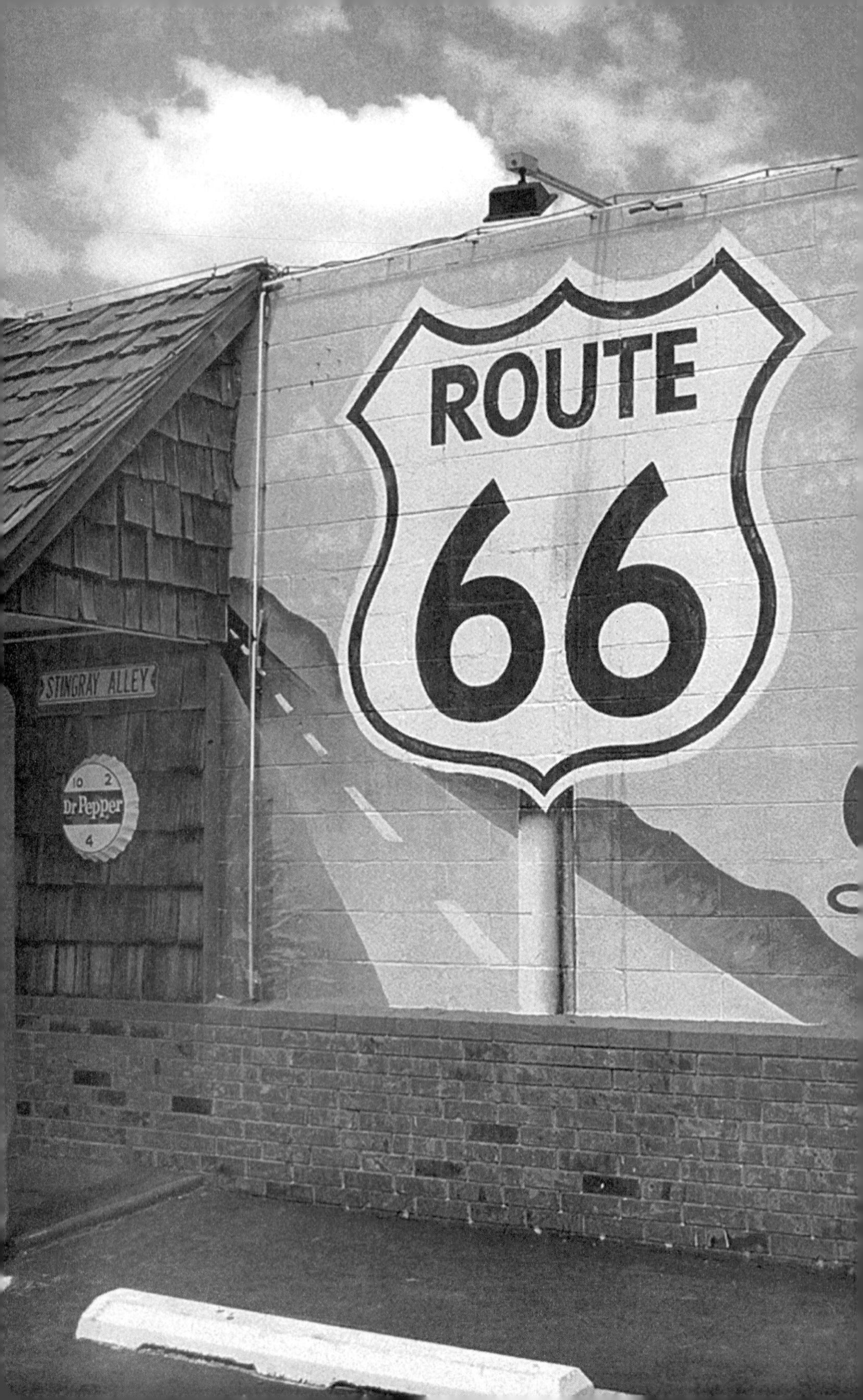
ROUTE
66
STINGRAY ALLEY
10 2
Dr Pepper
4

Over the years, thousands of individuals have tied their futures and livelihoods to Route 66—individuals who made their livings preparing meals, providing motel rooms, or perhaps offering whimsical diversions to the cross-section of America passing by their doors.

To those individuals, this book is gratefully dedicated.

—DREW KNOWLES

FOREWORD

Like so many people who have traveled it in recent years, Drew Knowles fell in love with the Mother Road. I don't mean "love" in the popular, overused sense, but a real love and respect for something very dear. Yet he is not just another enamored router. Far from it. He has spent many years on and off the road digging into every nook and cranny so he could write this important guide.

As Drew takes you down America's most legendary highway, he tempts you with just enough historical details to make you want to search for more. He shares his secrets for finding unmarked stretches so you can become an informed explorer. He challenges you to travel beyond the route itself so you can enjoy even more of our country's texture.

If you read and use this guide, there is a very good chance you will change your attitude towards motoring. Rather than simply driving to a location, your trip will become the destination. In fact, this attitude is relatively new in our country. When I was growing up, nearly every trip we took was a series of dots and dashes. You dashed from one dot to the next, then bragged about how quickly you got there. The advent of super highways was our dream come true. So were franchise operations because you could always count on them to be the same. This was what we wanted and it was what tourists from other countries came to see. But today, every country in the civilized world has more than its share of these "modern" conveniences.

Enter the "Heritage Tourist." These foreign and domestic tourists are more interested in experiencing the roots of America than the rides at its theme parks; and what better way to do that than to travel Route

66—the route to our roots. As it passes by vintage motels, bustling cafés, colorful trading posts, and through picturesque villages, three time zones, dozens of cultures, and numerous geographic and weather changes, the old road is a microcosm of historic roadside America that every age can enjoy.

So, it's time to do something different. Pack up the car, put this guide in the glove box, strap that water bag on the front, and get ready for a serious love affair.

David Knudson
Executive Director
National Historic Route 66 Federation

INTRODUCTION
by Michael Wallis

I was fortunate to grow up in the 1950s within easy striking distance of Route 66. Throughout the heyday of that fabled highway that Steinbeck appropriately dubbed "The Mother Road," my family, like so many others, used the artery of concrete and asphalt to our advantage.

It was a time when just the act of getting there was an important part of the vacation experience. We didn't want to be gypped out of a single moment, so we made the drive an indispensable component of the overall trip. There was an assortment of manmade and natural attractions to visit, tourist traps to survive, detours to avoid, and truck stop meals to consume.

Times may have changed, but Route 66—the highway some folks believed dead and gone—is alive and kicking like never before.

The old road (at least a major percentage of it) survived the attempts of five interstate superslabs that tried in vain to take its place. Today's rendition of Route 66 is a grizzled veteran—tried and true—but with the allure and prestige of an aging celebrity. Some time ago the highway achieved American icon status, and not just because of the physical roadbed or all the historical and cultural treasures that litter its shoulders from Chicago to Santa Monica. The road is a much-more-than-remarkable example of commercial archeology, diverse natural and fabricated attractions, and gentle curves tailor-made for a purring Harley or speedy Corvette.

Most of all, Route 66 is about people. That is what the road has always been about, and that is why it remains active and relevant to this day.

It is inspiring to realize that Route 66 truly is America's highway, just as it has been ever since 1926. Other venerable roads, longer or older than Route 66, crisscross the land, but the reality is that none of them measures up to the Mother Road. Not even close. Through the years, this celebrated highway has persevered, despite attempts to do away with it. Route 66 has become a destination in and of itself.

Although it seems there is something for everyone on Route 66, there are some exceptions. It is not a road for those who like cookie-cutter culture, food in Styrofoam boxes, or sprawling shopping malls filled with indistinguishable people pawing through look-alike merchandise. Even though franchise restaurants, chain stores, and homogenized fast-food joints have invaded the old highway, the true Route 66 crowd does not fully embrace them.

Route 66ers want kitsch that often is so bad it is good. They go for window decals, refrigerator magnets, salt and pepper shakers, and the other kinds of merchandise sold at the best tourist traps. They crave real hash browns, milk shakes, and berry pies made from scratch and on premises. They like nothing but open road ahead of them. They do not mind taking chances.

Since 1990, when the Route 66 resurgence really began, tens of thousands of enthusiasts from around the globe have discovered that this road is not just another American highway. Nor is it a romanticized corridor of nostalgia that only allows people to return to the so-called good old days. True, Route 66 serves as the definitive symbol of certain key segments of the nation's past, but it is also very much part of the present, as well as of the future.

Today, people from around the globe continue to take the open road—the free road. I enjoy showing these travelers the distinct layers of history along the highway. Their numbers are growing. I meet with them in diners and curio shops, at Smithsonian lectures, in university classrooms, and all along the old road. Through these many people and their enthusiasm, my sense of pure adventure and my passion for the highway and its people remains strong. The old road has again become an important part of the nation's cultural scene. Route 66 fans range from

commercial archeologists, historians, and American culture buffs to motorcycle club members, students, and the RV crowd.

Still, after they have listened to my stories and words of advice, every traveler needs a good guidebook to help show them the way.

Through the years, there have been many books published about Route 66, including guidebooks that have helped legions of travelers traverse the Mother Road.

This particular book, so carefully written by Drew Knowles, is unlike any other. Drew's writing is as smooth as a cup of fresh custard and captures the adventure and excitement of traveling the open road.

The *Route 66 Adventure Handbook* exposes a true slice of America—a nation of movement and energy. This book shows us people living in secret corners and hidden towns that can still be found if travelers merely dare to exit the interstate highway. To do that, they have to believe that life begins at the off-ramp. Then, with the windows rolled down and the radio playing, they can open their eyes to the past and, just maybe, discover something of themselves.

It is a journey worth taking.

Enjoy the ride.

Michael Wallis
Author of *Route 66: The Mother Road*

AUTHOR'S PREFACE

wrote this book because it's exactly what I need to take with me whenever I travel Route 66, and it is my sincere hope that it can be of similar service to you in your own explorations of the Mother Road.

I began driving, exploring, and photographing what remains of U.S. Route 66 back in 1992. Some might call it an obsession, but it's a passion that has stayed with me ever since, with no apparent end.

I live near Fort Worth, Texas, a considerable distance from the nearest portion of the Route, and so the time that I spend on the Mother Road is precious and comes at irregular intervals. Over the years, my knowledge of Route 66 has gradually expanded by exposure to many things: books and periodicals; conversations with people who live, work, or travel extensively on Route 66; documents on the world wide web; and, of course, my own travels, during which I've spent thousands of hours and taken thousands of photographs.

The problem I had, which this volume seeks to solve, is this: each time I get out on the Mother Road, there are many things I'd like to see and experience myself that I might only have heard or read about up to that time. Invariably, while out exploring the Route, there are things I remember to investigate, but there are others that I lack sufficient time for, or that I simply forget about until after I've returned home. This book solves that problem by putting all of that Route 66 information in one volume, which I can easily take along and refer to, so that each Mother Road excursion can be as jam-packed as possible.

This latest edition has some new features that I'm confident you'll appreciate. More than 60 maps have been added to assist you in getting around some of the more challenging Route 66 towns, and in many cases I've added navigational boxes with specific instructions. The majority of photographs you see are new to this edition as well, and are more plentiful than ever.

My sincere hope is that the *Route 66 Adventure Handbook* will be of valuable service to you as you do your own explorations of Route 66, and that those explorations cause you to appreciate America's Main Street as much as I do.

See you on the road!

Drew Knowles
Fort Worth, Texas

ABOUT THE 1957 ATLAS

Throughout this book, you will see mention of something I refer to as "my 1957 atlas." It's a 12 by 16-inch paperbound road atlas, published by Rand McNally in 1957 and containing individual road maps for all fifty states (plus Canada and Mexico).

It was in 1956 that President Eisenhower signed the bill that launched what we today call our Interstate Highway System. The bill also started the slow decline of the *old* system of interstate highways, of which U.S. Route 66 was a part. Therefore, my 1957 atlas depicts Route 66 and her sisters at their zenith, just before our nation's roadbuilding energies were diverted to the creation of a decidedly different type of highway.

I obtained my treasured 1957 road atlas at a local antique mall/flea market, and it has been invaluable to me in my quest to explore everything Route 66 has to offer. To peruse its pages is to take a step back in time, and that's been a journey well worth taking.

WHAT IS ROUTE 66, ANYWAY?

n the early years of the twentieth century, America was crisscrossed by a collection of disorganized and poor-quality roads (often no more than dirt paths). That was considered adequate when most travel occurred via horse-and-buggy or railroad. However, the development of the automobile—and especially its mass-production in the 1910s—fueled a demand on the part of the American public for more and better roads.

Construction of more and better roads did begin; however, it occurred at a local or regional level, and so development was spotty and haphazard. Naming and marking conventions also varied considerably, making cross-country travel confusing at best.

In 1926, the now-familiar numbered federal highway system was launched. This facilitated the marking of highways consistently across state and regional boundaries. Furthermore, in order to qualify for federal funding and inclusion in the new scheme, highways had to meet standards for surface quality and other criteria. In the beginning, the U.S. highways—including Route 66—were established as such, simply by posting the well-known black-and-white numbered shields at strategic points along preexisting roads to act as guides. The roads thus connected, then became part of a "route," even though they had not been originally built as such.

Numbers ending in zero, such as 60, were reserved for the major coast-to-coast routes (as they still are in today's interstate system). The highway between Chicago and Los Angeles, considered to be of lesser importance, was designated U.S. 66.

That highway, which we now commonly refer to as Route 66,

began its ascension into America's cultural lore when John Steinbeck made mention of it in his famous 1939 novel, *The Grapes of Wrath*. It was there that he gave the route one of its many nicknames, "the Mother Road." The highway received another boost in public awareness when, just after World War II, Bobby Troup penned his popular song "(Get Your Kicks on) Route 66" while driving to California for a shot at a career in show business. At about that same time, Jack Rittenhouse, realizing that the post-war years would mean increased auto travel in America, published his *A Guidebook to Highway 66* (see bibliography).

During the late 1940s and throughout the 1950s, America became a much more mobile society, and lots of people began to have first-hand experience using Route 66 either on business, while taking family vacations, or simply moving their households. It was during those years that Route 66 experienced its most prodigious growth, and simultaneously gained its reputation for tourist traps such as snake pits, trading posts, and roadside zoos. Countless Americans today still have fond memories of family trips to Disneyland and other Southern California destinations via the Mother Road.

Then, in the early 1960s, a national television series was produced, called simply *Route 66*. Although the series was seldom filmed on the highway for which it was named, it served to reinforce the highway's place in popular culture, and in fact is indicative of the status the highway had already achieved.

Beginning in the late 1950s, the United States began building a new set of cross-country highways that would change highway travel profoundly. For a variety of reasons, the new highways (which we now refer to as "interstates") were constructed as limited-access freeways, with only a relatively small number of access ramps, and no roadside driveway access whatsoever. This was the death knell for small roadside businesses all over the country, including those flanking Route 66.

The entire length of Route 66 was functionally replaced by a series of interstates paralleling it—in some cases only yards away from the older highway, but in the majority of cases making it next to impossible for the modern motorist to gain access to the multitude of businesses left high-and-dry.

An adventure on Route 66 is an opportunity to see exactly what those interstate highways cast aside so many years ago.

Phillips
66

FIRE-CHIEF
GASOLINE
TEXACO

SLOW
AVOID SPLASHING
PEDESTRIANS

BOUNCE

5¢

ola

DRINK NuGrape
SODA

CONTAINS GRAPE JUICE CERTIFIED FLAVOR
IMITATION GRAPE FLAVOR CANE SUGAR FRUIT ACID

YOU
CANT
FORGET

STAMPS

WHY TRAVEL ROUTE 66?

You're wearing a pair of tight, ill-fitting shoes. Sure, they're stylish, and they look pretty sharp with that suit of clothes you're wearing, but the fit is not right. They're confining. Furthermore, it's been a long day and you've been in those shoes so long, and become so acclimated to their shortcomings, that you've stopped paying attention to them. You've repressed your pain and forgotten what it feels like to be barefoot on a soft, cool carpet of green grass.

Now take off those shoes. Right away, good things begin to happen. The blood vessels in your feet begin to open up, allowing an influx of fresh oxygen and nutrients. The pores of your feet open up and bre-e-e-ath for the first time in a long time. Even the rhythm of your own breathing becomes less strained, and your mind is sharpened. You flex your toes with enthusiasm and think: "Ahhh, now that's more like it!" And you wonder how you could have put up with your discomfort for so long.

If you've never driven old Route 66, you're in for a similar sensation. And the analogy is far more apt than you might imagine.

For decades now, highway travelers—you included—have been subjected to an onerous set of circumstances which are, by and large, passively accepted. Furthermore, this condition has been accepted for so long that many of us have either forgotten that things weren't always this way, or—even scarier—may never have known anything different.

That set of ill-fitting restrictions I'm referring to is of course part and parcel of today's Interstate Highway System. Now, before you accuse me of wrongly condemning America's most ambitious peacetime engineering project in its history, hear me out.

Admittedly, the interstates—like the ill-fitting shoes—are not entirely without practical benefits. They are, after all, designed with graceful, high-speed curves, and enable us to travel from point A to point B in minimal time. We accomplish this with greater fuel efficiency, thanks to the ability to move with unvarying speed. And, a limited-access highway is safer from the standpoint that there are no driveways for irresponsible motorists to pop out of unexpectedly. These qualities are quite attractive, particularly to the long-distance truckers among us.

But what are those features costing us? That snazzy pair of oxfords does have a few important drawbacks. Did you ever stop to think of what a tremendous misnomer the word "freeway" is? There's not much freedom in interstate travel. Consider that you are shielded and encapsulated against the world at large. Sealed in your fast-moving mobile cocoon, your perception of the world is distorted. You are cut off from sound and smell by your tightly sealed windows. Open the window, and the buffeting and roaring of the air will cut you off from your senses just as effectively. Visually, the interstate corridor offers only the barest glimpse of the

surrounding countryside. Your visual stimulation is often limited to mile markers, exit signs of uniform appearance, and perhaps a swath of trees to block your view of anything outside the world of the superslab. This isolation is partly due to the enormous amount of land which America's interstates have taken as their own. There are enormous swaths of acreage on both sides of the interstate, in the medians, and still more locked up in the countless clover leafs, flyovers, and other interstate-grade interchanges. All of that empty acreage contributes to the interstate traveler's isolation from his or her surroundings.

Furthermore, there are restrictions which make it *unlawful* to attempt to squeeze a little more gusto from the experience. There are minimum speeds which must be maintained, preventing you from taking advantage of whatever paltry visual stimuli might actually be available. There are also prohibitions against non-emergency stopping or slowing, and against turning your vehicle around. No wonder it's hard to stay awake.

Ah, but Route 66. Now there's highway travel for you. Kick off your shoes, because the above restrictions do not apply.

On Route 66, there is healthy stimulation for all the senses, and conditions encourage you to take full advantage. Sensory experience is in no way out-of-fashion on the Mother Road. Smell the new-mown hay and the honeysuckle. Hear the clamor of children playing softball in a nearby park, or the tolling of a church bell. Feel the breeze on your face and know that the coolness signals a change in elevation, or even a new climate zone.

Visually, the difference is even more dramatic. There are schools and stores and mountains and crosswalks and downtowns and trains and depots and rivers and billboards and murals and cafés and menus and humanity.

Don't forget: you can pull over and stop at almost any time to savor it a little more. You can travel Route 66 by bicycle, horseback, or even on foot, so as not to miss a single nuance—don't try doing that on the interstate!

A few words about the concept of efficiency—the maximum of

one thing with a minimum of another. An efficient automobile is one that goes maximum miles on minimal fuel; an efficient apartment is one with maximum amenities in a minimum amount of space. Significantly, the thing which is maximized ought to be something desirable, while the thing which is minimized should be something either undesirable or expensive. I think that the two examples cited above—the auto and the apartment—fulfill this requirement.

One of the knocks against Route 66, which eventually led to its demise, was a call for increased efficiency. The interstates are considered efficient because they transport us with a maximum of speed in a minimum amount of time. That's well and good. But my point is this: the interstates have had some unforeseen and undesirable side effects, because at the same time that they minimized the *amount* of our time in getting to our destination, they also minimized the *quality* of our time on the road by placing us in an experiential vacuum.

That quality of experience is what you'll put back in your life when you kick off those shoes and travel Route 66.

GET THE MOST FROM YOUR ROUTE 66 ADVENTURE

Ask several people what you should bring with you on your Route 66 Adventure, and you'll likely get several different answers. One well-meaning friend might mention such practical travel items as maps, a compass, pen or pencil, notebook, camera, and sunglasses. Another person's suggestion might emphasize such things as proper footwear, layers of clothing, and sunblock. Someone else might recommend an ice chest with bottled water and plenty of trail mix. Oh—and don't forget your mobile phone and credit cards.

I travel with most of those things, too. But there is one thing which is far more important than all of the above *combined* when it comes to getting the most enjoyment out of your trip on old Route 66. And that one thing is a Spirit of Adventure. I never take a road trip without it.

In a nutshell, I urge you not to plan to take charge of your Route 66 experience too precisely; instead, plan for the Adventure on Route 66 to take charge of you.

As much as possible, I encourage you to simply "go with the flow." Don't set an itinerary which requires you to make it to city "X" by a certain time of a certain day. Keeping to such a schedule will inevitably cause you to hurry through certain portions of your journey, and there's no way of knowing how much you'll miss by doing so.

Move as the spirit moves you; pause and take in the sights and the sounds of your Adventure as they present themselves to you. Your reward will be a trip like no other.

Dare to dare. Try new food and drink, meet some strangers, turn down a road just because it looks interesting or because you're curious what's there. This is the stuff of which lifelong memories are made.

Things can change rapidly out on Route 66. What you see today might be gone tomorrow or soon after. Keep your camera loaded and ready and use it liberally. Film and processing expenses are cheap compared to the other costs of your trip, such as food, lodging, and fuel. This is even more true if you shoot digital, since digital storage media are reusable. Don't scrimp, and don't worry whether the resulting photographs will be worthy of a museum exhibition or not. If you don't consider yourself an artist, then be a documentarist. Just record what you see that interests you. It's far too easy to think to yourself: "Well, it's been standing there for 50 years now; I'm sure it'll be there for a few more." Sadly, too often this is not the case. Don't fall into that trap. This is a lesson I've learned again and again over the years, both on and off Route 66.

Bring this book with you. Your navigator can read aloud from it as various points in your journey are reached. Even if you elect to skip a certain side trip, the modest background information can enrich your trip in unexpected ways, sometimes by giving you an appreciation of other features of the countryside.

Incidentally, I certainly don't expect you to take in every feature that I've chosen to make mention of in this *Handbook*. Just pick out some of the ones which most tickle your fancy, or are most compatible with other attractions you intend to visit, and leave the rest for some other time. A continent is not fit for properly exploring in one outing.

Be cognizant of the fact that the information about various features and attractions is not meant to be authoritative. My objective is primarily to whet your appetite for investigation and exploration. If I provide too much detail in this *Handbook*, it may lessen your own desire to find out more on your own. The key is for you to experience things first-hand, not simply to absorb someone else's research.

Similarly, the lists of attractions and trivia associated with various places are not meant to be complete—they constitute more of a random sampling. How could one hope to compile a list of all of the noteworthy events or personalities associated with Chicago, for example? One of the

limiting factors I've used is to eliminate some of the more commonly-known attractions which are either already familiar to most people or are featured prominently in published visitors' guides to the areas in question.

Another point about things changing rapidly in 66-land: it took years for me to travel all of the route, and things have been changing the whole time. I have witnessed the disappearance and/or destruction of many distinctive features over the years. Do not be surprised if you find that by the time you use this handbook on your own Adventure, not everything will remain as I've described it. Just consider that a part of the Adventure, and let it make the Mother Road that much more precious to you.

A Spirit of Adventure. Please don't waste your time on Route 66 without it.

HOW TO USE THIS HANDBOOK

This handbook is here to fulfill one objective—to help you get the maximum possible enjoyment from your Adventure on Route 66. That's all. With that in mind, here are a few simple suggestions:

Don't keep your head buried—either in this book or in any other. That's why it's not designed as a "guide" focused on intricate maps and turn-by-turn descriptions that require close scrutiny. I've tried to keep the navigational information short and to the point. Most of the time, you can follow what's left of Route 66 on your own after reading the "How to Find Route 66" section of this book. That way, you won't miss anything due to trying to drive and read at the same time—plus, it's obviously much safer that way!

Keep this book close at hand at all times. What this book *does* have is a wealth of information on nearby attractions, historical background, fun trivia, and side-trip ideas. As you approach a new town or other landmark, have your navigator (if you've got one) read aloud some of the information from that area, so that both of you will know what to be on the lookout for and can make decisions on whether you're "passing through" or want to stop and take in some of the nearby features more fully. Some towns will have simple maps showing where some of those local attractions can be found. If you're traveling alone, you can just pull to the road's shoulder or into a friendly-looking driveway and quickly read about the nearby attractions yourself. That's one of the real advantages of Mother Road driving versus interstate driving—on Route 66, it's okay to slow down, pull over, smell the roses, etc.

You're the boss, so customize your trip based on your own passions and interests. Don't slavishly follow anyone's advice, not even mine. This road trip adventure is all about *your* enjoyment, right? That means that after you've briefed yourself on the area you're entering, make some personal decisions about the things that most intrigue you. For some people, that will mean making it a point to seek out each and every architectural treasure mentioned in this entire handbook. But your own tastes might run more toward historic sites or natural wonders or trivia or folk art or whatever—there's something for everyone. So spend *your* time doing what *you* enjoy the most. Ignore the rest, or save it for your *next* Route 66 safari.

Immerse yourself. As you travel Route 66, remember that you are surrounded by the remnants of an enormous support system developed for the transcontinental motoring public in the mid-twentieth century. I urge you to make full use of it. That support system included—and *still does* include—motels, cafés, fuel stations, general stores, and roadside attractions of every description. While this book *does not* attempt to offer a list of these support-system establishments—they are, after all, subject to frequent change—you should nevertheless take advantage as the need arises. Many of those old Route 66 businesses today have a marginal bottomline, and would sincerely appreciate your patronage. The other support resource I encourage you to make use of is comprised of the local residents and business operators all along the Route. Inquire locally for advice or directions to local attractions, and I know you'll be pleasantly surprised at the helpfulness of the response. There is also a generous listing of visitors' bureaus, chambers of commerce, and other professional groups in the Travelers' Services section of this handbook. Use those agencies to find out even more local information.

Enjoy!

HOW TO FIND ROUTE 66

U.S. 66 no longer officially exists. The emphasis is on the word "officially." The numerical highway designation system adopted in the 1920s was a system in which pre-existing roads were linked together by being given the same number. A traveler could, then, by following signs bearing that number, arrive at any of the destinations on that highway's route, or gain access to any of the other numbered highways which crossed paths with it. When a given route is no longer needed, for whatever reason, the signs can be removed and the route is no longer recognized as such.

But in most cases, the road itself remains. Although it may no longer carry the federal designation, it is unusual for the pavement to actually be removed and the ground returned to nature. Often, the road is re-numbered by the state or county in which it occurs; other times, the older roadway serves duty as an access road to the limited-access thruway, which may have brought about its obsolescence.

Officially, Route 66 ceased to exist when the federal highway authorities ordered the signs removed. But keeping in mind that the route was created in 1926 by the installation of signs marking the way, the only thing preventing a traveler from using the old road today is a lack of knowledge on where to find it without the benefit of all those signs at every turn—thousands in all.

While this book does include plenty of maps and other navigational guidance, it will *not* tell you exactly where each and every turn ought to be made in order to drive old Route 66. Other writers have already attempted this. As the old adage goes, "Give a man a fish and he eats for a day; teach a man to fish and he feeds himself for a lifetime." Similarly, my objective here is to share with you sufficient basic knowledge to be able to fend for yourself. A significant advantage to this strategy is that this knowledge will apply for years to come, with little or no regard to how local conditions might change over time. Another advantage is that you will begin to see and discover other old routes in your travels which have undergone the same processes of construction, use, upgrade, re-routing, bypassing, and de-certification as Route 66. I think you'll find that some of those other routes, though not as famous as the Mother Road, are also worthy of exploration, and you'll be well-equipped to do so.

HOW TO FISH

In the broadest terms, Route 66 ran (or runs) southwestward from Chicago, Illinois to Los Angeles (technically Santa Monica), California. The next thing for you to take note of is which modern-day highways currently carry that same Chicago-to-Los Angeles traffic. Look at a road map of the overall continental United States if you have one. Today's traffic is borne by a huge network of interstate highways. It turns out that Route 66 was replaced by not one, but five modern highways, none of which bears the number 66. The series which supplanted Route 66 is: I-55 from Chicago, Illinois, to St. Louis, Missouri; I-44 from St. Louis across the state of Missouri and all the way to Oklahoma City, Oklahoma; I-40 from OKC to Barstow, California; I-15 from Barstow to San Bernardino, California; and I-10 from there to the Pacific coast at Santa Monica. This is the general corridor in which you'll be traveling in order to experience Route 66.

This brings us to the first rule in learning to fish: be on the lookout for secondary roads which more or less parallel the interstate highways mentioned in the paragraph above. This goes for roads which take us to a destination city—a city formerly on old Highway 66—and not necessarily a road which literally runs alongside the freeway within sight of it. The main narrative section of this book points out most of those Route 66 towns. Your strategy, then, in keeping to the old route, should be to avoid the interstate when possible, and move from one town to the next using secondary roadways. In many cases, this is authentic Route 66 pavement.

The second consideration is the simplest and most obvious: the placement of "Historic Route 66" signs. In the last several years, the eight states along Route 66 have made great strides in getting the old road marked. Unfortunately, there are considerable gaps in sign placement, so that relying solely on them will get you off-course fairly quickly in many cases. However, you'll find that by keeping on the lookout for those friendly brown-and-white signs, you'll more easily keep to the route and be able to enjoy the sights and sounds thereof, without having your nose perpetually buried in a mile-by-mile guide or map. In places where the old road has been buried or otherwise obliterated, and you are forced to use the interstate, quite often the next exit which includes a stretch of Route 66 will have the Historic 66 symbol on the big green exit sign. This enables you to travel a minimum amount of the sleep-inducing superslab before returning to the central theme of your trip.

Figure A
Examples of Business Loop sign (green & white)
and Historic Route 66 sign (brown & white).

Very closely related to the foregoing is the third fishing strategy: "business loop" routes. Again, this is helpful when you have been forced to use the interstate for a distance. In many of the larger cities on Route 66, the old route through town will be designated as "Business Loop X," where the "X" stands for the number of the interstate that supplanted 66. For example, in the city limits of Albuquerque, New Mexico, and Amarillo, Texas, the path of Route 66 is marked with green signs designating it Business Loop I-40. Similarly, in Springfield, Missouri, Route 66 is marked Business Loop I-44. Keep in mind that in larger cities such as these, the path of Route 66 in most cases changed several times over the years. The alignment marked in this way is typically the last alignment of 66 prior to its demise as an official route. The earlier alignments will go either unmarked, or may bear the brown-and-white "historic" signs. Exploration is the order of the day.

Some of the rest of our fishing tips are a little more subtle, and will draw upon your powers of reasoning and observation a little more. This makes locating a vintage stretch of old 66 all the more satisfying, however.

For reasons of economy and expediency, most routes of any kind are established along the paths of previously-existing routes. Just as immigrant trails often followed older trade routes of Native Americans or trappers, Route 66 and others like her were constructed along right-of-way corridors established earlier by the railroads. Railroad tracks, then, are often an excellent guide to where the earlier alignments through a region are to be found. Given a choice between two alignments which will eventually reach the same destination, in most cases the one physically following the railroad tracks more closely is the older route. Over time, as the highway has been widened or otherwise upgraded, the newer alignment tends to be placed farther from the tracks. An instructive example of this can be found along the stretch of Route 66 between Sayre and Erick,

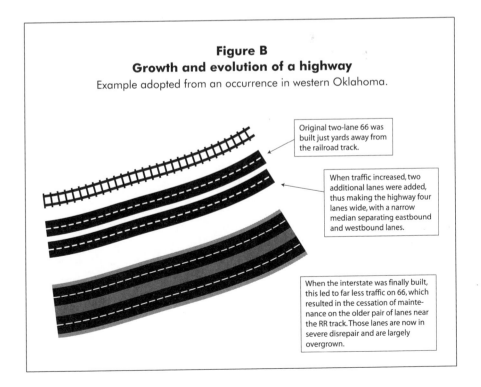

Figure B
Growth and evolution of a highway
Example adopted from an occurrence in western Oklahoma.

Original two-lane 66 was built just yards away from the railroad track.

When traffic increased, two additional lanes were added, thus making the highway four lanes wide, with a narrow median separating eastbound and westbound lanes.

When the interstate was finally built, this led to far less traffic on 66, which resulted in the cessation of maintenance on the older pair of lanes near the RR track. Those lanes are now in severe disrepair and are largely overgrown.

Oklahoma. Two lanes of Route 66 were originally c onstructed just a few yards to the south side of the railroad right-of-way. Later, the highway was increased to four lanes by the addition of a median and two east-bound lanes further still to the south. Then, when Interstate 40 was constructed, it was placed much farther south. The presence of I-40 resulted in diminished traffic on the older highway, and it was downgraded to two lanes by ceasing maintenance on the oldest two lanes near the railroad track. This is what the visitor sees very clearly today in traveling these several miles in western Oklahoma, and it's one of my favorite features. It's as though one can literally read the historical journal of the highway in this area.

Another tip-off to the location of old Route 66 has to do with some of the ancillary structures associated with it. In more urban areas, this means being observant of buildings—and building remains—which seem to have travelers' needs as their focus. Examples are motels, cafés, and gasoline stations, which originate in the era when the old road was

in its development (1930s) and growth (1945–55) stages. In small towns that were not crossed by other major highways, this is often simple. In larger cities, which may have been hubs for more than one major highway, it becomes more difficult to discern one from another, especially in light of the fact that multiple routes would often follow the same streets for a portion of their journey through town.

In more rural areas, bridges can be an excellent indication of a Route 66 alignment. The federal highway system, Route 66 included, was originally formed in the 1920s from pre-existing roads. Shortly thereafter, efforts were undertaken to improve these roads, many of which were not even paved at first. In the late 1920s and throughout the 1930s, many small bridges were constructed during the process of improving the country's network of highways. The bridges constructed during this period are not only often quite distinctive in design, they also sometimes bear a small plaque or medallion indicating the year of construction. Many of these were projects of the Works Progress Administration, and, in keeping with their dates of origin, exhibit an almost Art Deco appearance. A case in point is that often there will be an access road on either side of the interstate, and you might suspect that one of these might be old enough to be Route 66. One of the clearest indications is the type of bridges built for each of the two candidates. Often, one of the two will have bridges which appear to be 60 or more years old, while the other will have bridges of a decidedly more modern, less embellished style. The latter may have been constructed at the time of the interstate's construction for practical reasons, such as access to properties on that side of the freeway.

Somewhat related to the last point about structures to be found on old 66 has to do with construction methods used in building the highway itself. Road-building methods in the early- to mid-twentieth century were not as advanced as in later years, nor were funds as readily available. This is evident in the fact that the older highways such as Route 66 appear to follow the contours of the landscape more closely than more modern roads. Route 66 tends to rise and fall with the shallow hills and depressions in its path, and also tends to curve around prominent geographic features, such as mesas. Modern highways—the interstates especially—tend to exhibit considerable modification of the terrain. Blasting of hills and filling of depressions occur more regularly, while curves tend to be fewer and more gradual than in the case of the older highways, such as 66.

This results in a very important fact: there are many, many miles of Route 66 which have literally been cut to pieces by the interstates. Because the old highway took more turns and curves, while the modern interstate is much more direct, old portions of legitimate Route 66 are often found on both sides of a stretch of interstate highway, having been severed by the straighter cut of modern building methods. So, sometimes you'll need to keep the superslab to your left, and then you might need to cross to the other side and keep it to your right awhile in order to travel authentic Route 66 miles.

Another structural difference you're sure to note in many parts of Route 66 is the use of sectioned concrete rather than the continuous asphalt so prevalent today. This leads to a reassuring *thump, ka-thump, ka-thump* as your tires repeatedly hit the expansion seams in the roadway. You will find some excellent stretches of this type. For me, it evokes a nostalgia for road trips long past.

Finally, one last indication of an old highway alignment. In some cases, when a section of the Mother Road was taken out of service, the pavement was actually taken up and hauled away, leaving a scar in the earth. There are several places between Chicago and Los Angeles where

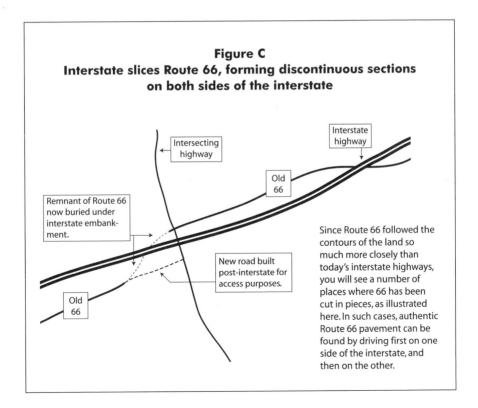

Figure C
Interstate slices Route 66, forming discontinuous sections on both sides of the interstate

Intersecting highway

Interstate highway

Old 66

Remnant of Route 66 now buried under interstate embankment.

New road built post-interstate for access purposes.

Old 66

Since Route 66 followed the contours of the land so much more closely than today's interstate highways, you will see a number of places where 66 has been cut in pieces, as illustrated here. In such cases, authentic Route 66 pavement can be found by driving first on one side of the interstate, and then on the other.

you can see evidence of this. In many cases, even decades later, the grass or other vegetation, which re-populates the old roadbed, exhibits a different color or texture than that on the undisturbed ground. This can be particularly pronounced in the more arid western portions of the route, where soil breakdown and other changes take place much more slowly than in the east. Keep your eyes peeled for swaths of vegetation that look just a little different than their surroundings, are one-to-two lanes wide, and alternately approach and diverge from the pavement on which you're driving. These are the ghosts of extinct roadways.

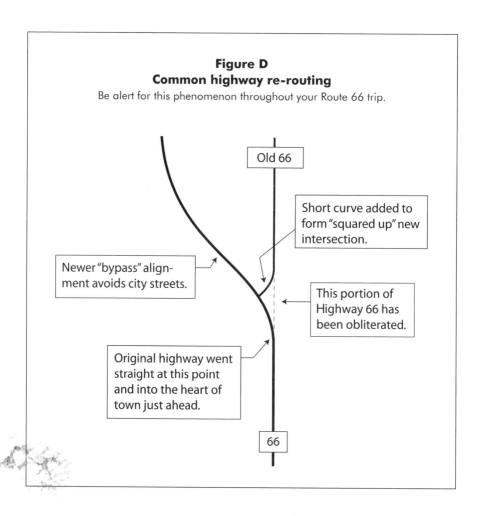

Figure D
Common highway re-routing
Be alert for this phenomenon throughout your Route 66 trip.

Old 66

Short curve added to form "squared up" new intersection.

Newer "bypass" align-ment avoids city streets.

This portion of Highway 66 has been obliterated.

Original highway went straight at this point and into the heart of town just ahead.

66

TO SUMMARIZE OUR FISHING TIPS:

- Be aware of the general direction and next destination town of the highway. Look for older, less-used roads which take you to that next Route 66 town.

- Look for, and take advantage of, the brown-and-white Historic Route 66 signs. These are found not only in rural stretches, but sometimes as a feature of an interstate exit sign.

- In larger cities, be aware that the green Business Loop signs often are used to designate old 66 through town, albeit only the most recent alignment. But also note that following these signs strictly will always return you to the interstate. As you near the interstate after having passed through such a city, be on the lookout for a more authentic route by way of which you could continue without the need to return to the interstate.

- Original stretches of highway are often very close to the shoulder of the railroad tracks in the area. As a general rule, the closer to the railroad, the older the alignment.

- Look for telltale period structures. The prime years of Route 66 occurred prior to the mid-1950s, so look for travel-oriented businesses (or buildings which used to house such businesses) dating from the same era. Other helpful indications include small bridges crossing ravines, especially if constructed in the WPA era.

- Look at the character of the road itself. Older highways such as Route 66 followed the lay of the land, rising and falling with the natural contours, with little or no evidence of large-scale earth-moving. Also be observant of the road surface itself; a road constructed of poured concrete may be vintage Route 66.

- Finally, look for telltale signs in the local vegetation for evidence of old roadbed that is either severely overgrown or has had the pavement completely removed.

Keep the above recommendations in mind, and in no time at all you'll be ferreting out old alignments of Route 66 like a pro. Now, let's get to it!

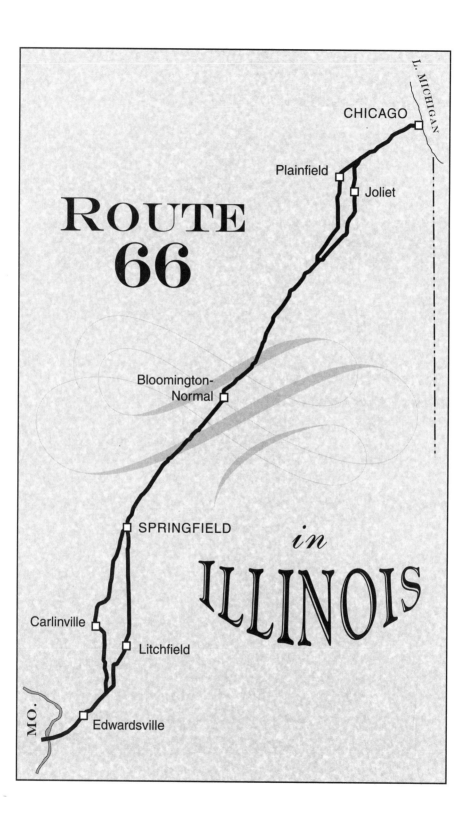

ILLINOIS

Route 66 begins in Illinois, near the shore of Lake Michigan. Of course, one can just as easily begin a tour of Route 66 from its western terminus in California, but there are good reasons not to. Traditionally, the Mother Road runs westward, from Chicago to Santa Monica, just as the United States of America has always been a westward-moving nation.

The U.S. began as a small grouping of states huddled along the Atlantic coast. To the west, the future states of Kentucky and Tennessee were wildernesses. Ohio and Indiana were settled by a few intrepid farmers for the value of their soil. Illinois was at that time considered the Northwest, and about as far west as any "American" semblance of civilization existed. Over the generations, more and more of that West has been tamed, and the outposts of civil society have moved westward as well.

Traveling Route 66 from east to west, then, you will be following the well-worn path of this country's very development. The countryside will unfold before you just as it did for the American people in their conquest of the continent several generations ago, almost as though you had mastered time travel. You will be richer for the experience, because you will come away feeling a kinship with the brave souls who pushed America's boundaries and made her what she is today.

Inseparable from the story of westward movement is the availability of water, both as transportation and as sustenance. The development of Chicago as the outpost of civilization it came to be was largely due to its being at the far end of a string of lakes and other navigable watercourses. For many reasons, water sources are conducive to settlement, while a scarcity of water is a severe hindrance to any development. It is no accident, then, that the largest cities on Route 66—Chicago, St. Louis, and Los Angeles—are located at the route's three largest water sources: Lake Michigan, the Mississippi River, and the Pacific Ocean, respectively.

As you move westward on Route 66, the story of water is one which the observant traveler will read all along the way. West of St. Louis, there is a gradual decrease in water availability and a simultaneous decrease in population density. The rivers that Highway 66 encounters are smaller, and the cities that dwell on the banks of those rivers are proportionately smaller as well.

CHICAGO

The famous Chicago fire of 1871, which may or may not have been caused by Mrs. O'Leary's cow, utterly destroyed the city. Afterward, the city made a conscious effort to rebuild using more durable materials and superior building methods so the new Chicago would stand the ravages of time and nature. More than a century later, the city continues to take pride in its architecture. If you are at all interested in the

> Route 66 in Chicago originally began at the corner of Lake Shore Drive and Jackson Boulevard, right at the edge of Lake Michigan. At the time, Jackson ran both east and west. These days, however, Jackson is eastbound-only, except for the portion between Lake Shore and Michigan Avenue. This means that, for westbound travelers, your first couple of blocks will be on Jackson, but then you'll have to jog over to Adams Street for several blocks. As always, when Route 66 splits onto two one-way streets, I recommend backtracking in the other direction so you don't miss anything you'll be sorry for later.

art and science of architecture, it is worth your while to take advantage of some of the countless tours available. Some of the most well-known tours take place on the water, and launch from either the Chicago River or Lake Michigan. Other tours, by bus, air, trolley, or bicycle, are also available.

Chicago was the scene of the World's Columbian Exposition in 1893, the grounds of which were designed by Frederick Law Olmstead, who also designed New York's Central Park, the Stanford University

campus, and other acclaimed outdoor spaces. It was at the 1893 Exposition that George Washington Gale Ferris introduced the now-familiar Ferris wheel. The original was 250 feet tall, and had 36 cars each with a capacity of 60 passengers. That original wheel was later moved and used at the 1904 fair in St. Louis. The two lions that graced the Exposition's Palace of Fine Arts building have since been made a part of the Art Institute of Chicago, near where westbound Route 66 begins.

The Exposition of 1893 made some other memorable or even permanent imprints. It was there that Cracker Jack was first introduced, later immortalized in the 1908 song "Take Me Out to the Ball Game." Little Egypt, otherwise known as Catherine Devine, scandalized the fair by performing the hootchy-kootchy in scanty attire (some say in the nude); the model for Aunt Jemima was a woman named Nancy Green, a cook who advertised food products at the Exposition; and visitors enjoyed the first-ever public use of electric lighting. The Exposition was also the scene where hot dogs were first served on buns. The vendor, A. L. Feuchtwanger, was handing out white gloves with the sausages so that his customers' hands wouldn't be scalded. To his initial dismay, the gloves were not being returned as he had intended, and so he began substituting bread instead.

Chicago once had a less-than-savory reputation as the home of the underworld. Gangland slayings were, for a time, not uncommon. The infamous St. Valentine's Day Massacre occurred in 1929 at the SMC Cartage Company at 2122 Clark Street. The building was demolished shortly after its use as the set for the 1967 film starring Jason Robards and George Segal.

Outlaw John Dillinger was gunned down by law enforcement officials on July 22, 1934, outside the Biograph Theater at 2433 N. Lincoln Avenue. Dillinger had just viewed a gangster film there called *Manhattan Melodrama*. There is a plaque to mark the occasion. The leader of the FBI contingent was Melvin Purvis, who committed suicide in 1960 using the same pistol given to him by his fellow officers to commemorate Dillinger's violent end.

Chicago played host in 1933 to the Century of Progress Exposition. It was there that Sally Rand made her splash by riding a white horse to the fair "attired," more or less, as Lady Godiva. Her main act consisted of an essentially nude dance routine, which included the strategic use of ostrich feathers. This caused such a sensation that she was able to parlay it into a career which lasted some 30 years.

The 1933 Exposition also brought the first aerial tramway, the first public demonstration of stereophonic sound reproduction, and the debut of Grant Wood's now-famous painting, *American Gothic*. A former student at the Art Institute of Chicago, Wood intended his painting as a sort of spoof of the Holbein style.

CHICAGO FIRE

The Chicago fire of 1871 is a well-known event. What most people don't know is that on the same date in nearby Peshtigo, Wisconsin, there was a "forest" fire that consumed more than a million acres and claimed 1,182 lives. That's more than four times the lives lost in the Chicago fire (250). Over 400 of the dead were buried in mass graves due to the fact that, in many cases, there were not enough survivors left to identify the bodies.

CHICAGO HOME-GROWN

Chicago gave birth to the mail-order catalog business about 100 years ago. This is the home of Sears Roebuck, Montgomery Ward, and Spiegel. Other famous commercial names centered here include Marshall Field, Hertz Rent-A-Car, Wrigley, Yellow Cabs, Kimball Pianos, Schwinn Bicycles, J. L. Kraft, and Oscar Mayer. It was Gustavus Swift, of Swift & Company meat packing, who made the famous remark that he used every part of the pig but the squeal. The Oscar Mayer wienermobile first appeared here in 1936. It was about the Chicago stockyards, and some of the deplorable conditions therein, that Upton Sinclair wrote his classic book *The Jungle*, which later resulted in the Pure Food and Drug Act of 1906.

In 1896, the zipper was invented in Chicago by Whitcomb L. Judson, who called it the "hookless fastener." The pinball machine was invented here in 1930 by the In & Outdoor Games Company. World-famous Twinkies were invented in nearby Schiller Park by James Dewar, manager of the Continental Baking Company's Hostess Bakery, also in 1930. Chicago was home to Scott Foresman and Company, publishers of the Dick and Jane readers, beginning in 1909. Brach's Candies originated in Chicago, and in 1977 the heir to the Brach fortune checked out of the Mayo Clinic and was never seen or heard from again—with a fortune estimated at 45 million dollars, she is considered the richest woman ever to have disappeared without a trace.

Ernest Hemingway and Edgar Rice Burroughs grew up in nearby Oak Park. Walt Disney was Chicago-born, but moved to Marceline, Missouri as a young child because the neighborhood here was considered too rough. Chicago was the birthplace of Raymond Chandler, creator of the Philip Marlowe detective character, and known for works such as *The Big Sleep* and *Double Indemnity*. Nat "King" Cole grew up in Chicago after moving here from Montgomery, Alabama, as a child. Dick Tracy was created in 1931 for the *Chicago Tribune* by Stephen Gould.

CHICAGO ATTRACTIONS

Following is just a small sampling of local offerings that you might find interesting if you plan to spend significant time in America's "Second City" and its immediate surroundings.

The **Chicago Water Works** is at Pearson Street and Michigan Avenue. The water tower was one of the few structures in Chicago to survive the 1871 fire. It now houses a visitor center where you can purchase half-priced day-of-performance theater tickets. There is also a gallery of photographs by some of Chicago's own native talent, as well as other welcome amenities.

The **Chicago History Museum** is the city's oldest cultural institution, having been established in 1856. The museum traces the city's development from outpost through the present day, with a permanent display pertaining to America in the Age of Lincoln. Also included is a passenger car from 1893, on which the public traveled to the World's Columbian Exposition that year. 1601 N. Clark St. at North Ave.

Dearborn Station, a National Landmark in the Romanesque style dating to 1885, has been converted to a mall and marketplace. S. Dearborn at W. Polk.

The **Charnley-Persky House Museum** is at 1365 N. Astor Street. The former residence was a joint project by Louis Sullivan and protégé Frank Lloyd Wright in the early 1890s.

Dating from the early 1880s, the **Pullman Historic District** is the country's first planned industrial community. Guided walking tours are available at 11141 S. Cottage Grove Avenue. Within the district are the Greenestone Church, the Hotel Florence Museum, and the A. Phillip Randolph Pullman Porter Museum Gallery. The Pullman Porter Museum features an outstanding collection of historical photographs.

The **Prairie Avenue Historic District** includes the Clarke House Museum, housed in the oldest residence in the city (1836). The Clarke House, designed in Greek Revival, stands at 1827 S. Indiana. The nearby Glessner House Museum is at 1800 S. Prairie.

The residences in the 3800 block of **Alta Vista Terrace** are a little bit peculiar. Each house on one side of the street has a twin (with only minor variations) on the opposite side of the street in exactly the same order. But, since the two series begin at opposite ends of the block, only in the center of the block do the designs directly across from one another match.

Chicago's **Hotel Intercontinental** started out in 1929 as the Medinah Athletic Club, and its world-class, lavishly-decorated swimming pool is where Olympic gold medalist Johnny Weissmuller did some of his training during his years portraying Tarzan on the big screen. 505 N. Michigan Ave.

The **Tribune Tower**, which houses the famous newspaper, was completed in 1925, following a design competition among several distinguished architectural firms. The building includes fragments of some 120 architectural icons from around the world embedded in its walls, including the Taj Mahal, Palace of Westminster, and the Great Wall of China. 435 N. Michigan Ave.

Accessible through a subway-like entrance across from the Tribune building is the **Billy Goat Tavern**, made famous by *Saturday Night Live's* "cheese-boiga" routine. 430 N. Michigan Ave.

Speaking of eateries, Chicago has myriads of them. But one of the more out-of-the-ordinary ones is the **Weber Grill Restaurant**, at 539 N. State Street. All meals are prepared on actual Weber-manufactured grills, much like the one you may have at home. They're fired by charcoal, just like yours, and you can watch your food being prepared in "backyard" fashion. Surrounding the patio is a railing made from Weber grill cooking grates.

The **Polish Museum of America**, at 984 N. Milwaukee Avenue, tells the story of Polish immigration to the new world, and to Chicago in particular, said to be the home of the largest Polish population in the world outside of Warsaw.

The **National Italian-American Sports Hall of Fame** pays tribute to those Italian-Americans making their marks in the world of sports. Inductees include the obvious, like Phil Rizutto and Rocky Marciano, but also some surprises such as Mary Lou Retton and Phil Mickelson. 1431

W. Taylor St.

The **International Museum of Surgical Science** is housed in a landmark lakeside mansion constructed by one of the heirs to the Diamond Match Company fortune. The museum, which launched in 1954, features more than 10,000 display items, and traces the art and science of surgery from its primitive beginnings to the present day. 1524 N. Lake Shore Dr.

The **Castle Car Wash**, in the North Lawndale section of town, is an early automotive business (1925) that resembles a crenellated medieval castle. 3801 W. Ogden Ave.

GREATER CHICAGO

Nearby **Oak Park** is the home of the **Frank Lloyd Wright Home and Studio**, at 951 Chicago Avenue. Oak Park features more than 20 of Wright's designs and, of course, tours are available.

Oak Park was also the boyhood home of **Ernest Hemingway**. His birthplace is at 339 N. Oak Park Avenue, and a museum containing first

Greater Chicago.

editions and the author's diary is just a short walk away at 200 N. Oak Park. Visitors are encouraged to begin their tour at the museum.

Within Greater Chicago is **Des Plaines**, home of the first franchised McDonald's restaurant. Their first restaurant, run by the McDonald brothers themselves, was in San Bernardino, California. This was the first one run by Ray Kroc, a former salesman who liked the McDonalds' concept and bought them out. Closed in 1983, it re-opened a couple of years later as the **McDonald's Museum** (400 N. Lee St.). Of course, McDonald's is the organization which started the demise of so many mom-and-pop enterprises, and so is actually antithetical to Route 66.

In the community of **Niles** is a half-size replica of the world-famous **Leaning Tower of Pisa**. It was constructed in the 1930s, and is located on the grounds of the local YMCA at 6300 W. Touhy Avenue.

THE BEGINNING OF ROUTE 66

Route 66 begins in downtown Chicago, by the shore of Lake Michigan. This end of Route 66 presents an immediate challenge, since eastbound and westbound lanes are actually on separate streets. Westbound 66 follows Adams Street, while eastbound 66 is a block to the south, on Jackson. Since you don't want to miss a thing, I suggest you drive on both streets to find as much of the old highway's flavor as possible prior to leaving downtown. Some of that flavor is to be found at **Lou Mitchell's Restaurant**, a downtown Chicago eatery since 1923, with its name spelled out in neon. It's at 565 W. Jackson, on eastbound 66. (Westbound travelers can turn left off of Adams at DesPlaines, then turn left again onto Jackson.) Don't stop at Lou's if you're on a diet—patrons munch on free Milk Duds while waiting to be seated.

The easternmost end of Adams Street has as its landmark, the **Art Institute of Chicago**, where countless American artists have had some of their formal training. The Art Institute, by the way, includes such famous works in its collection as Edward Hopper's *Nighthawks* and Grant Wood's *American Gothic*.

When you're ready to leave Chicago and Lake Michigan, begin your adventure by proceeding west on Adams Street. Like all of the larger cities on Route 66, Chicago itself will not reveal much in the way of that Mother Road feel that you are looking for—at least not when compared with the hundreds of smaller towns ahead of you. Cities like this were plotted out in the days well before automobile travel, and so you and your car do not feel entirely welcome here.

Westbound Route 66 angles left (southwest) at Ogden Avenue, which is named for Chicago's first mayor, William B. Ogden. He took office in 1837, at the time the city was first incorporated. At 3801 W. Ogden, at the corner of Hamlin Avenue, is **Castle Car Wash**, which is an interesting sight.

Continuing on Ogden, you will pass through the communities of Cicero and Berwyn.

CICERO

Here in Cicero once stood a large "muffler man" figure holding a hot dog in front of Bunyon's. In 2003, that figure was removed and relocated to Atlanta, Illinois, for more prominent display.

Cicero's Hawthorne Race Course is now the home of the **Chicagoland Sports Hall of Fame**, at 3501 S. Laramie Avenue.

BERWYN

There's not a great deal to differentiate Berwyn—it's suburban Chicago. For many years, the

"Paul" as he stood in Cicero at Bunyon's—since relocated to Atlanta, Illinois.

Cermak Plaza Shopping Center stood out for its varied collection of public art, including works with titles like *Bee Tree*, *Millennium Fountain*, and *The Embrace*. Sadly, most of the artwork has, in recent years, fallen into utter disrepair or been removed completely. North of Route 66 at the corner of Cermak and Harlem.

LYONS-McCOOK

On what was once Highway 66 in Lyons is the **Hofmann Tower**, a circa-1908 concrete structure built by a local brewer as part of a recreational park, which today is home to the **Lyons Historical Commission Museum**. As of this writing, the museum has been closed indefinitely due to deterioration of the building. Barry Point Road at Millbridge. Also in Lyons is the **Chicago Portage National Historic Site**, sometimes referred to as "Chicago's Plymouth Rock." 4800 S. Harlem Ave.

A short time after turning onto Joliet Road, you'll be forced to enter I-55. Interstate 55 follows the course of primary 66, which went towards, but ultimately bypassed, the town of Plainfield.

For a time, Route 66 split into two separate routes northeast of Plainfield. The rightmost fork was the primary route at the time my 1957 atlas was printed, and went towards the city of Plainfield. The left fork was designated ALT 66, and headed south toward Joliet. Even at this early date, Route 66 was being realigned in such a way as to bypass most cities and their associated traffic. The older ALT 66 at this time passed directly through towns such as Joliet, Elwood, Wilmington, and Braidwood. At the same time, the map shows the newer primary route passing near, but not through, Plainfield and other towns, much as I-55 does today. The two alignments later converged again just southwest of the town of Gardner.

Both Plainfield and Joliet were on the Lincoln Highway (U.S. 30), an east-west artery, that passed through here. So whichever path you take (and I recommend you explore both), it is here that you cross one of many routes of significance on your way west on 66. The Lincoln Highway was established in 1915, and was the first American transcontinental highway conceived with automobile travel in mind. Later, in the 1920s, when such interstate routes were designated with numbers, the Lincoln Highway officially became U.S. 30, but lovers of history still refer to it more commonly by its original name.

PLAINFIELD

If you enjoy hot rods and custom cars, Plainfield has them. This is the home of **Midwest Hot Rods**. They can either work with what you've got, or you can tour their inventory. E. Main Street near Penny Lane.

ROMEOVILLE

Keep an eye out for the **White Fence Farm**, a sort of grand catering enterprise right beside the highway. They even have kiddie

From I-55, exit Joliet Road toward Romeoville, where you'll soon merge with Highway 53 for the run into town.

rides and a petting zoo on-site. There was a very large fiberglass chicken on a flatbed truck parked on the grounds the first time I passed through here. 1376 Joliet Rd.

Between Romeoville and Joliet is the **Stateville State Prison**. The grounds cover a huge, well-manicured expanse, and when you first glimpse it you'll be excused for thinking you've come upon a university campus of some prestige.

Part of the décor at White Fence Farm.

JOLIET

Continue into Joliet on Highway 53, which will entail a left turn at Ruby Street and across the Des Plaines River.

Once nicknamed the City of Spires due to its many houses of worship (some 122 at one time), Joliet has in recent years taken a liking to gaming, and is now very much a center for casino gambling. Even the local **Joliet Prison** has what might be called spires, though.

Among Joliet Prison's more notorious prisoners were the duo of Leopold and Loeb, who in 1924 murdered their victim solely for the challenge of committing the perfect crime. In the world of fiction, Joliet Prison gave John Belushi's character his nickname, Joliet Jake, in the movie *The Blues Brothers*. You can drive by Joliet Prison and take a look at its depressing walls at 1125 Collins Street. The first prisoners were received here in 1858.

Another building that I'm sure has been joked about as looking like a prison is **Joliet Central High School**, which was built in 1901, and has what some would call a Gothic flavor. In 2010, restoration work was completed on the four original 109-year-old front doors, with plans to tackle the other 41 exterior doors in the near future. 201 E. Jefferson St.

In the past few years, Joliet has begun billing itself as the "Gateway to Route 66." The idea has merit since, as mentioned earlier, there's not so much of the Mother Road flavor to be had in Chicago. Roadies from overseas, in particular, seem interested in the small-town experience that begins here in this area.

In 1940, the **Dairy Queen** ice cream chain was established, with the first store being in Joliet. The now-familiar confection was actually first offered to the public two years earlier in a special taste trial in nearby

Joliet, Illinois.

Kankakee. Today, you can
indulge the same impulse
at **Rich & Creamy**, a walk-
up ice cream stand at 920
N. Broadway. The place
even includes figures of
Jake and Elwood Blues,
which were installed on
the roof a few years ago.

JOLIET ATTRACTIONS

Popularly known as the
Jewel of Joliet, the **Rialto
Square Theater** is a re-
stored 1926 vaudeville
theater on the National
Register. It contains the
largest hand-cut chande-
lier in the U.S. The inner
lobby area was fashioned

The Rialto is a truly luxurious theater,
sometimes called the "Jewel of Joliet."

after the Hall of Mirrors at
the Palace of Versailles; tours are available. 102 N. Chicago St.

Take a free tour of blast furnace ruins at **Joliet Iron Works Historic Site**. The site is also an access point for the 12.5-mile **Illinois &
Michigan Canal Trail**, which connects Joliet's City Center to the Centennial Trail in Cook County. On Columbia Street, one-tenth mile east of the
Ruby Street bridge.

Explore Joliet history at the **Joliet Area Historical Museum**,
where there is a permanent Route 66 exhibit and welcome center. It's at
204 N. Ottawa Street, in a former Methodist church building, where old
66 crossed paths with the Lincoln Highway.

In the South East Neighborhood Historical District is the **Jacob**

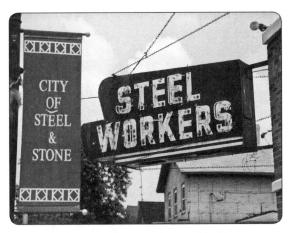

Joliet was once a center for the steel industry.

Henry Mansion, an 1873 40-room manor house decorated in lavish style, that today specializes in weddings, receptions, and similar events. The house is especially well-turned-out at Christmastime. At 20 S. Eastern Avenue, in what was once called "Silk Stocking Row."

ELWOOD

This is a very small community just south of Joliet. Is this where the inspiration came from for the name of the other Blues Brother, Joliet Jake's sibling, Elwood?

WILMINGTON

Wilmington has been nicknamed the Island City for the fact that the Kankakee River runs through town, forming an island, which is home to Island Park.

Wilmington is known among Route 66 fans as the home of the **Gemini Giant**. He's one of those giant figures, formerly a muffler man, who used to populate American highways in the 1950s and '60s. This one has been decked out like an astronaut and stands in front of the Launching Pad Drive-In restaurant, where he has been attracting attention since 1965. The shape of his helmet is a bit unusual, perhaps a nod to the Coneheads of *Saturday Night Live*.

Fans of architectural curiosities might want to drive by the octagonal **Schutten-Aldrich House**, at 600 Water Street. It dates from 1856,

MUFFLER MEN

Once plentiful across the American landscape, the Gemini Giant at Wilmington is a notable example of what are commonly referred to as "muffler men." Over twenty feet in height, they proliferated in the late '50s to early '60s as roadside icons for automotive muffler shops. Early on, some owners of these figures "personalized" them by customizing the clothing or even the facial features according to whim. As in the case of the Gemini Giant, in later years the oversized muffler held in the figure's hands was often replaced by something else—in this case, a model rocket.

At the Launching Pad, Wilmington, Illlinois.

and is reputed to have sheltered runaway slaves as a part of the famous underground railroad. The house is a private residence, so please be respectful.

FURTHER AFIELD

About halfway between Wilmington and Kankakee to the southeast is the **Kankakee River State Park**, consisting of over 2,700 acres strung out along 11 miles of the river. This area takes its water seriously, with canoe rentals, an annual fishing derby, and the Kankakee River Valley Regatta each Labor Day. 5314 W. State Route 102.

Leaving Wilmington, you're still on Highway 53, and you'll have the railroad tracks running right alongside to let you know you're on an early alignment of highway.

BRAIDWOOD-GODLEY

Through these neighboring towns, there are two versions of old 66 (Washington and Front Streets) separated by a set of railroad tracks right in between.

Route 66 slices through the southeast corner of Braidwood. There is an annual cruise held here each August, sponsored by the 1950s-flavored **Polk-A-Dot Drive-In** restaurant, located at 222 N. Front Street.

Godley is a tiny village right on the Will County-Grundy County line.

BRACEVILLE

According to my atlas, the town of Braceville was just west of Highway 66 in 1957. Today it sits in a narrow corridor between old 66 and I-55 just to the west.

GARDNER

Gardner's Route 66 claim to fame was the Riviera Roadhouse just north of town, built in 1928, which also featured a streetcar-cum-diner in the back yard. Unfortunately, the Riviera fell victim to a fire in 2010.

Gardner has a sort of "bypass" loop that skirts the southeast side of town and is easy to follow, but I recommend you enter town on Washington Street and meander through downtown, just as old 66 once did. The town of Gardner features a two-cell jailhouse dating from 1905.

 After Gardner, Route 66 runs directly alongside Interstate 55 toward Dwight.

DWIGHT

In 1940, Eleanor Jarman was serving a 199-year sentence at the women's prison, now called Dwight Correctional Center, for her involvement in several hold-ups. On the eighth of August, the "Blond Tigress" escaped, never to be seen or heard from again.

On old Route 66 itself (*not* the bypass), near the corner of Chippewa, is a retired service station now displaying a collection of vintage gasoline pumps and signage.

DWIGHT ATTRACTIONS

The **Ambler-Becker Texaco**

Approaching Dwight, be on the alert for a left turn just as the road you're on starts peeling away from the railroad track. That left turn takes you on the early alignment directly toward downtown, where there's much to see. The main highway will completely bypass the town of Dwight.

DWIGHT
ILLINOIS

Pizza restaurant with automotive heritage in Dwight.

Station is a 1930s-era building restored in 2007, now serving as the town's visitor center. It's at the junction of Illinois 17 and an alignment of old 66 on the west side of town.

Downtown at the old **Keeley Institute** (now the Fox Development Center) are five Tiffany-style windows, each of them portraying one of the five senses. Next door is the **First National Bank**, designed by none other than Frank Lloyd Wright around 1905. Nearby is an impressive Romanesque railroad depot listed on the National Register, now housing the **Dwight Historical Society Museum**. The **Bank of Dwight** dates from 1855, and features a mural in the interior by Viennese artist Oskar Gross. Also notable is the windmill on the library grounds, which dates from 1896.

Roadside in Dwight, Illinois.

Once a dilapidated wreck, this station has been beautifully restored by dedicated volunteers. Odell, Illinois.

Each September, Dwight hosts a basset hound parade called the "Waddle," which benefits **Basset Rescue**, an organization specializing in finding homes for neglected or abused dogs.

 Shortly after passing the Mt. Olivet Catholic Cemetery south of town, you'll find yourself running right beside I-55 again.

ODELL-CAYUGA

When I first passed through Odell in the 1990s, the old fuel station here was sagging and dilapidated. But thanks to the efforts of donors and volunteers, Odell's **Standard Station** has since been restored for your enjoyment. Don't fail to stop and take some photographs.

> Just as you did at Dwight a little earlier, be on the lookout for a left turn that keeps you parallel to the railroad tracks—that's the old route that'll take you through the heart of town.

Newly-painted advertising barn near Cayuga, Illinois.

A few years ago, a tunnel was discovered (or re-discovered) that used to run beneath Route 66 so that school-children and churchgoers could cross the busy street safely. Today, you can plainly see the entrance. Odell is small enough that you can take some time and thoroughly explore most of its streets.

Between Cayuga and Pontiac is a **restored barn** bearing a Meramec Caverns advertisement. For years now, it has been unlawful to create "new" advertising barns, due to some people's opinions about Highway Beautification. Existing barns such as this one are "grandfathered" under the law, and so can remain and in some cases even be restored. However, as such barns age and are removed, whether by natural or man-made forces, they cannot be replaced. Thus their number continues to diminish year after year.

PONTIAC

The first thing you'll see coming from Cayuga is the **Old Log Cabin Restaurant**. This is the place which has gained some renown for not giving up when the highway was re-aligned and they found that the new Route 66 was at their back door. The owners actually picked up and rotated the building toward

> You know how to do this now—as you approach the northern outskirts of Pontiac, the road you're on will start to wander away from the railroad tracks. Be alert for a left turn that more closely follows the railroad tracks in order to maximize your adventure. At that junction is the Log Cabin Restaurant.

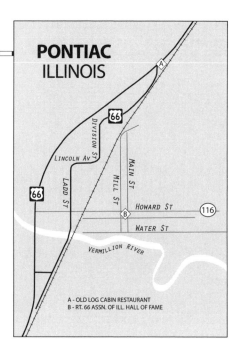

PONTIAC
ILLINOIS

A - OLD LOG CABIN RESTAURANT
B - RT. 66 ASSN. OF ILL. HALL OF FAME

the new road and barely missed a beat. The older roadway can be seen behind the present orientation, near the railroad tracks, as befits an early highway alignment.

At the state prison here in Pontiac, inmates manufactured Route 66 shields to meet public demand following the highway's decommission in Illinois in 1977.

PONTIAC ATTRACTIONS

The **Route 66 Association of Illinois Hall of Fame & Museum** was established here in 2004, in the old city hall/firehouse complex at 110 W. Howard Street. Recently added to the museum's collection are several artifacts from the now-demolished Wishing Well Motel, which for years did business in suburban Chicago. Included are both the original sign and the

iconic wishing well itself. By the time you read this, the museum will have already taken possession of Bob Waldmire's modified school bus, on which the artist logged many Mother Road miles and even lived in at times. Bob passed away in 2009, but his postcards and other artwork are still popular all up and down the

Pontiac, Illinois.

route, and he even left a partially-completed mural at the museum.

In 2009, a group called the Walldogs painted several murals scattered throughout town. One year later, the town showed its appreciation by opening the **International Walldog Mural and Sign Art Museum** at 217 N. Mill Street. The museum pays tribute to the history and evolution of mural and sign art.

The **Jones House** is the second brick home built in Pontiac, completed in 1858. It bears the name of Henry C. Jones, newspaper publisher and founder of the Pontiac Light, Heat and Power Company. The house is owned and operated by the Livingston County Historical Society. 314 E. Madison.

The **Catharine V. Yost Museum & Arts Center**, 298 W. Water Street, is a Queen Anne-style home from the 1890s, containing most of the Yost family possessions, some of which are much older than the house itself.

In the fall of 2010, it was announced that a collector of **Pontiac automobiles** and memorabilia would be moving his collection here and creating a museum, but with no clear timetable. Pontiac car dealerships closed permanently at the end of October 2010.

A couple of miles south of town on the highway stands a former state police headquarters that is shaped like a pistol when viewed from the air. From ground level, it features curved corners and glass block.

CHENOA

Chenoa is home to the **Matthew T. Scott Home** at 227 N. First Avenue. This was the home of Matthew T. and his wife Julia Green Scott. Matthew

Chenoa, Illinois.

was an enterprising farmer, businessman, and town founder, and his wife Julia held office in the Daughters of the American Revolution. Organized in 1890 and chartered by Congress in 1896, membership in the DAR is open to "any woman 18 years or older, regardless of race, religion, or ethnic background, who can prove lineal descent from a patriot of the American Revolution."

LEXINGTON

Lexington has an old neon sign announcing your arrival. On the north side of Lexington, Route 66 fans have created a sort of **"Memory Lane"** exhibit, with a stretch of old 66 roadway

> There's an old alignment of Route 66 close to the railroad tracks called Memory Lane, but it's only open to auto traffic during special events. You can pay a visit, however, by turning east on Wall Street for a couple of blocks.

set aside and enhanced with period billboards and even a Burma Shave

sign. If you'd like to get out of your car while in Lexington, try Koch's Depot, an antique store whose main building is an old railroad depot relocated to the downtown business district. The Koch family used to run the Lexington Café, which operated right on 66 for years.

The **Patton Cabin** is a log structure, parts of which date from 1829. It was used as an official polling place as early as 1831, and is the oldest building in the county.

Downtown Lexington, Illinois.

A long-retired stretch of Route 66 in Lexington, Illinois, is now the town's "Memory Lane."

Originally located about a mile and a half to the southeast, the cabin was reassembled in Keller Park (off N. Cherry Street) in 1969.

TOWANDA

There's a former gasoline station here at Towanda, which has an exaggerated sloping roof over the pump islands. At the time of my first trip through here, it was serving duty as a night club. Each subsequent time I see it, it appears to be serving a different purpose.

Towanda, Illinois.

I've seen an old postcard picturing something called the Asian Arts Gift Shop here in Towanda. It consisted of Polynesian-style huts elevated above the ground on piers.

In recent years a walking/biking path has been set up beside the newer bypass alignment of 66 in this area called **Route 66 Linear Park**. Towanda is small, so explore it thoroughly; there are fragments of old 66 on both sides of the main alignment.

BLOOMINGTON- NORMAL

When two towns have to coexist this closely (they share the same Main Street), it's natural for a rivalry to develop. Normal is home to Illinois State University, and Bloomington has Illinois Wesleyan College.

Bloomington seems to be able to claim more famous sons. These in- clude Adlai Steven- son, whose home is at 901 N. McLean; the fictional Colo- nel Henry Blake, from *M*A*S*H*; author and pub- lisher Elbert Hub- bard, who perished on the *Lusitania*; and Pawnee Bill, a.k.a. Gordon W. Lillie, who pro- duced Wild West

Unfortunately, Route 66 has been broken up where it enters town from the northeast. Although the route used to follow the railroad tracks for a fair distance in the early days, the downtown alignment was bypassed many years ago and some of the old alignment has been obliterated. To- day you're faced with a "stair-step" effect if you want to stay close to the more colorful early alignment. From Shelbourne, try taking a left at Henry, a right onto Pine, then left on Linden, right on Willow, and left onto Main Street.

Bloomington, Illinois.

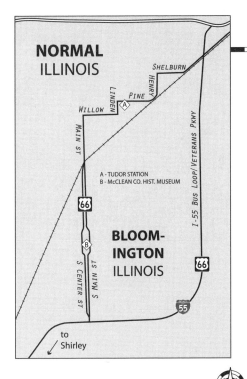

NORMAL
ILLINOIS

A - TUDOR STATION
B - McCLEAN CO. HIST. MUSEUM

BLOOM-
INGTON
ILLINOIS

to
Shirley

The route in Bloomington is split between north and southbound streets, with Center Street carrying the westbound traveler and Main Street carrying eastbound traffic.

shows in the first decade of the 1900s, similar to what Buffalo Bill became famous for. Bloomington is also the birthplace of the Republican Party, which was organized here at a convention in 1856.

NORMAL ATTRACTIONS

At 305 Pine Street (between Walnut and Oak) stands a **Tudor-style gas station** from the 66 era, which has been placed on the National Register of Historic Places. It's unusual in that it includes a caretaker's apartment upstairs.

Check out the Art Deco-influenced **Normal Theater**, which first opened its doors in 1937. It's on the National Register and has been fully restored to its original beauty. 209 W. North St.

Normal also has a one-room 1899 schoolhouse you can tour. The **Eyestone School** is at the corner of College Avenue and Adelaide Street.

BLOOMINGTON ATTRACTIONS

Bloomington is home to **Beer Nuts**, at 103 N. Robinson Street. Invented in the 1930s, and originally called "Virginia Redskins," Beer Nuts were a rousing success from the get-go. You can't actually see them made here, but you can visit the gift shop and see a video about them.

Also in Bloomington is the **David Davis Mansion State Historic Site**. The home, named Clover Lawn, is a 20-room Italianate villa at 1000 E. Monroe Street. The home was built in 1872 for U.S. Supreme Court

David Davis Mansion, Bloomington, Illinois.

Justice David Davis. Decorated by his wife, Sarah, the home features original furnishings and stencil-work. It also has features which were quite luxurious at the time, such as indoor plumbing and a central heating system. You are urged to allow at least 90 minutes to tour this gem.

The **McLean County Museum of History** is at 200 N. Main Street in the former courthouse, which was constructed in 1901–03. The museum includes a "hands on" area where visitors can experience such age-old tasks as beating a rug and pushing a steel plow.

The **Prairie Aviation Museum** includes several restored aircraft, a collection of Charles Lindburgh memorabilia, and also offers flight simulation. 2929 E. Empire Street, at the Central Illinois Regional Airport.

At the south end of town, just after Center and Main Streets rejoin one another, turn right onto I-55 Business Loop (S. Veterans Parkway) to continue your journey west. Many travelers enter I-55 just outside town and then exit in a few miles near the town of Shirley. However, if you want to stay off the superslab, then from S. Veterans Parkway turn right onto Beich Road, pass under I-55, then continue on Beich as it turns left and hugs the interstate on the opposite side for the trip into Shirley.

SHIRLEY

At Shirley we have the **Funk Prairie Home** and the **Funk Gem & Mineral Museum**. The home was originally built in 1863–64, and includes the first-ever electric kitchen island (added a bit later, of course). The mineral museum is a collection of gemstones, fossils, and petrified wood accumulated by Lafayette Funk II, Illinois State Senator and cattle king, and lo-

A subtle reminder that cross-country travel did not always involve automobiles. Shirley, Illinois.

cated on the same 27-acre property. 10875 Prairie Home Lane, east of town. Tours are by prior arrangement, so call ahead at 309-827-6792 for an appointment and detailed instructions for getting there.

Leaving town, Route 66 is tightly sandwiched between I-55 to the left and railroad tracks on the right. A few miles past Shirley, look for a right-hand turn that takes you across the tracks into the sleepy community of Funk's Grove. There you'll see an old tiny railroad depot (relocated from nearby Shirley) and the remains of a small country store.

FUNK'S GROVE

The Funk family has been tapping trees and making what they call "sirup" for well over 100 years. Stop in and pick some up.

Funk's Grove, Illinois.

Restored railroad depot, McLean, Illinois.

McLEAN

One of two towns by this name on Route 66 (the other being in Texas), the Illinois McLean is home to the **Dixie Travel Plaza**, a truck stop that started life as a much more humble travel amenity in 1928. Across from the Dixie is a small railroad depot that has been restored. You'll leave town on the highway that parallels the railroad tracks.

ATLANTA

Atlanta was at one time called Xenia, as evidenced by the modest Xenia Park in the heart of town.

Heading into Atlanta, the railroad tracks are on your right. After the road begins to veer left and away from the tracks, look for a right turn to take you through the heart of downtown (Sycamore Street, which will turn into Arch Street).

ATLANTA ATTRACTIONS

At the town center of Atlanta, check out the distinctive **library**, which has been converted to a museum. It is eight-sided and has a clock tower standing beside it, which came from a nearby school building. The circa-1909 Seth Thomas clock, unlike most of its electrified peers, is still

wound by hand. 100 Race St.

Atlanta was fortunate enough not long ago to host a sort of **mural**-making festival. You'll see a number of buildings throughout the town that have had artwork added to their sides. This project was spearheaded by a group of signmakers calling themselves Letter-Heads. Look for the giant **"muffler man"** who was moved here from Bunyon's in Cicero.

The town also boasts of the circa-1904 **J. H. Hawes Grain Elevator Museum**, which is "standing on its original site" and is further described as a "skyscraper of the prairie." The museum is set up to actually demonstrate some of the arcane workings of the place, so you may want to take in the tour and lecture. I'll

This former library is now a museum. Atlanta, Illinois.

bet every grade-schooler around here remembers coming here on a field trip. 301 SW Second St.

Atlanta's latest attraction is the restored **Palms Grill Café**, a combination restaurant and museum at 110 SW Arch Street. You can't get lost in a town like this, so I recommend doing some exploring.

LAWNDALE

Just a very small community beside Route 66 where the highway crosses Kickapoo Creek.

LINCOLN

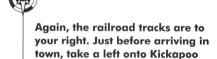

This is said to be the only town named for Lincoln while he was still alive, and on hearing of this plan, he is attributed with the remark that he never knew of anything named Lincoln that amounted to much. He was personally involved in drawing up the legal papers establishing the town, and he actually practiced some law here in the 1850s. For a time, there were actually two separate towns, Postville and Lincoln, which were officially merged in 1865.

> Again, the railroad tracks are to your right. Just before arriving in town, take a left onto Kickapoo Street.

LINCOLN ATTRACTIONS

While in Lincoln, look for **The Mill** restaurant at 738 S. Washington on the far side of town. The Mill dates from the early days of the route (1929), and featured a lighted, revolving Dutch-style windmill. A couple of years ago, a

The Mill is currently undergoing restoration. Lincoln, Illinois.

group spearheaded by concerned citizens began the arduous task of restoring the building, with plans to turn it into a museum.

Lincoln is now home to the **World's Largest Covered Wagon**,
recognized as such by the Guinness Book of Records. The wagon was
built several years ago by a man recovering from heart surgery, and after
completion was displayed in the Divernon area with a huge figure of
Abraham Lincoln in the driver's seat. It now has a permanent home on
the grounds of the Best Western Lincoln Inn, at 1750 Fifth Street.

Reconstructed in 1953 on the site of the original is a *replica* courthouse at the **Postville Courthouse State Historic Site**, 914 Fifth Street.

Signs like this were once plentiful on Route 66. Lincoln, Illinois.

The original, constructed in 1840, was frequented by Abraham Lincoln during his years of practicing law in the area. In 1848, however, the county seat was moved to Mount Pulaski, and a new courthouse was erected there. The old Postville Courthouse was acquired in 1929 by Henry Ford, who dismantled it and reassembled it at his Greenfield Village complex at Dearborn, Michigan. Many years later, in the 1950s, the replica you see today was created. Incidentally, Greenfield Village is of interest in itself, having more than 200 historic buildings of all sorts spread over an 81-acre tract.

At the **Heritage In Flight Museum**, barracks that once housed German prisoners-of-war are now a museum filled with aircraft and other artifacts dating as early as World War I. At the Logan County Airport.

Check out the **downtown monument** depicting a life-sized, ear-to-ear watermelon slice, commemorating the day in 1853 when the future president christened his namesake community with melon juice. The monument was erected in 1964, through the combined efforts of the local Kiwanis, Rotary, and Lions Clubs.

FURTHER AFIELD

Southeast of Lincoln (or due east of Springfield if you prefer) is the city of **Decatur**. It was in Decatur that the Lincoln family first settled after coming to the state from Indiana. Here stands the courthouse where the young man first earned a reputation as a trial lawyer, and there is a memorial statue marking where he gave his first political speech. Decatur was also the original home of the Chicago Bears professional football team.

Scattered through Decatur are several Lincoln statues: *Finding the Biggest Man*, at 101 N. Water Street; *Lincoln's First Speech*, N. Main at Merchant Street; *Wake Up Lincoln*, at 130 N. Water Street; and *The Railsplitter Candidate* and *Troosting Lincoln*, both on S. Park Street across from Central Park.

The **Macon County History Museum and Prairie Village** is at 5580 N. Fork Road. Local history is exhibited, including a train depot, print shop, and a log courthouse dating from 1830, in which Lincoln is said to have tried some cases.

The **James Millikin Homestead** is at 125 N. Pine Street. The home was built in 1876 in an ornate and rather Gothic style, which contrasts sharply with the Frank Lloyd Wright-inspired designs with which it is surrounded. The home has been fully restored and is listed on the National Register. Open weekends.

At 420 W. Eldorado Street is the **Hieronymus Mueller Museum**. The Muellers, a family of German immigrants, played a significant role as inventors in both the nineteenth and twentieth centuries. They either invented or improved such things as plumbing fixtures, roller skates, soda fountains, auto parts, and munitions.

Leaving Lincoln, you'll rejoin I-55 Business Loop. But just before merging onto Interstate 55, you should take a left turn onto a frontage road that closely follows the railroad tracks toward Broadwell.

BROADWELL-ELKHART

Broadwell is the former site of the **Pig-Hip Restaurant and Motel**. The owner, Ernie Edwards, had turned it into a museum post-retirement, but unfortunately it burned down in 2007. Today there is a large monument stone with a commemorative plaque. Continue to parallel the railroad tracks through Elkhart.

Broadwell, Illinois.

WILLIAMSVILLE

The **Williamsville Historical Museum** was fashioned from a pair of railroad cars and is located at 104 S. Elm Street. Next door is the old railroad depot, which is now home to the town library.

    Die Cast Auto Sales specializes in automotive miniatures. They're housed in a vintage gas station at 117 N. Elm.

The railroad tracks are to the left. Take a left turn onto Taylor Street in order to explore downtown. However, not only does "old" Route 66 not pass completely through town due to fragmentation, even the newer bypass alignment has been broken off. You'll need to backtrack toward the middle part of town and enter Interstate 55 using Stuttle Road to leave Williamsville and continue on your way west.

Celebrating 66 in Williamsville, Illinois.

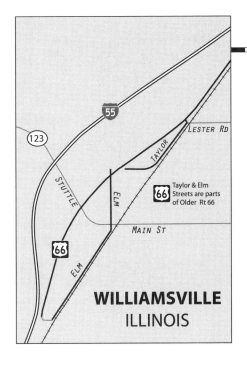

**WILLIAMSVILLE
ILLINOIS**

(Map labels: 55, 123, LESTER RD, TAYLOR, STUTTLE, ELM, 66, Taylor & Elm Streets are parts of Older Rt 66, MAIN ST, 66, ELM)

 After passing through and exploring Williamsville, you'll be forced to enter the interstate for a short distance; exit again at the I-55 Business Loop in order to pass through the town of Sherman.

SHERMAN

You probably won't be able to easily tell from the highway where Sherman's business district is. If you want to see it, make a left turn onto E. Andrew Road and then a right onto First Street, where you'll find a small central district of only about four square blocks.

After passing through Sherman proper, you'll encounter **Carpenter Park**, which includes a quarter-mile section of pre-1936 Mother Road pavement at its eastern edge. That stretch of road has been closed to vehicular traffic since that time, so it's more of an archaeological site for Route 66, including some bridge abutments where it crossed the Sangamon River. After Carpenter Park, you'll be entering Springfield via N. Peoria Road/N. Ninth.

SPRINGFIELD

The Illinois state capital was moved here from Vandalia in 1857, by a group which included Abraham Lincoln. Today, Springfield is still the center of the Lincoln universe, as well as being nearly the exact

There is a very early (pre-1930) alignment through town that leaves the city on what it is now Highway 4. However, because that alignment was superceded so early, most roadies traverse Springfield via the later alignment, which uses 5th and 6th Streets downtown and has more surviving Route 66-era places of business.

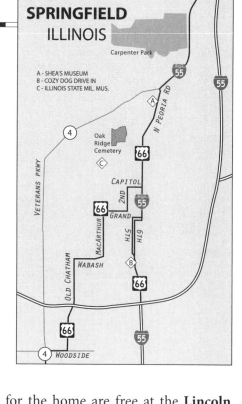

SPRINGFIELD
ILLINOIS

Carpenter Park

A - SHEA'S MUSEUM
B - COZY DOG DRIVE IN
C - ILLINOIS STATE MIL. MUS.

geographic center of the state (the precise center being about 28 miles northeast, in Logan County).

Springfield boasts more Lincoln sites than any other city, which is not at all surprising when you consider that the man lived and worked here for many years before departing to pursue the presidency. Several of these Lincoln sites can be taken in rather conveniently via the Springfield Trolley Tours.

"The only home Mr. Lincoln ever owned" is at Eighth and Jackson Streets. Tour tickets for the home are free at the **Lincoln Home Visitors' Center** at 426 S. Seventh. Lincoln's law office (the **Lincoln-Herndon Law Office**) is at Sixth and Adams Streets. The railroad depot here in Springfield is where Lincoln gave his eloquent departure speech before leaving permanently to assume the presidency. And, the Lincoln family tomb is at **Oak Ridge Cemetery** (north of downtown on Walnut Street). There, you can walk the solemn halls of the mausoleum and rub the nose of his bronze likeness for luck, as many before you have. The Oak Ridge Cemetery even

Final resting place of our 16th president, Springfield, Illinois.

Festivities at the Old State Capitol, Springfield, Illinois.

includes a souvenir kiosk where you can indulge your lust for more Lincoln memorabilia. Topping it all off, the **Abraham Lincoln Presidential Library and Museum** opened in 2004, and houses the largest collection of Lincoln artifacts ever assembled (112 and 212 N. Sixth).

Springfield, Illinois.

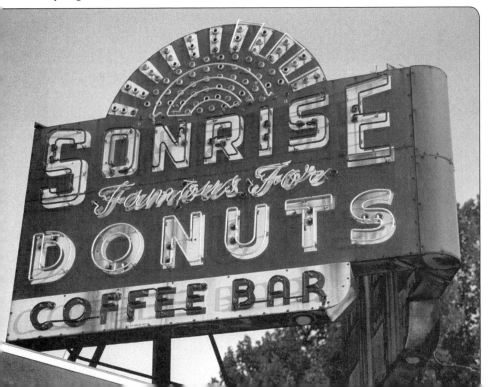

For Route 66 followers, the hands-down centerpiece of Springfield is the **Cozy Dog Drive-In**. Ed Waldmire, who established a small chain of restaurants here, invented the corn dog while serving military duty at Amarillo, Texas (also on Highway 66). After the war, he started serving his invention—which he originally wanted to call the "Crusty Cur"—in his hometown of Springfield, in 1949. Today, the Cozy Dog on Route 66 (just north of its original location) is still open, and still run by members of the Waldmire family. 2935 S. Sixth.

Route 66 devotees will also want to stop at **Shea's Gas Station Museum**, where you can satisfy your urge to pore over restored gas pumps and other petroliana. 2075 N. Peoria Rd.

SPRINGFIELD ATTRACTIONS

The **Illinois State Military Museum** salutes the Illinois National Guard through exhibits of uniforms, equipment, weaponry, and photographs housed in a Civilian Conservation Corps structure. By far the most notable item in the museum's collection is the wooden leg worn by General Santa Anna. The story goes that the general and a small group of his men were having a lunch of roasted chicken when an Illinois detachment surprised them. The general had just time enough to mount his horse and escape, but was forced to leave behind his artificial leg and the remains of the chicken. Fortunately for him, he had a spare one just like it elsewhere—the leg, that is. 1301 N. MacArthur Blvd.

In front of the Illinois Exhibits building at the state fairgrounds is a 30-foot-tall statue of a clean-shaven Abraham Lincoln entitled *The Rail Splitter*. It was created in 1968 by Carl W. Rinnus, a Springfield native.

The **Old State Capitol State Historic Site** is where President Lincoln delivered his famous "house divided" speech, and where he lay in state following his assassination in 1865. It was also the scene of the 1858 Lincoln-Douglas debates. On E. Adams, between Fifth and Sixth.

The **Dana-Thomas House**, at 301 E. Lawrence Avenue, is a 1902 Frank Lloyd Wright-designed home with most of the original furnishings, including art glass. It is considered one of his earliest experiments in

Springfield, Illinois.

what was later to become famously known as his Prairie Style. On October 8th each year, citizens turn out to celebrate the birthday of the lady of the house, socialite Susan Lawrence Dana, with an open house, live music, etc.

The **Executive Mansion** is the nation's third-oldest, continuously-occupied governor's residence. Many rooms are open to public viewing, including the state dining room, library, ballroom, and the Lincoln bedroom. 410 E. Jackson St.

The **Vachel Lindsay Home** is the birthplace of the native Springfield artist and poet, who resided here until his death—by suicide—in 1931. Near the governor's mansion, at 603 S. Fifth.

The **Oliver P. Parks Telephone Museum** houses a collection assembled by a long-time Ma Bell employee. At last count, there were 117 phones on display here, including such classics as wooden wall-mounted phones, candlestick models, early coin phones, and even a switchboard. 529 S. Seventh St.

The interior of the **Lawrence Memorial Library** was designed by Frank Lloyd Wright, and has been restored to its original luster at 101 E. Laurel Street.

The **Route 66 Twin Drive-In Theater** shows two features nightly (in season) beginning at dusk. The theater is on the south side of town, at 1700 Recreation Drive. The theater is actually part of a larger recreational complex called **Knight's Action Park**, which includes a water slide, driving range, picnic areas, pedal boats, and more.

Back on 66: Leaving Springfield, you have a treat—two distinct Route 66 alignments are here to enjoy. The more modern route takes you south out of town paralleling I-55, through towns including Divernon, Litchfield, and Mount Olive. This was the course of the highway during most of its years of existence. However, there is an older alignment, passing through Auburn, Carlinville, and Gillespie—and today bearing the number 4—which carried traffic in the 1920s. In fact, that road predated Route 66 and was a major thoroughfare in the area years earlier. Because of the very early realignment (1930), the older highway does not have much surviving 66-era road architecture, and is harder to follow. However, it is certainly worth driving, as it is easier to imagine yourself in an Illinois long gone. If you follow Highway 4, keep alert for a section of very old brick-paved roadway, just over a mile long, north of Auburn.

The narrative immediately following takes you on the older alignment along Highway 4. If you choose to take the more modern route through Litchfield (my personal preference), you can pick up the account for that segment at the town of Glenarm.

CHATHAM-AUBURN

Between Chatham and Auburn, be on the lookout for a right turn onto Snell Road, and then a left onto Curran. This is an example of an old section of highway that predated Route 66, then became part of 66 from 1926 to 1930, and then was bypassed in favor of a more direct alignment to the east. The bricks were not added to the roadway until 1932. According to the Auburn Historical Society, the first paved streets in town did not occur until 1928.

One of Auburn's esteemed sons was Emil "Dutch" Leonard, a major league baseball pitcher for 20 years in the 1930s, '40s, and '50s. He is buried in the town cemetery.

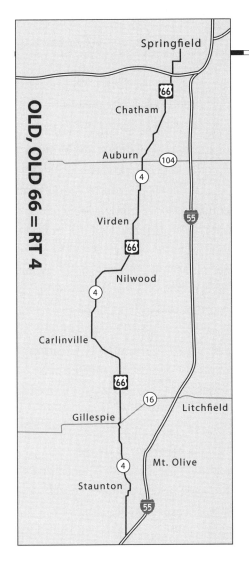

OLD, OLD 66 = RT 4

Springfield

Chatham

Auburn

Virden

Nilwood

Carlinville

Gillespie

Litchfield

Mt. Olive

Staunton

THAYER-VIRDEN-GIRARD

Girard was lobbying hard to win "Single Best Town in America," a contest sponsored by Kraft Foods in 2010. Although they were among the finalists, Girard ultimately lost out to Three Lakes, Wisconsin. While in Girard, consider a stop at **Doc's Soda Shop**, a circa-1880 former pharmacy, now a pharmacy museum and soda fountain. 133 S. Second St.

NILWOOD-CARLINVILLE

Nilwood is known for its stretch of old concrete highway that has turkey tracks imprinted in it. There are enough tracks to suggest the turkey was not just crossing the street, but dancing or shadow-boxing instead.

Carlinville's downtown square and adjacent areas are part of a historic district recognized since 1976. The town's spiritual center is a gazebo where a series of concerts is held during the summer months.

CARLINVILLE ATTRACTIONS

The **Million-Dollar White Elephant Courthouse** (Macoupin County Courthouse), at 200 E. Main Street, is said to have cost more than 10 times its original estimate, taking more than two years to build and 40 years to pay for. It has some rather overwrought features, such as iron doors, some weighing in at over a ton, and all interior trim is made of either iron or stone. It was at one time the largest courthouse in the United States. The courthouse project also included a new **jailhouse**, and it, too, has some interesting features, such as a crenellated roofline and leftover cannonballs embedded in the walls (construction was completed in 1869, not long after the Civil War). The jailhouse, amazingly, was still in use as recently as 1988.

Nearby is the **Loomis House**, a former 50-room hotel, which was designed by the same architect as the courthouse and jail (above). The Loomis has been preserved and today contains a number of local businesses.

More on the pragmatic side is Carlinville's **Standard Addition**, a housing subdivision comprised of one of the largest aggregates of Sears Roebuck catalog homes to be found anywhere—more than a hundred of them. This fact has led to the publication of a number of books and documentaries in recent years.

The **Macoupin County Historical Museum** is in the 1883 Anderson Mansion, which features a stained glass window purchased at the 1893 Columbian Exposition in Chicago. A schoolhouse, church, and blacksmith shop are also on the property. 920 W. Breckenridge St.

There is a small **stone marker** in front of the United Methodist Church in Carlinville, marking the spot where Abraham Lincoln delivered a speech in 1858 while campaigning for a Senate seat against Stephen A. Douglas. At the Corner of S. Broad and E. First.

GILLESPIE-BENLD-SAWYERVILLE

These three communities share a mining heritage—at least three coal mines were established in this area to serve the needs of the railroads in the first decade of the twentieth century. A paved recreational path—the Benld-Gillespie Bike Trail—connects these two towns along what was once an Interurban rail line. To find it in Gillespie, turn left on Clark

Street from Highway 4 (south side of town) and go about 2 ½ blocks. The trail entry is on the right.

The town of Benld's strange name comes from the first five letters of the name Ben L. Dorsey. He and his son of the same name are buried in the city cemetery.

STAUNTON

In 1923, Staunton High School was defeated by Gillespie High in football by a score of 233-0. Staunton is home to **Henry's Rabbit Ranch**, with a sign that spoofs the billboard at the Jackrabbit Trading Post many miles to the west in Arizona. Look for the Campbell's

Part of the collection at Henry's Rabbit Ranch, Staunton, Illinois.

Staunton, Illinois.

"Humpin' to Please" truck trailer, along with lots more roadie stuff on display. Also adding to the ambience is **VW Ranch**, a display of four-wheeled rabbits up-ended in homage to the Cadillac Ranch in Texas. By the way, they really do raise rabbits here—the four-*legged* variety. The sign for the **Stanley Cour-tel**, a tourist lodging that succumbed to the wrecking ball in greater St. Louis, has found a more or less permanent home here at Henry's. 1107 Old Route 66.

If you've been following the old alignment, Highway 4, then the next town you'll come to is Hamel. You'll need to skip ahead—it comes immediately after the Glenarm-to-Livingston section covered below.

If you elected to skip the old Highway 4 alignment in favor of the more modern route out of Springfield, that narrative—Glenarm through Livingston—follows.

Map showing route from Springfield to Glenarm, Illinois, featuring Lake Springfield, E Lake Shore Dr, Route 66, Interstate 55, New City Rd, and the towns of Glenarm and Springfield.

SPRINGFIELD-to-GLENARM ILLINOIS

GLENARM

A nearby park (north and west of town, off Covered Bridge Road) features

The conventional way to get to Glenarm is along the most modern Route 66 alignment, which runs right beside I-55. However, if you're interested in something a little more "off the beaten path," you can use an alignment older than the modern I-55 corridor but newer than the Highway 4 corridor explained earlier. In either case, your first step is to leave southbound I-55 at Exit 88. Then, turn either right (onto a late 66 frontage road) or left (onto Lake Shore Road), depending on your preference. See Glenarm-area reference map.

the restored Sugar Creek Covered Bridge and shady picnic grounds.

Near Glenarm, Illinois, is a small park which includes this covered bridge.

You'll be forced to enter I-55 at Interchange 82 to continue on your way, but you'll be able to exit again at Interchange 80 for the town of Divernon.

DIVERNON-FARMERSVILLE-WAGGONER

All three of these communities are just to the west of the highway. Divernon has a nice, quiet little town square, which features a few vintage advertising murals on some of the buildings. Look for the Mother Road-era **Art's Motel** at Farmersville and for the **Our Lady of the Highway** shrine south of Waggoner.

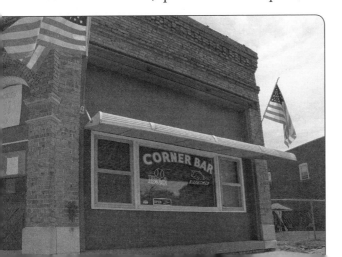

Divernon, Illinois.

Farmersville, Illinois. This sign has been repainted since the photograph was taken.

LITCHFIELD

The **Sky View Drive-In Theater** has been in continual operation since 1951, right on 66 on the outskirts of town.

A longtime Route 66 stopping-place is the **Ariston Café**, which has been in business in the present location since 1935. The first restaurant was in Carlinville, established in 1924, on the old alignment of the route (Highway 4). When Route 66 was re-routed around 1930, the family started up anew in Litchfield—across the street from the current location—and then moved one last time in '35. When Route 66 was realigned yet again (from the street in front to the one in the rear), the Ariston simply added some signage on the back side for the new traffic flow.

North of Litchfield, you should be traveling on the western frontage road. Cross over to the east side of the interstate via County Road 1600 N./N. 16th Avenue. Turn south toward Litchfield, where both Sherman Street and Columbian Boulevard carried Route 66 traffic.

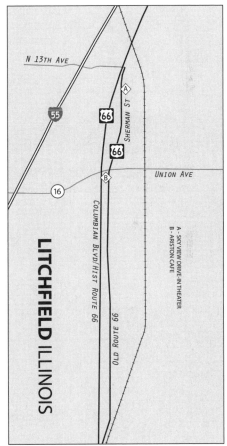

A still-operating drive-in theater, Litchfield, Illinois.

The Ariston Café has been serving locals and travelers alike since the 1920s.

Litchfield, Illinois.

MT. OLIVE

Be sure to stop and see the **Russell Soulsby Shell Station**, a restored jewel originally constructed in the 1920s. The town's cemetery in the northwest corner of town includes the gravesite of **Mother Jones** (Mary Harris), the famous mining activist and labor organizer of the same era, who died in 1930.

Between Litchfield and Mt. Olive, you'll be traveling old Route 66 with the railroad tracks immediately to your left. Look for a left-hand turn just as the main highway begins to veer away from the tracks to keep you on 66 into the heart of town.

MT. OLIVE
ILLINOIS

Soulsby Station, Mt. Olive, Illinois.

LIVINGSTON

By the time 66 was realigned to take in Livingston, it was no longer standard highway practice to take the motorist through the central part of town. Route

At the I-55 Exit 41 interchange, you'll need to cross from the eastern frontage road to the western frontage road, which will take you to Livingston.

66 only nudged Livingston along its southeast edge, just as the interstate does today. After exploring Livingston, continue on the west frontage road toward Hamel.

HAMEL

Keep an eye out for the St. Paul Lutheran Church, with its **blue neon** cross, before you reach Hamel proper. Across the highway from the church is a Meramec Caverns barn, a good view of which is to be had from the Church Road overpass. **Scotty's Roadhouse** started serving highway travelers in Hamel in the 1930s, under the name Tourist Haven, with sleeping accommodations upstairs. Rumor has it that Al Capone and some of his minions stayed here back in the day. 108 S. Old Route 66, south of the Highway 140 junction.

 Continue southwest on Route 66 (now marked Highway 157/Hillsboro Avenue) to Edwardsville.

A crossroads near Hamel, Illinois, includes this message from long ago.

EDWARDSVILLE

The unassuming town of Edwardsville was the scene of some social experimentation in the late 1800s. **LeClaire Village** was a test community founded by industrialist N. O. Nelson

In Edwardsville, Route 66 continues under the guise of Highway 157, entering town from the northeast on Hillsboro, then cutting westward on Vandalia and St. Louis, and finally leaving town headed southwest via West Street and N. Bluff Road.

on the principles of profit sharing and Britain's cooperative movement, and survived as such into the early years of the twentieth century. In the 1930s, it was annexed by the city of Edwardsville, and is now listed as an official historic district. The area is roughly bounded by Longfellow Avenue on the west, Madison on the east, Hadley on the south, and Wolf on the north.

The **Madison County Historical Museum & Archival Library** is housed in the 1836 Weir house with period furnishings, historical costumes, and other exhibits. 715 N. Main St.

FURTHER AFIELD

Directly south of Edwardsville, via Highway 159, is the city of **Collinsville**. Called the Horseradish Capital of the World, the town holds a

Edwardsville, Illinois.

horseradish festival each spring, with horseradish-eating contests, cook-offs, and a horseradish toss competition.

This mosaic adorns the side of a pharmacy in downtown Edwardsville, Illinois.

Collinsville is also the home of the **world's largest ketch-up bottle**, at the old Brooks Foods plant. Built as a water tower, the bottle is about 70 feet tall and stands atop a 100-foot base. Brooks left town years ago, but the bottle replica, constructed in 1949, remains. Local legend states that red-headed offspring may result when pregnant women pass too closely. 800 S. Morrison Ave.

Just west of Collins-ville is **Cahokia Mounds State Historic Site**. Located here are the ruins of a prehistoric city, inhabited from AD 700 to 1400, which covered nearly six square-miles. There are several mounds here, the larg-est of which is called Monk's Mound and is approximately 100 feet high. There are also remains of a sort of wooden stockade, which has been nick-named Woodhenge, due to its astronomical similarity to the world-famous Stonehenge. Partial reconstruction of the site allows for dramatic effects

Collinsville, Illinois.

at the time of the equinoxes. Cahokia is considered the largest prehistoric society on this continent north of Mexico.

Further west is the town of Cahokia. The **Cahokia Courthouse**, originally constructed as a residence in about 1740, was completely disassembled in 1901 and displayed at the 1904 World's Fair across the river in St. Louis. It was then sold at auction and relocated to Chicago, where it was reassembled and stood for many years. In the 1930s it was reacquired by the citizens of Cahokia, and reassembled in 1939 on its original foundation with the aid of historic photographs. (At First and Elm Streets.) The courthouse is actually part of the Colonial Cahokia State Historic Sites complex, which also includes the Jarrot Mansion and the Martin-Boismenue House. The **Jarrot Mansion** was completed in about 1810, and is the former home of one of Cahokia's most prominent citizens. (124 E. First St.) The **Martin-Boismenue House** (1790) is a rare surviving example of French-Creole construction, also on First Street. Both the Jarrot and the Martin-Boismenue hold open houses twice per year; at other times, an appointment for a tour can be arranged by calling 618-332-1782.

Old 66/Highway 157 forms a junction with University Drive east of Mitchell. It's here that you'll have the option of taking eastbound Chain of Rocks Road, which will take you through Mitchell, and also on to the well-known Chain of Rocks Bridge.

MITCHELL

What's left of the **Bel-Air Drive-In Theater** is out on the outskirts of Mitchell next to the Highway 111 junction. The screen is gone; only the marquee remains, and who knows for how long.

Further west in Mitchell, be on the lookout for the **Luna Café**, an authentic roadhouse that predates Route 66, with a neon martini glass incorporated into its sign. 201 E. Chain of Rocks Rd.

If you intend to visit the Chain of Rocks Bridge, be advised that

En route to the Chain of Rocks Bridge, near Mitchell, Illinois.

just west of the Luna Café the road encounters a pretzel-like interchange with I-270, which can be confusing. As a stranger to the area, it could take you more than one attempt to get to the bridge.

According to my 1946 map of Illinois, Route 66 split at the town of Mitchell, with "City 66" veering southwest through Nameoki, Granite City, Madison, and Venice, with a subsequent crossing of the river into the central city of St. Louis. That road is still driveable, and named Nameoki Road/Highway 203. The simple "66" designation belonged to what is now Highway 270, which bypassed urban St. Louis in favor of a beltway route. This is the favored route today, which in the old days crossed the Mississippi via the Chain of Rocks Bridge. You can continue west to Chain of Rocks Bridge, but it no longer carries vehicular traffic over the Mississippi.

Granite City was once known as Six Mile, due to its distance from the Mississippi River. The **Old Six Mile Museum** is housed in the old Emmert-Zippel mansion dating from the 1830s. 3729 Maryville Rd.

The Chain of Rocks Bridge now carries foot and bicycle traffic over the Mississippi River. West of Mitchell, Illinois.

FURTHER AFIELD

Lovers of petroliana may want to take a side trip to Wood River, Illinois, less than 10 miles north of Mitchell. There you'll find the **Wood River Refinery Museum** (formerly the Shell History Museum) in what was formerly part of a refinery on State Highway 111. The complex dates from 1918, when it was operated by Shell Oil Company; after some 80 years, ownership passed to Phillips Petroleum. In addition to the usual pumps, globes, and advertising examples, the museum has on display a number of authentic vehicles, such as an oil tanker and fire truck, which actually saw service at the refinery.

The community of Wood River also is proud to be home to several Sears catalog homes, though of course not as large a collection as Carlinville. If you're interested, check with the folks at the **Wood River Museum and Visitors Center**, at 40 W. Ferguson.

The Illinois prairie is now behind you. Just ahead is the mighty Mississippi River. And beyond that, you and Route 66 will get much better-acquainted.

MISSOURI

Long before there were roads in the modern sense, there were river-roads. Look at any map of any country and be reminded that the older, more established cities—if not on a coastline—were founded

on the banks of rivers, whose currents and near-frictionless surfaces made for quicker and more economical transportation than did the available land-based modes of transport. Yet while rivers have been conducive to transportation and settlement along their lengths, they have at the same time presented barriers to movement where bridges have been few and far between. And so arises their age-old role as natural borders.

The Mississippi is just such a barrier-road, fostering settlement and commerce while at the same time creating a sort of natural pause in America's relentless westward movement. As you cross the Mississippi River, you pass over one of the North American continent's most vital arteries, one which served to nourish and sustain generations of mankind

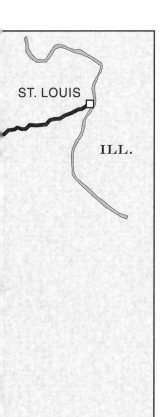

long before the invention of asphalt and the proliferation of the internal combustion engine. What is more, you leave behind the older and more established portion of the American experience, and you pass both physically and spiritually into one of America's most important chapters, that of westward expansion.

Missouri—first at St. Louis, then later at Independence—was long the staging ground for that westward impulse. Situated at the threshold of an enormous, uncharted wilderness, this was the last bastion of civilization and the last chance to prepare and outfit for the rigorous journeys that lay ahead. As Chicago is the starting point for Route 66, so Missouri is the starting place for the famous migratory trails of history that made settlement of the West a reality: the Overland, the Oregon, and the Santa Fe Trails all had their origins here on a Missouri riverbank. And, under the sponsorship of President Thomas Jefferson, a corps led by Meriwether Lewis and William Clark set out from here on their Voyage of Discovery in 1804, eventually finding their way to the Oregon coast.

As for U.S. Highway 66, its crossing of the Mississippi River into the Show-Me State occurred at several places over the years. Today, you will likely want to avoid the older alignments, which crossed the river directly into the central part of St. Louis.

Unfortunately, those alignments of the highway pass through sections of the city in which one does not always feel safe. For that reason, and also because urban alignments tend to fragment over time and be very hard to follow, you are better-advised to approach St. Louis via the "bypass" route, which used to take the traveler across the **Chain of Rocks Bridge**.

Today, the bridge is closed to auto traffic, but it has been turned into a recreational attraction open to pedestrians, and is also the scene of frequent special events. The bridge is just south of Highway 270 and Riverview Boulevard, and is touted as "the world's largest bicycle and pedestrian bridge." This is appropriate. Earlier in its history there was a popular park named Riverview, which sat near the end of the Chain of Rocks Bridge on the Missouri side of the river. There, St. Louisans gathered for picnics, skating, swimming, and softball. **Riverfront Trail** now connects the bridge with the **Gateway Arch** to the south. Up on the bluff overlooking the bridge and the site of the old park, there used to be a fairly elaborate amusement park called **Fun Fair Park**. Fun Fair Park and its sundry attractions failed to survive the competition from Six Flags Over Mid-America, which opened in the early 1970s, just to the west near Eureka.

Opened to traffic from 1929 until the late 1960s, the former toll bridge with the distinctive bend in the middle was used in the filming of 1981's *Escape From New York*. It is here that Adrienne Barbeau's character meets her demise, while Kurt Russell makes his escape.

Today's Mother-Roader crosses the Mississippi just a little north of the Chain of Rocks Bridge on Highway 270. This modern-day loop highway has replaced the old route for several miles along here. Exit Highway 270 at Highway 67 and go south to follow the course of 66 as it once skirted the city. Head due south on 67 until you meet up with the city alignment of 66 at Watson Road, now numbered 366, near the community of Kirkwood. Turn to the east there in order to take in some of what St. Louis has to offer, before continuing your 66 odyssey west.

ST. LOUIS

The city of St. Louis attained what many consider to be its high-water mark in the first decade of the twentieth century. In 1904, the city hosted the World's Fair and summer Olympic Games. The fair was timed to coincide with the centennial of the Louisiana Purchase. The following year, 1905, St. Louis had the dubious distinction of being the city with the first recorded auto theft. At the end of the twentieth century, St. Louis was the fastest-shrinking major city in the U.S., declining by more than 12 percent in population during the 1990s.

The 1904 World's Fair (or St. Louis Exposition) enjoyed a number of distinctions, having played a role in the evolution of ice cream, hamburgers, and iced tea. It was there that ice cream

Route 66 took several paths around and through St. Louis over the years. As with other urban areas, 66 originally passed through the downtown business district, but later was re-routed to avoid central-city congestion by creating beltline or bypass routes. For most of its life, U.S. 66 was marked to offer the driver two or more choices in traversing the area, depending on his or her objectives. There's plenty to do and see in St. Louis, so today's roadie will want to stray from the standard alignments anyway.

was first served in cones when a Syrian immigrant named Ernest Hamwi came to the rescue of an ice cream vendor who had run out of serving dishes. By the end of the fair, it was reported that several vendors were selling ice cream in folded waffles.

That same fair was also the scene of the mass introduction of the hamburger on a bun, a development which had originated just a little earlier in New Haven, Connecticut. And, an Englishman named Richard Blechyden, tea concessionaire, determined that the weather was simply too hot for his tea to sell well. His solution was to ice it down, thus creating the decidedly un-English iced tea.

The 1904 fair was held at **Forest Park**—then the nation's largest urban park, at over 1,300 acres—which is still very much a part of present-day St. Louis. Forest Park contains the St. Louis Zoological Park, the St. Louis Art Museum, and the Missouri History Museum. There are also some giant turtle sculptures on the south side of the park. Judy Garland starred in a 1944 musical entitled *Meet Me in St. Louis*, which portrayed the year the world came to visit the city (the title song, "Meet Me in St. Louis, Louis," actually dates from the year of the exposition). It was during the filming of that movie that Judy Garland became romantically involved with her future husband, Vicente Minelli.

Charles Lindbergh's famous airplane, *Spirit of St. Louis*, was so named because his backers for the trans-oceanic flight consisted of the *St. Louis Globe Democrat* newspaper and a group of local businessmen who wanted to promote their city as a center of aviation. Lindbergh had earlier approached the American Tobacco Company with the idea of naming the craft for their Lucky Strike Cigarettes (he was already named "Lucky" Lindy by that time), but the company refused to back the venture. There is a replica of the *Spirit of St. Louis* at the **Missouri History Museum** (Forest Park, Lindell at DeBaliviere). This replica was manufactured by the same firm that made the original, and it was used in the Jimmy Stewart movie, *The Spirit of St. Louis*.

In 1907, St. Louis became the home of the first gasoline station chain, the American Gasoline Company.

Betty Grable, pin-up girl par excellence during World War II, was from St. Louis and lived at the Forest Park Hotel. Vincent Price graduated from St. Louis' Country Day School. Miles Davis and Chuck Berry both were born here. And another St. Louis native, the moody T. S. Eliot, won the Nobel Prize for Literature in 1948; then, well after his death, one of his lighter works, *Old Possum's Book of Practical Cats*, inspired the Broadway musical comedy *CATS*. You will be amazed at the number of St. Louisans who have made it big in the world and have been inducted into the city's **Walk of Fame** on Delmar Avenue (see Attractions, below).

Here in St. Louis, there's a Route 66 institution still going strong which you simply must pay a visit to: **Ted Drewes Frozen Custard**, at 6726 Chippewa. The building itself is an important landmark, but the crucial thing is that here is a business that still believes in the older values of quality product and personal service. They've never "sold out" for a fast buck, and their adoring public appreciates it. Their list of mouth-watering toppings is printed right on the side of the building to stoke your anticipation. Stop by some morning before opening time and watch the people begin to flock in from all over. In no time at all, the place will be mobbed, and it happens virtually every day. And check to see if there's still a mannequin peering out from one of the upstairs windows.

Ted Drewes' Frozen Custard is still a popular stop for both roadies and St. Louisans, as it has been since the heyday of Route 66.

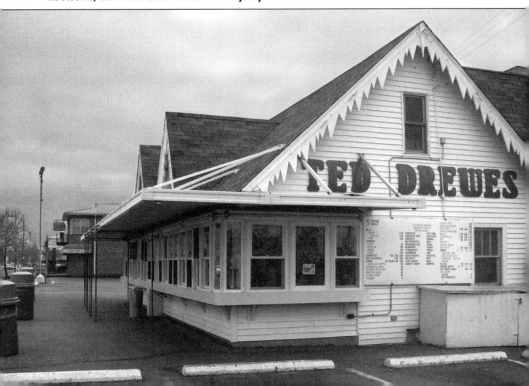

Before leaving St. Louis and hitting the road once again, consider going down to the riverfront area that the Highway 270 alignment avoided on your way in. The **Jefferson Expansion Memorial** includes the Gateway Arch and the Museum of Western Expansion at its foot. Eero Saarinen's famous 630-foot archway aptly symbolizes the area's role as gateway to the West. The arch contains a pair of elevator-trams that swivel as they ascend to the top, sort of like a ferris-wheel car, constituting a feat of engineering in and of themselves. There is a terrific panoramic view from the top of the arch, and there is also a film, *Monument to the Dream*, which details its construction (the arch was completed in 1965). The adjacent museum, which is as large as a football field, presents information about the Louisiana Purchase and the Jefferson-sponsored Lewis and Clark expedition. Also part of the memorial complex is the **Old Courthouse**. This building originates from 1839, and was the site of the early trials of the Dred Scott case, which was ultimately decided by the United States Supreme Court in 1857.

Elsewhere downtown, the old **Union Station** railroad depot has been nicely converted to a luxury hotel and eclectic shopping venue.

ST. LOUIS ATTRACTIONS

At 6504 Delmar is the **Blueberry Hill Café**. You can spend considerable time here just admiring the great memorabilia on display, including posters, album covers, and vintage toys, but a more "gut" reason to come is for the extraordinary burgers. The Blueberry Hill also plays host to the largest annual dart tournament in the United States, with approximately 500 entrants each year.

Also on Delmar Avenue, just down the street from the Blueberry Hill, is an indoor arcade where the clock from the city's demolished **Route 66 Drive-In Theater** is on display. At 6605 Delmar is **Fitz's American Grill and Bottling Works**, where you can enjoy your meal and watch Fitz's Root Beer being bottled at the same time. The equipment dates from the 1940s, and is visible from the main dining area.

In the 6100 thru 6600 blocks of Delmar is the **St. Louis Walk**

of Fame. There are stars embedded in the sidewalk on both sides of the street honoring nearly a hundred men and women who have a St. Louis connection, and who have made an impact on the world at large. They run the gamut from Yogi Berra to Josephine Baker, from William Burroughs to Virginia Mayo. The same stretch of Delmar became the home of the **Delmar Loop Planet Walk** in 2009. It's a walkable (2,880 feet) "model" of the solar system, where the representations of the sun and planets are proportionally spaced according to their real-world relationships.

During prohibition, local brewery Anheuser-Busch sold non-alcoholic brews from the **Bevo Mill**, a replica of a Dutch-style windmill built in 1916. The Bevo still stands, and was recently refurbished for its new life as a special-events venue. 4749 Gravois Rd. Across the street, at 4746 Gravois, is the **Miniature Museum of Greater St. Louis**.

St. Louis' **City Museum** is located in the heart of the loft and garment district, and is more offbeat than its name would imply. It is housed in the International Arts Complex, which was formerly the home of the International Shoe and Rand Shoe companies, two of the leading shoe manufacturing firms of yesteryear. Included among the exhibits is the Tiny Trailer of Tragedy, once owned by Elvis and Priscilla Presley, as well as the world's largest pair of underpants. The museum has also added a rooftop water park. 701 N. 15th St.

Formerly on display at the City Museum, but since relocated to the Brown Shoe Company headquarters, is the **Shoe of Shoes**. It consists of hundreds—perhaps thousands—of cast-metal life-size shoes welded together in the shape of one enormous woman's pump. This city used to be so well-known for its shoes that at one time wags used to say of St. Louis: "First in shoes, first in booze, and last in the American League." Of course, that was when the St. Louis Browns were still playing America's pastime. At Maryland Avenue and Topton Way in the suburb of Clayton (west St. Louis).

Faust Park includes an 1820 estate home, historical village, butterfly house, and a restored Dentzel carousel on property that was formerly owned by the second governor of Missouri. 15185 Olive Blvd.

Anheuser-Busch Brewery, the world's largest, has tours, beer tastings, and brewing demonstrations. And don't forget the world-famous Clydesdales. 1127 Pestalozzi St.

Calvary Cemetery covers more than 400 acres and includes the gravesites of such notables as playwright Tennessee Williams, General William Tecumseh Sherman, and Dred Scott. There is also a large crucifix marking the location of a mass grave. At the time of the cemetery's establishment, earlier burials of Native Americans were collected and reinterred at that spot. 5239 W. Florissant. Adjacent to Calvary is **Bellefontaine Cemetery**, where explorer William Clark and other notables are buried.

The **Ulysses S. Grant Historic Site**, at 7400 Grant Street, was the Grant family residence from 1854 to 1858 and known as White Haven. Adjacent to it, at 10501 Gravois, is **Grant's Farm**, a ranch with free-roaming animals, an 1856 log cabin, breeding Clydesdales, and a fence made from Civil War rifle barrels. The property was purchased by the Busch family (brewers) in 1903.

The **Campbell House Museum**, the first home built in the elegant Lucas Place neighborhood, has been restored to its 1880s prime and is open for tours Wednesday thru Saturday. The home still has many of the original furnishings, including some of the family carriages. Corner of 15th and Locust.

Canine lovers won't want to miss the **American Kennel Club Museum of the Dog**. The permanent collection includes a great many oil paintings and other works of art devoted to man's best friend, some by household names like William Wegman. Rotating exhibits have included matchbook cover art portraying dogs. 1721 S. Mason Rd.

The **Eugene Field House & St. Louis Toy Museum** is at 634 S. Broadway. Son of a prominent attorney, Mr. Field was known as the Children's Poet, as well as Father of the Personal Newspaper Column. His former home now features the Field family possessions, a book collection spanning 250 years, and antique and collectible toys.

The **St. Louis Car Museum** has more than 150 legendary vehicles on display. 1575 Woodson Rd.

The **St. Louis Fire Department Museum** has a unique and extensive collection that includes leather fire buckets, glass "hand grenade" extinguishers, and insurance-company-issued fire plaques dating to the 1700s. 1421 N. Jefferson Ave.

Take a tour of the **Samuel Cupples House** on the grounds of St. Louis University. The 42-room mansion was built in 1888, and features gargoyles, ornate stonework, and 22 fireplaces. It also boasts Tiffany glasswork and other decorative arts dating from the fifteenth century onward. On the third floor is a special exhibit, the Turshin Fine Arts Glass Collection of American and European Art Glass. 3673 West Pine Mall.

Also open for tours is the **Scott Joplin House State Historic Site**, at 2658 Delmar. Here Joplin and his wife kept a modest flat, circa 1902. There is a music room with an operating player piano so visitors can experience first-hand the type of ragtime piano that Joplin used himself. West of Jefferson Avenue.

The **Cherokee-Lemp Historic District** is a south-side neighborhood with two nineteenth-century mansions (the Lemp and the DeMenil), as well as the **Lemp Brewery**, which was once the largest in the world. The Lemp Mansion (now an inn and restaurant) is said to be haunted by the spirits of four family members who committed suicide in the house, and a fifth who died there under the proverbial "mysterious circumstances." The district is bounded by the streets of Cherokee, Lemp, Utah, and DeMenil.

Jasper's Antique Radio Museum has over 10,000 radios in its collection, making it the largest in the world. The owner, Jasper Giardina, has the stated goal of finding, repairing, and restoring any radio that he crosses paths with. You'll see everything from fully-restored examples to basket cases fresh from the attic, and everything in between. Many are for sale. 2022 Cherokee St.

Here's an unusual attraction: the **Delta Dental Health Theater**. Dental "instructors" combine education and entertainment using a set of 16 three-foot-tall fiberglass teeth. The teeth light up from within as each is described, and you'll be shown exactly the right technique for brushing—using a really large toothbrush, of course. Admission is free; the theater is located at 727 N. First Street.

Open only on the first Saturday of the month, the **Compton Hill Water Tower** was built in 1898, in a style described as French Romanesque.

The observation deck offers a 360-degree view after a climb of 198 steps. S. Grand Boulevard at Russell.

The **Kemp Auto Museum** specializes in Mercedes-Benz automobiles, with specimens as early as 1886. 16955 Chesterfield Airport Rd.

The **Moto Museum** is a collection of motorcycles representing more than a dozen countries of manufacture. 3441 Olive Street, across from St. Louis University.

FURTHER AFIELD

Just northwest of St. Louis is the city of **St. Charles**. There is a visitors' bureau at 230 W. Main Street. The central business district was named the "Williamsburg of the West" by a national magazine.

St. Charles is where Lewis and Clark began their long journey of discovery after camping here in the spring of 1804. You can see the departure point for Lewis and Clark's expedition—Bishop's Landing—at the **Lewis & Clark Boat House and Nature Center**, 1050 S. Riverside Drive. Replicas of the vessels used in the voyage can be seen on the lower "boathouse" level, while the museum level above has extensive exhibits of other kinds.

In the St. Charles historic district, at 200-216 Main, is the **First Missouri State Capitol Historic Site**. This federal-style row house is where the territorial government met in 1821–26 to reorganize into a state system of government. Sessions were held here until the new capitol building in Jefferson City was ready for use in October of 1826. Included are legislative chambers, two residences, a dry goods store, and a carpentry shop, all of which have been restored to period appearance.

St. Charles is also home to the Missouri Wing of the **Commemorative Air Force** (CAF). The CAF is dedicated to preserving WWII-era aircraft in flying condition as "a tribute to the men and women who built, serviced, and flew them in the defense of democracy." This is the same organization formerly known as the Confederate Air Force; the name was changed for the sake of political correctness, but of course they never had anything to do with the War Between the States, anyway. Stop in and browse the collection of vintage warplanes on Thursdays and Saturdays.

If you've still got some time to spend in St. Charles, there's the **Shrine of St. Rose Phillippine Duchesne** at 619 N. Second Street, site of the first free school west of the Mississippi River. It was established in 1818 by Missouri's only saint, who was canonized in 1988.

Heading back out on our tour of Route 66, the next stop is a suburb on the southwest edge of St. Louis known as:

KIRKWOOD

Kirkwood, while once a distinct community, has been more or less absorbed by its sprawling neighbor, St. Louis. There is a very nicely restored railroad station in the old Kirkwood business district. The downtown business district in general has also undergone some nice work to make a pleasant, pedestrian-friendly area.

A few blocks south of the railroad depot is the **Magic House**, a children's museum that now occupies a former mansion built by George Lane Edwards, a director of the St. Louis Exposition, in 1901. 516 S. Kirkwood.

There is a **Frank Lloyd Wright** residence—one of only five Wright-designed structures in the entire state of Missouri—at 120 N. Ballas, in the Sugar Creek area of Kirkwood (just off Dougherty Ferry Road). Tours are available, but must be arranged in advance by calling 314-822-8359. Built in the 1950s, the house is particularly notable in that it is virtually 100 percent authentic, right down to the original furnishings.

Kirkwood is also home to the **Museum of Transportation**, at 3015 Barrett Station Road, not far from the junction of 270 and Dougherty Ferry Road. The museum has an automobile pavilion, as well as several tracks of locomotives and other railroad stock for you to tour and enjoy. The autos include a 1963 Chrysler Turbine, and a custom-built aluminum car made in 1960 and used in the Bobby Darin movie *Too Cool Blues*. Among the railroad exhibits are the last steam locomotive to operate in

One of the many interesting displays at the Museum of Transportation, Kirkwood, Missouri.

Missouri, a wooden caboose, a complete passenger train, a tank car, and the "Big Boy," the world's largest-ever steam locomotive. Also on display are a tow boat and a C-47 military transport, which flew in the Second World War. But most important to Route 66 fans is the fact that the museum now includes the façade from one of the **Coral Court Motel** units, on exhibit inside. The Coral Court was a very special example of highway architecture from the heyday of postwar travel, and it stood not far from here until "redevelopment" took it in 1995. Thankfully, a small part of it has been preserved for your enjoyment. Built in 1941 of glazed hollow brick and glass block in the Streamline Moderne style, the Coral Court, even when new, was evocative of another time. Legend has it that bank robbers once stashed loot in the hollow walls of one or more units, of which the Coral Court once boasted more than seventy.

TIMES BEACH

This was a planned community that was established in about 1925, just on the eve of the birth of the federal highway system. Lots were sold or given away by the *St. Louis Star-Times* newspaper as part of a promotion, hence the name. What happened at Times Beach, however, shouldn't happen to anyone. Residents were forced to evacuate decades later when it was determined that the ground on which the community sat had been contaminated with dioxins, which had been present in the materials used to spray on the roads for dust control. That evacuation occurred in 1982. Fortunately, the site was the object of cleanup efforts for years, and has since been turned into the **Missouri Route 66 State Park**, with trails, picnic areas, and river access. The visitor center includes Route 66 exhibits, and is housed in a vintage roadhouse building that dates to 1936. Exit 266 from I-44.

EUREKA

West of Eureka is **Six Flags Over Mid-America**, one of those large-scale theme parks which adds immeasurably to the traffic in this area. South of I-44 at

After visiting Route 66 State Park, leave the interstate again at Exit 264 and cross to the south side. Follow W. Main Street out of town toward Allenton.

Exit 264 in Eureka is the **Black Madonna Shrine and Grottos**. Built by a Franciscan brother entirely by hand, the grottoes are "dedicated to the Black Madonna, Our Lady of Czestochowa, Queen of Peace and Mercy." These ornamental works of faith have become known far and wide. 100 St. Joseph's Rd.

Founded by Dr. Marlin Perkins of *Wild Kingdom* fame, the **Endangered Wolf Center** (formerly Wild Canid Research Center) has since 1971 sought to protect and preserve endangered wolf species through educational programs and captive breeding. 6750 Tyson Valley Road, east of Eureka at I-44 Exit 269.

ALLENTON-PACIFIC

When it's time to leave Allenton, cross to the north side of the railroad tracks to I-40 Business Loop/66.

In this vicinity is the Al-Pac Motel (Allenton-Pacific, of course!). About a mile east of Pacific is the **Red Cedar Inn**, a café and former hotel that first started serving travelers on this stretch of road around 1934. In recent years the city has flirted with the idea of taking over the Red Cedar Inn, now closed, for a community museum or similar endeavor, but the idea has not gotten off the ground. One of the more distinctive features of Pacific is the presence of some prominent bluffs along the north side of the highway. These were considered interesting enough that they found their way onto many an early postcard of the

Near Allenton, Missouri.

area. There are several cave-like cavities that resulted from silica mining.

Now closed, the Red Cedar Inn has become the focus of local preservation efforts. Pacific, Missouri.

GRAY SUMMIT

This town is best known for its association with Ralston-Purina. Just north of Gray Summit, on County Road MM, is **Purina Farms**. This compound holds canine events through most of the year, which include agility trials, herding competitions, all breed shows, and racing. One of my personal favorites is the Jack Russell Fun Days, sponsored by the Missouri Earth Dog Club. These dogs are incredibly enthusiastic about racing around, rooting things out of holes in the ground, and just all-around cavorting. Aside from being fun for pets and owners alike, many of the events presented at Purina Farms are educational as well. There are workshops in dog-obedience training, for example. You can also learn to milk a cow or operate a simulated pet-food manufacturing machine.

Just across the interstate from Gray Summit is the 2,500-acre **Shaw Nature Reserve**, an extension of the Missouri Botanical Garden, where prairie flora and fauna are preserved, and a visitor center, historic home, and several miles of hiking trails await.

VILLA RIDGE

Near Villa Ridge is the **Gardenway Motel**, a colonial style motel that probably graced the front of many a postcard in its prime. Notice the glass-block detailing in the roadside sign. A little further to the west is what remains of the Tri-County Truck Stop.

West of the Tri-County is the **Sunset Motel**, which has a unique sunburst-style sign, whose neon was restored and ceremonially re-lit in 2009.

Villa Ridge, Missouri.

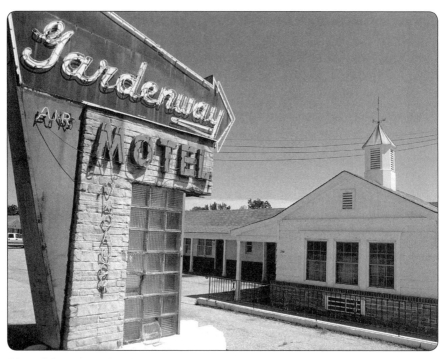

West of Gray Summit, Missouri.

Sign at the former Diamonds Restaurant, near Villa Ridge, Missouri.

ST. CLAIR

This town was formerly known as Traveler's Repose, but it's said the townsfolk grew tired of being thought of as a cemetery. There used to be a motel here with an eye-catching sign, the Arch Motel, overlooking the superslab. For many years, St. Clair was the home of Ozark Rock Curios, a purveyor of interesting geological specimens to Route 66 tourists.

The **St. Clair Historical Museum** contains 23 exhibits, including Native American artifacts and mining-related items, as well as a Victorian parlor, doctor's office, and general store. The museum is housed in a former Odd Fellows Hall, at 280 Hibbard Street.

Between St. Clair and Stanton, if you follow the road paralleling the railroad track (W. Springfield Road) on the south side of I-44, you'll be taken on an old alignment of the highway through Anaconda. The town is about midway between St. Clair and Stanton, and was named Morrellton when my 1946 road map was printed. By the time my '57 atlas was printed, the town had been completely bypassed by the new alignment, and it bore the current name of Anaconda. Unfortunately, that road no longer continues to Stanton.

Alongside the highway just east of Stanton formerly stood the Ozark Court Motel, which had a distinctive sign featuring a prancing deer.

STANTON

This community is best known as the gateway to the **Meramec Caverns** to the south.

Former motel with a distinctive sign near Stanton, Missouri.

STANTON ATTRACTIONS

You'll want to stop in for a look at the **Antique Toy Museum**, near I-44 Exit 230 (State Highway W). There are thousands of first-rate antique and collectible toy cars, trucks, tractors, trains, etc., as well as dolls, doll houses, and doll furniture. There are even a few full-size antique trucks on the premises for the really big boys in the family (including one nicknamed the Big Mack Attack).

A neighbor to the toy museum is the **Jesse James Museum**, a true roadside attraction. The central focus of this museum is that Jesse James didn't really die of a gunshot wound in 1881 as the authorities have been telling us all these years—he actually lived to a ripe old age under another name and died in 1952! There are even wax figures of the conspirators in this diabolical plot to mislead the public. The museum staff will enthusiastically heap evidence upon you of their version of Jesse's life, such as a list of physical traits (scars, etc.) shared by the original Jesse and the mystery man who survived until well into the Route 66 era.

Also very near the two museums above is **Riverside Reptile Ranch**, where you can see a wide variety of native and non-native snakes and other reptilians.

FURTHER AFIELD

Just a few miles south and east of Route 66, via Highway W, is one of the route's most widely-known attractions, **Meramec Caverns**. In fact, a trip to Meramec Caverns is more a required pilgrimage than a side trip for anyone traveling the Mother Road. That's largely because clever marketing made this cave almost a part of any trip down 66.

Lester Dill opened Meramec Caverns commercially in 1935, and managed successfully to portray his caverns as a former hideout of Jesse James, even though the evidence for this is fairly thin. Secondly, he paid to have the sides and roofs of barns all over the country painted with his "logo" so that motorists far and wide were made aware of Meramec Caverns. The barns dotted the countryside not just along Route 66, the

Part of Meramec Caverns, a traditional tourist destination on Route 66, near Stanton, Missouri.

highway that takes one there, but on roadsides all over the Midwest (some estimates place the number at around 350). Thirdly, each visitor to Meramec Caverns became an advertisement for the attraction. That's because the Dill clan pioneered the bumper sticker. Youngsters were paid to ensure that each vehicle in their parking lot left with a Meramec Caverns tag tied to their rear bumper. The combination of these strategies made Meramec Caverns not just one of the best-known caves in the country, but one of the most-recognized attractions of any kind whatsoever.

Inside, in addition to the usual underground formations, there is a neon sign proclaiming "Jesse James Hideout," and nearby is Loot Rock, where facsimiles of Jesse and his gang divide the spoils of their latest heist. Also included is a moonshiners' cave. The tour climaxes with a light show projecting the Stars and Stripes onto a structure called the Stage Curtain—the largest such formation in the world—while Kate Smith belts out "God Bless America."

Adjacent facilities include a motel, campground, gift shop, restaurant, and canoe rentals (with shuttle service).

Note on barn painting: Well-informed roadies will know of an attraction near Lookout Mountain, Georgia, that began featuring painted barns back in 1936. The barns, once numbering about 900, covered 19 states with the See Rock City motif. About 80 of those barns remain, according to recent count, and Rock City itself is still going strong.

Very near Meramec Caverns as the crow flies is the much lesser-known **Fisher's Cave** on the grounds of Meramec State Park. However, you'll need to approach it via Highway 185 from a junction just east of Sullivan. Visitors use hand-held lanterns to explore these caves during a 90-minute tour on paved walkways. This cave is said to have been in use since the 1860s, when then-governor Thomas Fletcher organized a celebration there. 2800 S. Highway 185.

Meramec and Fisher are just the first of several caves which will be in striking distance of Route 66 as we sweep through Missouri. For cavers, Missouri is a paradise. At last count, there were more than 5,400 *registered* caves in the state.

 Leaving Stanton, use the S. Outer Road (not Springfield Avenue). The road will hug the interstate all the way to Sullivan.

SULLIVAN

George Hearst, whose son William Randolph later made his name in the publishing business, was born on a farm near Sullivan. George made *his* fortune in

> Old Route 66 becomes E. Springfield Road. At Elmont, you'll need to turn right and then left on the service road on the west side of the freeway.

mining. In the **Odd Fellows Cemetery** on N. Church Street is the grave of Jim "Sunny" Bottomley, Hall of Fame baseball player for the St. Louis Cardinals.

BOURBON

The main street through town is marked "OLD HWY 66." The town slogan? "Make Our Bourbon Your Bourbon." The town's water tower has become a popular photographic subject.

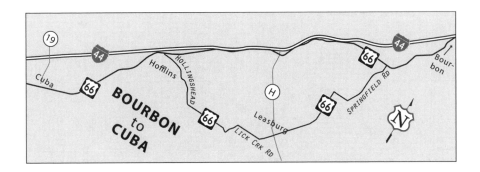

 About two-thirds of the way from Bourbon to Cuba, right where the railroad track sidles up close to the south side of I-44 and just east of Exit 210, is the site of a town called Hofflins. A full-fledged town in the 1940s, my 1957 atlas chose to omit it completely. That atlas shows U.S. 66 in this vicinity as already a four-lane divided highway. That highway growth nearly on its doorstep—along with the concomitant traffic— likely made Hofflins unlivable for its residents. Today, little remains.

After Hofflins, old 66 wanders away from the interstate and towards the town of Cuba.

CUBA

Cuba has adopted the nickname "Mural City," thanks to more than a dozen outdoor artworks scattered through the town. One of those murals adorns the side of a restored Phillips 66 station at the corner of Washington and Franklin Streets. The station is at an intersection known locally as the "Four-Way." Washington Boulevard is the former U.S. 66, while Franklin Street is Highway 19,

Downtown Cuba, Missouri.

The Wagon Wheel still serves travelers passing through Cuba, Missouri.

the first designated "scenic route" in the state.

The most important feature of Cuba to a Route 66 traveler is the **Wagon Wheel Motel**, which not only is still in operation, but looks every bit as inviting as the day it opened for business. If you haven't stayed in a good old-fashioned mom-and-pop motel yet on this trip, this is an excellent place to do so, since the current ownership is intent on restoring it to a really nice condition. If you'll be moving on, then just stay around long enough to snap a few photos and appreciate the one-of-a-kind sign, with its neon-trimmed wagon wheel suspended over the road.

The **Crawford County Historical Society Museum** occupies a two-story 1934 building at 308 N. Smith Street, across from the library. Just north of town on Highway 19 is the **Highway 19 Drive-In Theater**, still showing films as it has since 1954.

Business is not what it used to be in Cuba, Missouri.

Fanning, Missouri.

FANNING-ROSATI

West of Cuba you'll encounter the small community of Fanning. A recent addition to the roadside is the Fanning U.S. 66 Outpost and General Store, which is home to the **World's Largest Rocker**. The Guinness-certified chair was erected in 2008, and is more than 40 feet tall.

The area around Rosati is known for its grape vineyards. Years ago, the area was thick with vendors offering grapes from small roadside stands. Today there are a number of operating wineries in the vicinity.

ST. JAMES

Finn's Motel draws travelers here with its neon sign, not far from the **St. James Winery**. Opened in 2009, the **Vacuum Cleaner Museum** is an offshoot of local vacuum maker Tacony Manufacturing. The museum

Route 66 becomes James Boulevard through town. After exploring St. James, drop down to Springfield Road—the old route toward Dillon and Rolla. Once you reach the Highway V junction, site of the Mule Trading Post, cross to the opposite side of I-44 and use the North Outer Road to continue.

exhibits models from as early as 1910, and the displays are organized

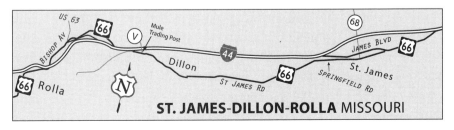

ST. JAMES-DILLON-ROLLA MISSOURI

by decade, with carpeting and furniture of each era adding to the atmosphere. #3 Industrial Drive, east side of town.

FURTHER AFIELD

About eight miles southeast of St. James via Missouri State Highway 8 is **Maramec Spring Park** [sic]. Maramec Spring proper is a National Natural Landmark, and it exudes some

St. James, Missouri.

96 million gallons of water each day from the base of a bluff. This spring used to provide the power for the Maramec Iron Works, established circa 1857, the ruins of which can still be seen within the park.

Leave St. James on Springfield Road, which becomes St. James Road as you approach Dillon (see the reference map). As you leave the vicinity of St. James and continue your southwesterly trek across Missouri, you are leaving the Big Prairie section of the state and climbing atop the Ozark Plateau. You will begin to see a change in the topology as you encounter exposed rock outcroppings more and more. The hilly Ozark region, which extends into northwestern Arkansas, is well-known as moonshine territory and home of the Hatfields and the McCoys.

DILLON

South of I-44, Dillon had already been bypassed by 1957 in favor of a faster, four-lane alignment in the corridor now occupied by the interstate. On the opposite (north) side of the interstate, on the frontage road, is **Route 66 Motors**. At the time I visited, they had an impressive array of signs on display outside, making an excellent photo-op. Also on hand were gasoline pumps, a power boat, and sundry vehicles in various stages

Near Dillon, Missouri.

of neglect or restoration.

The **Mule Trading Post** is still in business near I-44's Highway V exit. The Mule moved here in 1957 from Pacific. In 2007, the Mule's proprietors added a giant hillbilly sign with rotating arms.

NORTHWYE

This village did not appear on my 1946 map, but evidently the U.S. 63/66 junction location spurred growth. By 1957, it was plotted by the cartographers. Now the location is home to **Memoryville USA**, an antique auto museum and gift shop, which also features a working automobile restoration workshop where you can see works in progress. Displays include a fully-restored 1938 Nash Lafayette formerly owned by radio personality Paul Harvey.

ROLLA

Named after the North Carolina capital, but spelled more phonetically, based upon a southern drawl. Rolla has a surprisingly active downtown, with the Ritz and Uptown theaters, Lambiel Jewelers, and Alex's Pizza keeping things going. It doesn't hurt that it's a college town.

The Missouri University of Science and Technology

Route 66 enters Rolla from the north along U.S. 63/Bishop Avenue, and for most of its life skirted the west edge of downtown. As always, I recommend exploring downtown, which has plenty to offer, before rejoining Bishop Avenue for parts west.

Downtown Rolla, Missouri.

is proud to be not-your-average university. They have their own mine rescue team and extensive mineral collection, and have created some works of art using high-pressure water-jet technology: a scale model of Stonehenge and a sculpture called *The Millenium Arch*.

ROLLA ATTRACTIONS

The **Dillon House** is a log structure which served as the area's first courthouse circa 1857. The logs used are 18 feet in length. Third and Main. The **Phelps County Jail**, built in 1860, is on the National Register. Park Street between Second and Third.

The **Totem Pole Trading Post** was moved to the west side of Rolla more than 30 years ago from its original location near Clementine. The carved totem pole, which used to adorn the roof of the old trading post, is now on display indoors at the present location. 1413 Martin Springs Drive, where 44 Business Loop meets I-44. The building really doesn't look anything like what you think a "trading post" should, with a huge modern overhang sheltering the gas pumps.

Mule Trading Post, eastern outskirts of Rolla, Missouri.

Leaving Rolla, you are heading into the heart of Ozark country. Keep an eye out for some curbed sections of the highway as you leave town headed west on Martin Springs Road.

The Rolla-to-Springfield portion of Route 66 here in Missouri roughly follows the infamous **Cherokee Trail of Tears**. There were a number of variants on the route of the forced march from Georgia to Oklahoma, and the Northern Route went through this very corridor, circuitous as it may seem. It began in 1838, when a combination of congressional maneuvering, along with some wholesale trickery, led to the expulsion of the Cherokee people from their homes in Georgia. That year, U.S. troops under the command of General Winfield Scott began rounding up men, women, and children and herding them hundreds of miles across the country. As implied by the name, many perished along the way.

In recognition of this fact, someone has paid tribute by building a stone gateway to his property, over which hangs a sign proclaiming simply "Trail of Tears." The work that went into this tribute is nothing short of astounding: there is the arched gateway, several walls, circular wheel-like formations, more arches, and obelisk-like objects, all constructed of thousands of stones piled upon one another. Keep on the alert as you pass through the area near Arlington.

DOOLITTLE

The town was named for air-racer and World War II hero Jimmy Doolittle of Alameda, California. Doolittle set a world speed record in 1932; in 1942, he led the famous attack on Tokyo and other cities by B-25s that were launched from the aircraft carrier U.S.S. Hornet. That raid, coming as it did only a few

Doolittle, Missouri.

months after Pearl Harbor, was a tremendous boost to American morale, and was later dramatized in the film *Thirty Seconds Over Tokyo*, starring Spencer Tracy. Doolittle also served in Italy, Germany, and North Africa during the war.

Before joining I-44 at Interchange 176, you can make a short side trip for something you really should stop and see. **John's Modern Cabins** was a tourist abode made up of a set of small wooden cabins. These were some rather primitive accommodations, as evidenced by the remains of an outhouse in the rear. Somewhat ironically, in the midst of this rather rustic encampment, a neon sign glowed in "modern" welcome. A stone's throw away from the cabins is **Vernelle's Motel**, which has a vacant convenience store of the vintage variety out front. John's and Vernelle's were bypassed many years ago, but a further realignment of I-44 just a few years ago isolated them even further.

ARLINGTON

On the bank of the Little Piney River, the town of Arlington has been pretty effectively cut off from highway traffic, and you might assume that this was a result of the replacement of U.S. 66 by Interstate 44. However, if you read Jack Rittenhouse's 1946 account of his passage through here, you learn that Arlington had already been cut off by that time due to earlier construction. He went on to state that the area was rumored to be earmarked for development of a resort. More than 60 years later, Arlington is a quiet place indeed.

Onyx Mountain Caverns is just to the west of the highway

Above: **Tribute to the Cherokee Trail of Tears, near Arlington, Missouri.**
Left: **Town center of Arlington, Missouri.**
Below: **Part of John's Modern Cabins, near Arlington, Missouri.**

between Powellville and Clementine, and appears as King Cave on some earlier maps.

CLEMENTINE

Rittenhouse stated that Clementine was "hardly a town," and it does not appear (nor does Powellville) on 1946 or 1957 maps of the region. At one time, this area was characterized by its numerous basket vendors arrayed beside the highway. Today, there is little to nothing left of these communities, other than a small cemetery that can be reached by taking Clementine Outer Road east from Exit 169.

  After Clementine/Exit 169, you will need to take Highway Z (south side of the interstate) in order to pass through the village of Devil's Elbow.

DEVIL'S ELBOW

The ominous name of Devil's Elbow comes not from any highway hazard, but rather from the fact that there is a severe bend in the Big Piney River here, which caused problems for those whose livelihoods depended on trans-

> The early Route 66 alignment was extremely convoluted, not only at the river crossing itself, but also for much of its eastern approach to the town. Looking at it closely, it's easy to see why the highway was straightened by construction of the Hooker Cut in order to facilitate the passage of trucks.

port of goods up and down the waterway. There is a 1920s-era bridge that crosses the river here, and carried Route 66 traffic in the highway's early years. However, the narrow bridge and twisting roads in the vicinity were considered a real problem during the war years when military materiel began being transported back and forth, and so the highway

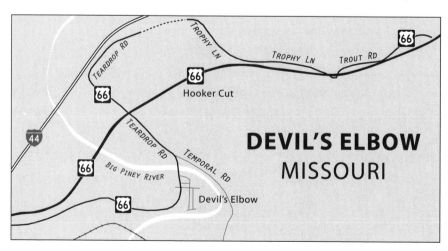

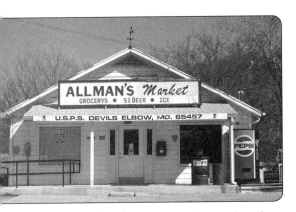

This store has for many years served as the post office for the small hamlet of Devil's Elbow, Missouri.

was re-routed for a straighter course. You can see the wandering course 66 took prior to the war era by looking at the reference map: old 66 followed Trout Road, Trophy Lane, and Teardrop Road to the town of Devil's Elbow. As a truck driver, that had to have been some headache.

The Munger Moss Sandwich Shop plied its trade here at the town of Devil's Elbow (at the location of the current **Elbow Inn**), but during the highway's re-alignment in the 1940s, both the town and the restaurant were unceremoniously cut-off, and so the proprietors moved to Lebanon and eventually established the Munger Moss Motel.

There is a combination post office and general store in Devil's Elbow, which has changed its name over the years from Miller's to Allman's to Sheldon's, but otherwise it has looked very much the same for decades.

 Continue on Highway Z (south side of freeway) to St. Robert.

ST. ROBERT

St. Robert is a young community by Route 66 standards, having been chartered in 1951. The town seems to have been engendered by the growth in local population, spurred by the establishment of Fort Leonard Wood during the Second World War. There is a small historical museum in the municipal center at 194 Eastlawn Avenue, Suite A.

The **Pulaski County Tourism Bureau**, at 137 St. Robert Boulevard, Suite A, has brochures describing three self-guided local driving tours: Fort Leonard Wood, Frisco Railroad, and Route 66.

FURTHER AFIELD

There is a turnoff for **Fort Leonard Wood** at Spur 44/Missouri Avenue. General Leonard Wood was quite an accomplished officer, and well-deserving of having an army post named after him. After the outbreak of the Spanish-American War in 1898, then-Colonel Wood and his friend Theodore Roosevelt recruited the 1st Volunteer Cavalry—the famous Rough Riders—of which Wood was the commanding officer. Meritorious conduct at the battles of Las Guasimas and San Juan Hill gained Wood promotion to brigadier general. After the war, Wood served as military governor of Cuba from 1899 to 1902, during which time he oversaw improvements in sanitation, education, and policing. He also served as governor over the Phillippines from 1921 to 1927. General Wood even ran for the Republican presidential nomination in 1920, narrowly losing that bid to Warren G. Harding.

At Fort Leonard Wood is the **John B. Mahaffey Museum Complex**. Included are exhibits honoring the army's Engineer Corps, Chemical Corps, and Military Police Corps. There is also information about General Wood's life and career, as well as an area set up as a replica of Fort Leonard Wood as it appeared during the 1940s.

WAYNESVILLE

The town is named for a revolutionary war hero, "Mad" Anthony Wayne. Located as it is just northwest of Fort Leonard Wood, Waynesville was the chief recreational center for troops training here during the war years. During that time, the streets were lined with bars, cafés,

Former hotel and stagecoach stopover, downtown Waynesville, Missouri.

and other businesses that tend to gravitate to young GIs. This was very much in evidence immediately following the war when our friend Jack Rittenhouse came through here.

Waynesville, Missouri.

During the Civil War, Union troops built a fort overlooking the city in order to protect the telegraph wires between St. Louis and Springfield. There is a historical marker at the fort's location, on Fort Street between Benton and Dewitt.

At Roubidoux Creek, Route 66 is carried by a five-span concrete arch bridge that was constructed in 1923 (pre-66), and widened in 1939. A large open field near the bridge served as a campsite for the Cherokees during the Trail of Tears march.

WAYNESVILLE ATTRACTIONS

Be on the lookout for **Frog Rock** (a.k.a. W. H. Croaker) jutting out of a hillside on the east outskirts of town. Locals decided the rock outcropping looked a lot like a frog, so it has been painted very nicely now to *really* look like a frog.

At 106 Lynn Street is the **Old Stagecoach Stop**, a two-story station that also saw duty as a wartime hospital and as a hotel during its 140-year history. It is on the National Register.

The **Pulaski County Courthouse Museum** is located in the 1903 courthouse. Themes include the Civil War, Trail of Tears, pioneer history, and Route 66. Open Saturdays on the town square. The **Talbot House** is one of the oldest in town, and it now houses an antiques shop, so you don't need to come away from your tour empty-handed. 405 North St.

After Waynesville, the highway is marked 17. Stay with it all the way to Buckhorn.

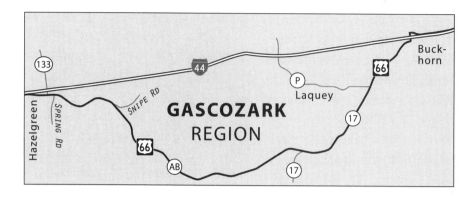

BUCKHORN-LAQUEY-HAZELGREEN

Historic 66 crosses I-44 (at Exit 153) here at Buckhorn under the guise of Highway 17. Buckhorn was named for the Buckhorn Tavern, a former stage stop on the old Wire Road, which displayed a set of antlers. Between here and the Highway 133 junction is an area called Gascozark.

Near Buckhorn, Missouri.

That name was coined by a developer in the 1920s, and is a hybrid derived from Ozark and Gasconade (for the nearby river). The old Gascozark Trading Post complex still stands, neglected and overgrown, near where Highway 133 crosses I-44, including some former tourist cabins. West of Hazelgreen, Route 66 crosses the Gasconade River on a steel bridge constructed in 1922 (south of I-44).

Continue on the south frontage road to interchange 135 (at Highway F), then cross to the north side of the freeway for the run into Lebanon.

LEBANON

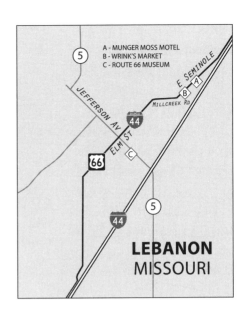

A - MUNGER MOSS MOTEL
B - WRINK'S MARKET
C - ROUTE 66 MUSEUM

LEBANON
MISSOURI

Lebanon is home to the **Munger Moss Motel**, which has a huge red porcelain-and-neon sign out front, which was manufactured just a little up the road by a firm named Springfield Neon. If you'll be staying the night in the Lebanon area, I highly recommend you do so here at the Munger Moss. The owners really care about Route 66 and roadies like you and me. The lobby is also a combination gift shop and vintage toy display.

Not far from the Munger Moss is **Wrink's Market**. Unfortunately, Glenn "Wrink" Wrinkle passed away in 2005. Wrink started operating the market in 1950, and kept it open until only a few weeks before his death 55 years later. After sitting idle for a time, the store was reopened by Glenn's son Terry, who maintains the family business today.

Opened in 2004, the LaClede County Library houses a great **Route 66 Museum** run by the Lebanon/LaClede County Route 66 Society, at

The Munger Moss Motel is a place every Mother Roader should plan to stay the night sometime. Lebanon, Missouri.

915 S. Jefferson. The old **LaClede County Jail** is on the National Register. 262 N. Adams.

A few miles east of Lebanon, **Nancy Ball-hagen's Puzzles**, at 25211 Garden Crest Road (I-44 at Highway F, Exit 135), is a must-stop for truly serious puzzle fanatics. There are literally thousands in

Roadside market, Lebanon, Missouri.

stock, and you can see a couple of hundred completed jigsaw puzzles on display. What's the biggest puzzle you can buy? It's a 24,000-piece monster that measures 14 feet across when completed.

FURTHER AFIELD

North of Lebanon (about 25 miles) via Highway 5 is **Camdenton**. A nearby park, **Ha Ha Tonka State Park**, includes the remains of a 100-year-old European-style **castle**. In 1905, a Kansas City businessman named Robert Snyder began construction of a three-story stone castle on 2,500 acres of land that he had acquired for its natural beauty. He intended to create a

The centerpiece of Ha Ha Tonka State Park is this stone ruin. Near Camdenton, Missouri.

retreat that would rival any in the world, and he spared no expense in its creation, hiring the most qualified artisans and obtaining the best materials available. Tragically, Snyder died suddenly in 1906, and the unfinished project was taken over by his sons. The property eventually included the castle, an 80-foot water tower, stables, and several greenhouses. In later years, the family came upon hard times and was forced to lease the property to someone who operated it as a hotel for some years. In 1942, more tragedy struck when a spark from a fireplace spread rapidly and gutted both the main house and the stable. Those ruins now stand stark and haunting atop a 250-foot bluff overlooking the Lake of the Ozarks.

The state of Missouri purchased the estate in 1978 and opened it to the public as a state park. The park's beautiful natural features confirm Mr. Snyder's good taste in obtaining the property. Today, park visitors can enjoy sinkholes, caves, a natural bridge, springs, and of course the famous ruins via some 15 miles of trails. The trails run the gamut from paved, "accessible" paths and boardwalks to strenuous, rocky climbs suitable for overnight backpacking. Some of the caves here—much as with others throughout Missouri—are said to have been used as hideouts by criminals during the 1830s. The Ha Ha Tonka (Laughing Water) visitor center features a relief map of the area carved from a block of stone.

Back on 66: from Lebanon, take Highway W (west side of I-44) to Phillipsburg.

PHILLIPSBURG-CONWAY-SAMPSON-NIANGUA

According to a 1946 oil-company road map of Missouri, the towns of Conway and Sampson were both Route 66 towns strung between

Pair of advertising barns near Phillipsburg, Missouri.

Phillipsburg and Marshfield, with 66 just barely missing Niangua. Considering the fact that the railroad tracks pass directly through the heart of Niangua, it seems likely that originally—in the 1920s–30s, perhaps—the early Route 66 did take in Niangua. By 1957, however, a new four-lane alignment had been constructed that bypassed all of these towns by a few miles and occupied the present-day I-44 roadbed through the region. Also by then, the village of Sampson was no longer deemed worthy of mention at all. All of these towns are still there, but you'll have to make a greater effort if you intend to see them. See reference map.

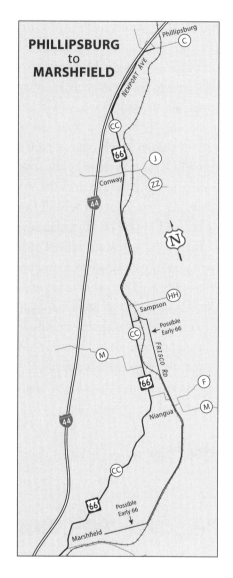

Not far from Conway, a new **Route 66 Welcome Center** was opened in 2009 at I-44's Exit 113. There's a neon sign based upon the iconic Munger Moss Motel sign in Lebanon, and aside from the expected indoor displays, there is a spacious picnic area with shelters that are made to resemble roadside businesses such as garages, gasoline stations, and diners.

MARSHFIELD

Marshfield is the hometown of **Edwin Hubble**, creator of the space-based telescope of the same name known for the corrective lens made especially for it. The town has a one-quarter-sized replica of the telescope occupying the west side of the courthouse lawn. At 219 S. Clay Street is the **Webster County Historical Museum**, housed in the old community library that was funded by the Carnegie Foundation in 1911. Outside the museum is a "Walk of Fame" honoring prominent citizens of Missouri.

County courthouse, Marshfield, Missouri.

Hidden Waters Nature Park includes springs that form the headwaters of the Niangua River and walking trails that pass other water features, as well as an assortment of gardens. There is also the **Callaway Cabin**, dating from 1853, one of the few structures to survive the tornado that struck the area in 1880.

HOLMAN-STRAFFORD

East of Strafford, near the small hamlet of Holman, is **Wild Animal Safari** (formerly Exotic Animal Paradise), one of those zoological parks in which you drive through in your car and view hundreds of animals in captivity, some of which may not even know it is they, not you, that are in the lockup. Denizens of this paradise include bison, lamas, and zedonks (zebra-donkey hybrid). Unlike most zoological parks of one kind or another, you are not forbidden to feed the animals here. In fact, there is animal feed for sale, so that you can toss some out of your car to entice the animals to approach more closely. There are also paddle boats and a petting zoo.

SPRINGFIELD

Established in the 1820s when pioneer John Polk Campbell carved his initials in a tree near the confluence of four springs, and soon thereafter known as the Queen of the Ozarks, Springfield won't disappoint the Route 66 traveler.

There are multiple Route 66 alignments, so exploration is strongly encouraged. The best-known versions enter Springfield on Kearney Street, turn south on Glenstone, and then head west again after turning onto either Chestnut or St. Louis. Both will take you through the heart of downtown. A later bypass routing continues further west on Kearney before turning south, thus avoiding downtown traffic. There are still a number of classic motels and other vintage businesses to excite your senses. Among the motels are the Rest Haven, Skyline, and Rail Haven, to name only a few.

Springfield has a special distinction. It was here in 1947 that Red Chaney opened the first hamburger stand with a drive-thru window—Red's Giant Hamburg. Red eventually retired, and his landmark was demolished in the 1990s, with more than a few nostalgic souls turning out for the occasion. There had been a song written about the place in 1982 called "Red's" and recorded by a Springfield band called the Morells. A photo of Red's place even appeared on the album cover.

Another business originating here in Springfield was Campbell's

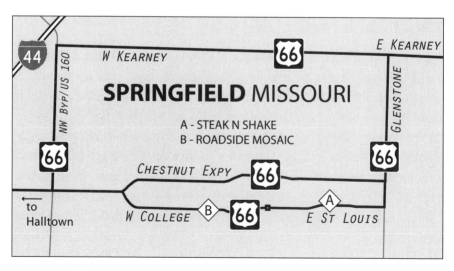

The Rest Haven Motel in Springfield, Missouri, sports a huge neon sign in excellent condition.

66 Express, the trucking firm which used Snortin' Norton, the "Humpin' to Please" camel, as its trademark.

The **Steak 'n' Shake** restaurant chain still has a sizable presence in Missouri, and in Springfield in particular there are a number of the earlier examples still extant. Their famous directive to Take Home a Sack (modified to Takhomasak) has been echoed many times over by famous burger chains nationwide: White Castle's "Buy 'em by the Sack"; White Tower's "Buy a Bag Full"; and Krystal's "Take Along a Sack Full" all encourage us to indulge the same impulse. The flagship restaurant at 1158 St. Louis Street will make you think you've time-traveled to 1960.

As you pass through town on what is now College Street, be on the lookout for a small embankment beside the road adorned with a Route 66-themed mosaic. The artwork was created by local artist Christine Schilling with the help of some young students. In 2010, Schilling began restoration of an advertising mural in downtown Springfield

Springfield, Missouri.

that was partially exposed when a vehicle collided with the building. The ad touts BEEMAN'S PEPSIN GUM, and is located on East Commerce Street.

SPRINGFIELD ATTRACTIONS

The town is widely known as the home of **Bass Pro Shops Outdoor World**, a veritable theme-park of a retail experience for the outdoor set. There's a 140,000-gallon game fish aquarium and a four-story waterfall. If

ED GALLOWAY

Nathan Ed Galloway was born in 1880 in Stone County, near Springfield, Missouri. From a very young age he showed a talent and propensity for wood carving.

Ed joined the U.S. Army and served in the Spanish-American War in 1898 before being assigned to duty in the Philippines. While there, he came into contact with creatures such as crocodiles and other reptiles that would inspire some of his later art.

After leaving the Army, Ed returned to Springfield and pursued his wood carving. He specialized in household objects such as hall trees and smoking stands, which he covered with intricate carvings of animals and other figures. He also fashioned many large-scale items from tree trunks; these, too, were often decorated with human and animal figures. Ed planned to be an exhibitor at the Panama-Pacific International Exposition in San Francisco, taking place in 1915. Tragically, a fire at his studio destroyed most of his work.

Ed managed to salvage a few pieces, including his sculpture known as *Lion in a Cage*, and began making his way west toward California for the exposition. It is said that he had been temporarily waylaid in Tulsa, Oklahoma, when his work was seen and admired by Charles Page. Page was a businessman and

that's not enough, check out the stuffed and mounted bears, the antique fishing gear, and the wildlife art gallery. 1935 S. Campbell Ave.

Next door to Bass Pro Shops is **World of Wildlife** (formerly the American National Fish and Wildlife Museum), featuring a myriad of authentic habitats, such as aquariums, aviaries, and even a swamp area. 500 W. Sunshine St.

The **Typewriter Toss** is held each April on Secretary's Day, just in case you thought that was a "holiday" you could live without. From a

---

philanthropist who had established a home for orphaned children in nearby Sand Springs. He offered Ed a job teaching woodworking to the boys at the Sand Springs Home. Ed remained in Sand Springs in that capacity for the next twenty-plus years.

From 1936 to 1937, Ed and his wife, Villie, bought several acres of land near Foyil, Oklahoma (Villie was from the Bushyhead area) and began the chapter of his life for which he is best known. Ed began building a stone residence on the property (completed in 1937) and a collection of large Native-American-inspired structures. The largest of those structures is a ninety-foot-tall totem pole bearing the date 1948, which took him eleven years to complete.

Ed also constructed his "Fiddle House," an eleven-sided building created expressly to house the growing collection of fiddles he carved during this time. That collection is said to have exceeded 300.

Ed seems to have been speaking to Mother Road lovers such as you and me when he said: "All my life, I did the best I knew. I built these things by the side of the road to be a friend to you."

Ed died of cancer on November 11, 1962 (Veteran's Day). His Foyil property was donated by his family in 1989 to the Rogers County Historical Society, which maintains the present-day Totem Pole Park.

height of 50 feet, the typewriters are thrown at a bull's-eye.

If pioneer history interests you, check out the **Gray-Campbell Farmstead**. Centered around the oldest house in Springfield (circa 1856), exhibits include a log kitchen, two-crib barn, family cemetery, and Civil War-era artifacts. There are costumed docents on hand to explain the history of the place. 2400

Springfield, Missouri.

S. Scenic, in Nathanael Greene Park. Also at Nathanael Greene Park is the **Mizumoto Stroll Garden**, with over seven acres of lakes, winding paths, and other traditional features of Japanese-style gardens.

At the **Missouri Sports Hall of Fame** you'll become acquainted with some of the great names that have called the Show-Me state home base: Stan Musial, Whitey Herzog, and Bob Gibson, to name only a few. There's even a cage where visitors can stand behind home plate while 100-mph fastballs come blazing in from the mound. 3861 E. Stan Musial Dr.

The **History of Hearing Museum** will take you back to the days of hand-held ear trumpets, and explains how the evolution of hearing-aid technology has improved lives. 628 E. Commercial St.

The restored **Jefferson Avenue Footbridge** was built in 1902, and is a favorite train-watching spot, passing as it does over several sets of tracks. At more than 500 feet in length, locals consider it their largest public sculpture, and in fact, it's the longest footbridge in the entire country. Commercial St. at Jefferson Ave.

The **Railroad Historical Museum** preserves railroading heritage with several different types of railcars on display. Opportunities for kids include exploring a locomotive cab and ringing the bell. 1300 N. Grant Ave.

Pythian Castle was originally constructed by the Knights of

Pythias in 1913 as an orphanage. It was commandeered for use by the U.S. Army during World War II, and is said to be haunted. Tours are available of the 55-room, 40,000-square-foot castle, and special events are held there frequently. 1451 E. Pythian St.

The **Calaboose**, at 409 W. McDaniel, was built in 1891 as a jail, but now serves as a police substation with a law-enforcement museum on the first floor.

Askinosie Chocolate makes chocolate and related products from scratch (beans!), and tours of the factory are available for a small donation. The building itself dates from 1894, and previously saw action as a carriage factory. 514 E. Commercial St.

Military memorabilia abounds at the **Air and Military Museum of the Ozarks**, including restored aircraft, a variety of military vehicles, dioramas, and flight simulators. You can even have your own personalized dog tags made. 2305 E. Kearney.

Civil War buffs will want to visit **General Sweeney's Museum**. An official site of the Civil War Trust, it's the only museum to focus on the trans-Mississippi portion of the conflict, and it houses more than 5,000 wartime artifacts. 5228 S. State Highway ZZ.

FURTHER AFIELD

Just northwest of Springfield you'll find **Fantastic Caverns**. Acclaimed as "America's Only Drive-Thru Cave," the tour takes visitors along the path of an underground river, in Jeeps, while the guides extol the considerable virtues of protecting the environment by powering the tour vehicles with propane. Furthermore, the cave was once owned by the Ku Klux Klan, who held meetings in one of the caverns here.

In contrast to the above, due north of Springfield via Highway H is **Crystal Cave**. Here, the operators have endeavored to provide a cave experience in a more natural state. There are no vehicles; instead, visitors clamber about on narrow paths and must negotiate tight spaces. Unusual features include Rainbow Falls, the Cathedral, fossil crinoids, and numerous Native American symbols.

The town of **Marionville**, southwest of Springfield on U.S. 60, has a reputation for **albino squirrels**. Keep your camera ready.

To the south of Springfield, via U.S. 65, is the town of **Branson**, Missouri. Though considered by many people of sound mind to be a tad overblown, Branson does have at least one redeeming feature—the **Branson Scenic Railway**, a restored Ozark Zephyr, plies the area and hearkens to the passenger service glory days of the 1940s and '50s.

To the northwest of Branson, via Highway 76, is a semi-Christian theme park called **Silver Dollar City**. The park sprang up due to the presence of nearby **Marvel Cave**, a subterranean attraction in the area since 1950. The theme park was officially established in 1960, and then received some additional notoriety when a few episodes of the *Beverly Hillbillies* television series were filmed there in 1967.

Head west out of Springfield on the Chestnut Expressway (Highway 266), which is Historic 66.

PLANO

In this vicinity is a masonry building just a few feet from the edge of the highway that is being taken over by vines and other vegetation. The interior is completely gutted and roofless. Inside, many small trees are growing, reaching for the windows and the sky.

Former casket-making shop, near Plano, Missouri.

If you have a detailed map of this region, you can see that the later version of Route 66 (present-day Highway 266 from here to Paris Springs, and Highway 96 from Spencer to northeast of Carthage) was plotted as nearly a straight line over the next 40 miles or so.

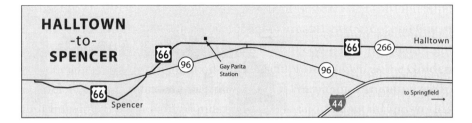

HALLTOWN

Established in 1833 and later named for merchant George Hall, Halltown is known for its antique shops, the largest of which is the Whitehall Mercantile. Amazingly, back in 1946 Jack Rittenhouse characterized Halltown by making mention of its antique shops.

PARIS SPRINGS-SPENCER-HEATONVILLE-ALBATROSS-PHELPS

Halltown, Missouri.

Coming up is one of my favorite stretches of old Route 66. Ahead of you now is a string of very small towns stretching between Halltown and Carthage. Highway realignments caused traffic to begin being diverted south of here, with the result that towns such as Albatross and Phelps had their lifelines pulled from them, and they became almost frozen in time.

As you pass through this section, I urge you to slow down considerably. Take your time exploring the communities of Paris Springs, Spencer,

Spencer, Missouri.

Heatonville, Albatross, and Phelps. You will see the ruins of convenience stores, tourist courts, and other structures, many of which look as though the owners left suddenly and never returned. You will also see some structures that have been assigned to new uses, such as a set of tourist cabins now being used as storage sheds.

What's left of Bill's Station, Phelps, Missouri.

Don't fail to stop at the Gay Parita station in Paris Springs. Gary Turner wants to meet you and talk for a while—no kidding.

Gary Turner's Gay Parita station, Paris Springs, Missouri.

RESCUE-PLEW-AVILLA

Between Rescue and Plew is a turnoff (YY North) to Red Oak. This reference will be more meaningful a short time later when you encounter the turnoff for Red Oak II just outside of Carthage.

RED OAK II

You won't find it depicted on a road map, but here it is anyway, created by a local artist northeast of Carthage. Red Oak II is a village (partly the original Red Oak) that was brought over from its original location more than 20 miles away and installed here, presumably to attract nostalgia-minded travelers—and it keeps growing. It features a multitude of

Part of the art-inspired community of Red Oak II, Missouri.

vintage structures, including a blacksmith shop, diner, general store, church, a couple of filling stations, and several residences, both occupied and otherwise. There's even a mock cemetery. 12266 Kafir Rd.

CARTHAGE

The famed Carthage marble is quarried here, and more than a few Carthaginians have made their living in the field. There is a home tour that begins and ends at the courthouse in the square (pick up a brochure at the chamber of commerce) and takes you on a drive to see several homes of Carthage's most prominent citizens. Constructed between 1870 and 1910, many of these residences were built by stone quarry and mine owners.

You can head into Carthage on current Highway 96 to Central Avenue, but there's an older alignment to the left (see map) that wanders to the eastern side of Kellogg Lake and includes some old tourist courts. For a time, that alignment then proceeded west on Java Street before joining Garrison north of town.

The **Jasper County Courthouse** itself was constructed in 1894–95. There is a mural inside depicting the history of the area, painted by

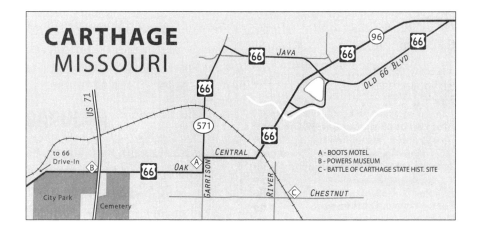

a local artist. In 2009, a Route 66 display was added that loosely resembles the former Boots Drive-In (see below). The courthouse also features a wrought-iron, cage-style elevator that is still in operation. Take a stroll around the town square,

Boots Motel, Carthage, Missouri.

which is lined with buildings dating from as early as the 1870s.

For a reminder of authentic Route 66, the **Boots Motel** is hard to beat. It's at 107 S. Garrison; you'll see it just as you make the turn from Central (left) onto Garrison. According to a local tourism brochure, Clark Gable once stayed at the Boots, in room 6. There used to be a Boots Drive-In & Gift Shop across the street in the streamlined building now housing a bank.

CARTHAGE ATTRACTIONS

The **Battle of Carthage Civil War Museum** is at 205 Grant. A mural, prints, historic relics, and souvenirs memorialize the battle and its participants. The Battle of Carthage was fought early in the war (1861), and was a victory for the Confederates, setting an early tone for the hostilities. The **Battle of Carthage State Historic Site** is also nearby, on the north side of E. Chestnut Road, near S. River Street.

Historic Phelps House, 1146 S. Grand Avenue, is a restored Victorian mansion (circa 1895) offering tours. Some of the furniture and fixtures here are originals. It has 10 fireplaces, each with different-colored tile, and a hand-operated elevator

Phelps House, Carthage, Missouri.

The 66 Drive-In is still in business on the west side of Carthage, Missouri.

serving four floors. The house is built of local stone.

Marlin Perkins, longtime host of the popular television series *Wild Kingdom*, grew up in Carthage, and there is a statue of him standing in the town's **Central Park**. Belle Starr also grew up here, in her father's hotel downtown, prior to the Civil War.

Local history is the focus at the **Powers Museum**, which has rotating exhibits on a variety of themes. Located at 1617 W. Oak Street (historic 66), the museum is on the former site of Taylor Tourist Park, later known as the Park Motor Court & Cafe. In 2005, the museum instituted what it calls its "Traveling Classroom Trunks" program for educators. The theme of one of these trunks is Jasper County highways, including Route 66 and other early auto trails.

On the western outskirts of town is the 1940s-era **66 Drive-In Theater**. This theater was restored in 1998, and re-opened exactly 49 years after its original grand opening in September '49.

One of Carthage's most-visited attractions is the **Precious Moments Chapel & Gardens**. The compound includes the chapel, ornamental gardens, a museum, gift shop, and snack bar. 4321 S. Chapel Rd.

CARTERVILLE

Route 66 enters Carterville from the north along Pine Street. According to Rittenhouse, Carterville in 1946 was already a virtual ghost town, with "boarded-up stores, empty buildings, and general air of desolation."

Furthermore, it offered no facilities for motorists. My 1957 atlas, however, still affords it the status of a viable highway community.

WEBB CITY

Webb City is well worth some exploration. Named for a local farmer, John Webb, who discovered lead in the area, the town's fortunes were tied to mining in its early days. There seems to be an identity crisis of sorts, though, in Webb City: the water tower is emblazoned "City of Flags," while a sign at the nearby park proclaims "Zinc City." I haven't found anyone who can explain the "Flags" moniker. Since the town was established in 1876, I'm a little surprised they didn't call themselves the "Centennial City."

Webb City has a large neon arrow that points in the direction of its business district, which is slightly off today's main highway,

Webb City, Missouri, has a neon sign pointing the way to its business district.

MacArthur Drive. Adjacent to the business district are some very nice older homes which are worth a walking tour. There are also some murals—one on the side of Bruner Pharmacy and another in Mid-Missouri Bank. At Ball and MacArthur Streets is a 105mm howitzer named Jeannie, said to have played a role in the liberation of France in World War II.

There is also a local park (**King Jack Park**) that features a large sculpture of a miner or prospector with pick in hand. The park also features a tiny train depot, which was moved there after having functioned

Among the many features of King Jack Park is this sculpture of praying hands on a hilltop. Webb City, Missouri.

as part of the interurban commuting system that was shut down in the 1930s—the depot now houses the Chamber of Commerce. There's even a streetcar that runs on special occasions. Overlooking King Jack Park is an enormous pair of praying hands, a sculpture created by artist Jack Dawson in the early 1970s. The body of water you see in the park is actually an old mining pit called Sucker Flats.

The **Clubhouse Museum** makes its home in a building constructed in 1910, used as a "clubhouse" for the employees of the local commuter railway. They don't keep set hours, but you can call ahead for a tour at 417-673-5866. 115 N. Madison St.

JOPLIN

Downtown Joplin features Wilder's Fine Foods, which has a terrific old neon sign. Joplin is also the hometown of actor Dennis Weaver.

JOPLIN ATTRACTIONS

There are multiple Route 66 alignments going both to and through Joplin, some of which are shown on the reference map. Also, as you'd expect, 66 took a stair-step route through town in its earliest days, touching Zora, Euclid, and Broadway on its way west. Ultimately, Route 66 left Joplin via W. Seventh Street.

The **Thomas Hart Benton mural**, called *Joplin at the Turn of the Century, 1896-1906*, is the last signed large-scale work by this Missourian. There are also sketches documenting the mural's progress. In the city hall at 602 Main Street.

Richardson's Candy House occupies the 60-year-old Rock Tavern building and still does things the old-fashioned way. Watch hand-dipped chocolates and divinity being made. Somehow I'm reminded of an *I Love Lucy* episode.... 454 Redings Mill Rd. (Hwy. 86 South).

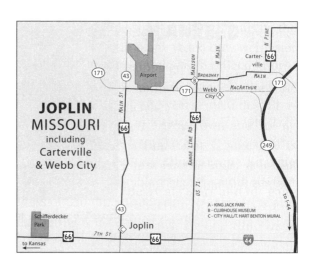

Exhibits at the **Dorothea B. Hoover Historical Museum** recall the Joplin of the 1870s, with antique dolls, a miniature animated circus, and a replica of a nineteenth century tavern. Schifferdecker Avenue at Fourth Street, in Schifferdecker Park. Also at Schifferdecker Park is the **Tri-State Mineral Museum**. The park is on the western outskirts of the city.

Grand Falls, with a 25-foot drop, is Missouri's largest waterfall. Riverside Drive, just south of town. 800-657-2534.

This monument stands at Schifferdecker Park, on the west side of Joplin, Missouri.

FURTHER AFIELD

The **George Washington Carver National Monument** is southeast of Joplin, and about 2.5 miles southwest of the town of Diamond on County Road V—his birthplace. Carver was born into slavery, but through hard work became the director of agricultural research at the Tuskegee Institute. There, his experimentation led to the development of more than 400 new products made from peanuts, cotton, and soybeans.

 Highway 66 leaves Joplin on W. Seventh, heading due west, and it's only a few miles to the Kansas border. Look ahead to the Galena, Kansas, reference map so that you make your turn prior to the state line and don't miss anything. The State Line Bar & Grill will remind you that you are passing into the Sunflower State.

Sign in downtown Joplin, Missouri.

KANSAS

 ansas has a reputation, at least among some of us, as epitomizing the safety and security of home. The impressions we form at an early age are slow to change, and many of us in twentieth-century

America have grown up with a picture of Kansas heavily influenced by the classic 1939 film *The Wizard of Oz*. Kansas was portrayed first as dull, then as a secure place to return to, but always—fundamentally—as *Home*. Perhaps this impression is reinforced by the fact that Kansas is so centrally located within the contiguous 48 states. The state of Kansas seems to be officially satisfied with this image, having adopted "Home on the Range" as its state song.

Even beyond that, stereotypes have a way of persisting. Someone who has never set foot in Kansas will tell you with great certainty that Kansas is a very flat, monotonous country, with nothing but wheat fields mile after mile after mile.

The view from just east of Galena, Kansas.

But in fact, Kansas is a place well worth getting to know. It's more diverse than most people realize, and it's far less a Home than it is a Crossroads. Numerous legendary trails traversed the state of Kansas en route to more remote objectives, such as California and Oregon, while others, like the Chisholm Trail, were laid out with Kansas as their destination.

A complete inventory of the historic tracks crisscrossing the state would be difficult to compile, but the list would have to include the Oregon Trail, which took settlers to Oregon Territory by way of Topeka; the California Overland Trail, which followed the same route during its passage through Kansas; the Santa Fe Trail, a trade route to the ancient capital passing through the longest dimension of the state and exiting near Elkhart; the Pony Express Route, along which mail was carried between Missouri and California; and the Chisholm Trail, the path of countless cattle and cowboys between the ranches of south Texas and the railheads at Abilene, Kansas.

Other trails in Kansas that are less known, but served their purpose in their own time, include the Parallel Road, the Ellsworth Trail, and the Pawnee Trail. And there have yet been others, including U.S. Route 66. Highway 66 was one of many such paths that only touched upon Kansas in order to reach someplace else.

Route 66—like so many of us—never gave Kansas a chance, never got to know her well. The path of Route 66 barely took a nibble from the southeast corner of the state—a mere 13 miles of road in a land of 82,000 square miles, 52,000,000 acres, and 2.8 million people. To appreciate Kansas from so meager a sample is to emulate the blind man who tried to envision the elephant by touching only its tail.

The Kansas that you see from Route 66 isn't a lot like the stereotype you expect. No amber waves of grain shifting in the breeze here. Southeast Kansas is mining country, and mining districts are not often candidates for scenic postcard views. This is a different kind of bountiful earth, one that yields its rewards grudgingly, and one that does not find its way easily into glossy tour guides.

But that's not to say this portion of Kansas is any less proud of what it is. Route 66 paid its respects here and departed; the people of

Kansas have gotten used to the idea and have moved on with their lives.

As you head westward into Kansas, past the State Line Bar & Grill, the first stop in the Sunflower State is:

GALENA

Formerly two distinct towns, Galena and Empire, Galena annexed the latter in 1911. The town is named for lead-bearing ore, which is plentiful in the area. Surprisingly to this traveler, Galena is a very popular name for American towns. At least 21 other states have—or have had—a town so named. Downtown Galena has a number of buildings with old advertising murals painted on the sides, that are becoming visible again due to weathering.

Just about four miles past Schifferdecker Park on the west edge of Joplin, turn right onto Front Street in order to enter Galena on the much-preferred older alignment.

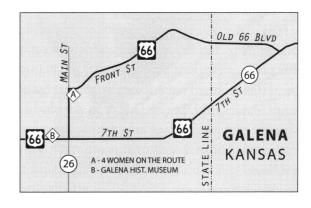

GALENA ATTRACTIONS

Entering Galena from the east along Front Street, you'll make a left-hand turn onto Main. On the southeast corner is an old gasoline station now called **4 Women on the Route.** They were honored as Route 66 Business of the Year in 2008, and serve today's Mother Road adventurers with a combination welcome center, gift shop, and snack bar. Usually parked on the property is the tow truck that supplied the inspiration for the "Tow Mater" character in the movie *Cars*.

Also on Main in Galena is **Route 66 Howard "Pappy" Litch**

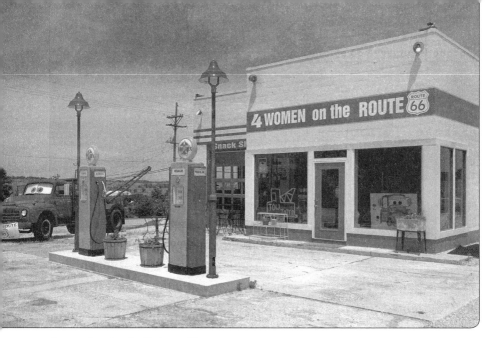

A popular stop in Galena, Kansas.

Park, named for a local citizen and historian. The park contains one of the original 1952 Will Rogers Highway plaques—this one was brought from a site at the Missouri-Kansas border—and is located on a plot of land formerly occupied by a federal highway weigh station.

The old Katy railroad depot, which is right on Highway 66 (319

Galena, Kansas.

This retired MKT (Missouri-Kansas-Texas) railroad depot now serves as the local history museum in Galena, Kansas.

W. 7th Street), now houses the **Galena Mining and Historical Museum**. Pappy Litch, for whom the park (above) was named, was one of the major forces in establishing this museum.

For a very short side trip, you can take Kansas Highway 26 south two miles from downtown Galena to **Schermerhorn Park**, in an area of the state called the Kansas Ozarks. There, you'll find a great-looking WPA-constructed building and stone terraces from the 1930s. Formerly a boy scout meeting place, the structure has now been transformed into a Nature Center. Also in the park is a cave—Schermerhorn Cave—which, like Meramec Cavern in Missouri, is reputed to have been a hiding place of outlaw Jesse James.

West of Galena, en route to Riverton, you'll cross the Spring River. At one time, covering several acres on the bank of the river was the **Spring River Inn**; a neon sign for it is still standing alongside the highway. The Spring River Inn started life as a private residence shortly after 1900, but then served stints as part of a country club, yacht club, and finally a restaurant before falling victim to a fire in the 1990s.

RIVERTON

This is truly the center of Route 66 in Kansas. The **Eisler Brothers Store** (circa 1925) is the de facto headquarters of the Kansas Route 66 Association, and serves not only as a general store, but also carries a wide array of roadie paraphernalia intended just for adventurers like you and me.

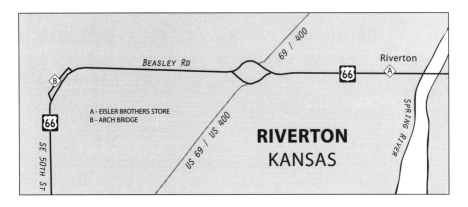

FURTHER AFIELD

Northwest of Riverton is the town of **Columbus**. There is a **clock tower** featuring a 1919 Seth Thomas movement still in operation. The clock was built using public donations as a memorial to servicemen of the First World War (known at that time as the Great War). 101 W. Maple Ave.

On the bank of the Spring River, Riverton, Kansas.

This bridge stands just west of Riverton, Kansas.

The nearby **Columbus Museum**, at 100 S. Tennessee Avenue, includes memorabilia from Merle Evans, hometown boy who for 50 years was a bandleader with the Ringling Brothers circus. Also at the museum is a ball of string which was featured on the *I've Got A Secret* television show in the 1950s.

A bit further north from Columbus is Scammon, home to the **Carona Depot & Railroad Museum**, with an extensive collection of memorabilia and equipment, including two restored railroad depots. 6769 Northwest 20th.

North of Riverton via U.S. 69/400 is the town of **Pittsburg**. Just north of Pittsburg on 69 is the **Mined Land Wildlife Area #1**, formerly a heavily mined area now converted for recreational uses, such as fishing.

Riverton, Kansas.

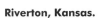

The car parked nearby gives a clear indication of the enormous size of Big Brutus. West Mineral, Kansas.

There is also a resident buffalo herd kept there. (Just to set your mind at ease, by "mined" they mean that ore excavation took place—as far as we know, there are no undetonated explosive devices in the area.)

While in Pittsburg, check out the **Crawford County Historical Museum** on Highway 69 between 20th and Atkinson, and the **Hotel Stilwell** (Seventh and Broadway), which was built in 1880 and is listed on the historic register. Pittsburg also hosts the **Old Time Tractor and Gas Engine Show** in June.

If you want to do even more exploring, turn west from U.S. 69 onto State Highway 102 to reach the town of **West Mineral**. Here stands **Big Brutus**, the second-largest power shovel ever built, standing 16 stories tall. With one scoop, its shovel could fill three railroad cars. One look at Big Brutus will erase any lingering doubts that this part of Kansas owes its livelihood to mining. Each June, West Mineral holds the Big Brutus **Miners' Day Reunion**, when veteran miners reconvene here to talk over old times. August gets even livelier, with the **Big Brutus Polka Fest** featuring dueling polka bands. Big Brutus is at 6509 NW 60th Street. The Big Brutus complex even includes RV and camping facilities.

 Back on 66: Just to the west of Riverton, the junction at U.S. 69/400 feels almost like a roundabout. Be sure to pass straight through it and exit onto Beasley Road. Further ahead is a restored arched bridge, sometimes referred to as the **Rainbow Bridge**, with a commemorative marker on a very short one-way leg of the highway. Curve left onto SE 50th Street toward Baxter Springs.

BAXTER SPRINGS

In 1863, at the height of the Civil War, Baxter Springs was the scene of a significant attack on Union forces by Quantrill's

> Enter Baxter Springs from the north on SE 50th Street, then turn left on Third, and then right onto Military Avenue.

Raiders. The Bill Quantrill gang raided a U.S. Cavalry wagon train near here on October 6th, and killed about 100 men. It became known as the Baxter Springs Massacre. The graves of many of those who died lie in the Baxter Springs National Cemetery on U.S. Highway 166 near Spring Valley Road.

Although some dispute the veracity of the tale, the local restaurant at 1101 Military Avenue (**Café on the Route**) is housed in a building that was formerly a bank robbed by Jesse James in 1876. In the 1870s, Baxter Springs was widely considered the toughest town in Kansas. **Murphey's**, another local restaurant, is also located in a former bank building that was the target of a robbery in 1914 .

BAXTER SPRINGS ATTRACTIONS

The **Baxter Springs Heritage Center & Museum** features exhibits on the Buffalo Soldiers, the African-American troops who were heavily involved in the resistance against Quantrill's Raiders. They got their nickname from the local Native Americans, who likened their coarse hair to that of the American bison. You can also pick up a numbered walking guide to the town, featuring such sites as a log school building dating from 1866; John Baxter's inn and trading post, from which the town eventually

On the grounds of the Baxter Springs Heritage Center, Baxter Springs, Kansas.

sprang; and a replica of Fort Blair, a Civil War-era army post (East Avenue at Eighth). On the grounds of the museum is a small historical marker commemorating the Black Dog Trail.

The **Fort Blair Historic Site** occupies the block bounded by Sixth, Seventh, East, and Military, and was a campsite for Union troops in 1863. There is an information kiosk and a log structure at the site.

The **Johnston Public Library** is housed in a building constructed in 1872, originally intended to be the county courthouse. Though it never served in that capacity, it has seen duty as a city hall, theater, and college. 210 W. Tenth. On the library's grounds is a monument erected by the Daughters of the American Revolution in 1931.

At Tenth and Military is a 1930 cottage-style filling station now serving as the town's **Route 66 Visitor Center**.

At Eleventh and Military is **Bilke's Western Museum**. There is a mural on the exterior depicting a longhorn cattle drive, and upstairs is a private collection of old saddles, spurs, and other cowboy-type gear.

At Fourteenth and Grant is the **Little League Baseball Museum**, featuring stars such as regional hero Mickey Mantle, who came from just across the border in Oklahoma. Mantle played a few years with the Baxter Springs Whiz Kids in the late 1940s. It was during that time that he hit a home run into the Spring River and was later approached by a scout for the New York Yankees. The rest, as they say, is history.

One mile west of town on U.S. 166 is a cemetery, which includes a section designated for Civil War veterans. That plot is bounded by a fence made of **cannon barrels** protruding from the ground.

FURTHER AFIELD

A few miles outside of town is a small monument at the point where the states of Kansas, Oklahoma, and Missouri all come together. The **Tri-State Marker** was constructed in 1938 by the Youth Work Administration. Go about six miles east of town on U.S. 166, then turn right just before the state line (Stateline Rd./SE 118th) and follow the road south. Note that this is a dead end.

A little west of Baxter Springs via U.S. 166 is the town of **Chetopa**, proud to call itself both the Catfish Capital and Pecan Capital of Kansas. The town holds an annual pecan festival the third Saturday in November. The **Chetopa Historical Museum** includes a collection of buttons made at a nearby button-manufacturing plant and information about Osage Chief Che-to-pah, for whom the town was named (419 Maple St.). The **Bath Funeral Home** at Seventh and Maple occupies a showpiece house built in 1875.

Further west via U.S. 166 is the city of **Coffeyville**. The **Dalton Defenders Museum** is dedicated to the memory of the local citizens who gave their lives in defending the town. On October 5, 1892 in Coffeyville, Kansas, the Dalton Gang tried to do what no one had ever done before: rob two banks simultaneously. The gang of five (some of whom were former residents of the town) split up and entered the Condon and First National Banks that morning. Some of the local citizens recognized them and went to the nearby Isham hardware store for weapons and ammunition. When the robbers emerged, they were met by armed citizens and a shootout ensued. All but one of the gang were killed; also killed were four of the eight town defenders. The museum, at 113 E. Eighth Street, also has exhibits pertaining to other local history, as well as mementos of Wendell Wilkie, who lived and taught school in Coffeyville. The Condon Bank building still stands and has been nicely restored.

Just a mile south of the shootout site, you can visit the Daltons' graves in **Elmwood Cemetery**. Emmett Dalton, the only survivor of the gang, returned to Coffeyville many years after the raid and placed a permanent marker over the graves.

Also in Coffeyville is the **Brown Mansion**. Completed in 1904 and incorporating some Tiffany-designed glasswork, the house is a three-story, 16-room residence built by one of the town's leading citizens, W. P. Brown, who made his money in the lumber and natural gas businesses. The home sits on U.S. 166 at the corner of Eldridge and Walnut. Guided tours are available (admission charged), and reservations can be made for private parties.

Located throughout Coffeyville are **murals** depicting facets of Coffeyville's history, including the Brown Mansion, the Perkins Building, Wholesale Grocery, Walter "Big Train" Johnson, and the Interurban.

At **Pfister Park**, housed in a 1930s-era hangar, is the **Aviation Heritage Museum**. The hangar was constructed in 1933 as a Works Progress Administration project, and was used until 1960, when the Big Hill Airport ceased operation. Vintage airplanes and memorabilia associated with the Coffeyville Air Base are on exhibit. 2002 N. Buckeye.

Route 66 travels under the guise of U.S. 69A as it moves south out of Baxter Springs. Shortly after crossing W. 30th Street, look on the left side of the highway at the empty lot that once was the site of the Twilight Drive-In. The theater was destroyed by a storm in the 1970s.

After sweeping across the Illinois prairie, crossing the mighty Mississippi, meandering through the Ozark region of Missouri, and then sampling the soil of Kansas, Route 66 is finally ready to enter that part of the country with which she is most intimately associated.

Prepare yourself. You are about to enter the Great American West.

OKLAHOMA

The pavement of Route 66 begins in Chicago, but the idea begins here in Oklahoma. When the Joint Board of State and Federal Highway Officials was establishing the system of numbered routes

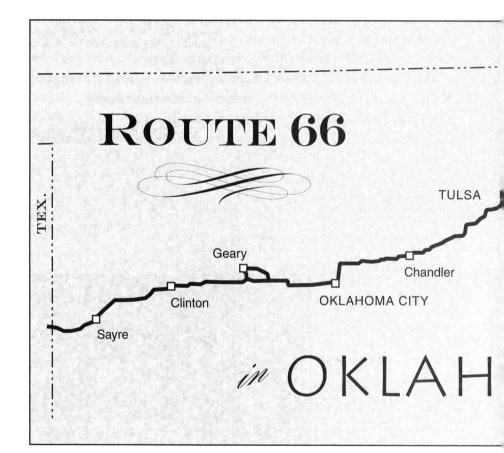

in the 1920s, Cyrus Avery envisioned a major such artery passing right through the heart of his own state of Oklahoma. And he worked long and hard to make it a reality.

It is no accident that Route 66 cuts such a long, sweeping swath directly through the center of Oklahoma. If you look at a map of the United States and draw a more or less direct line from Chicago to Los Angeles, that path will miss the state of Oklahoma entirely. Even allowing for the curvature of the earth not apparent in such a map, the most logical path for such a highway would pass through very little of Missouri, none of Oklahoma, and directly through the heart of Kansas. Indeed, if the highway had been plotted along already-established trails through middle America, such as the Santa Fe Trail, that path, too, would have made Kansas, but not Oklahoma, a prominent part of the route.

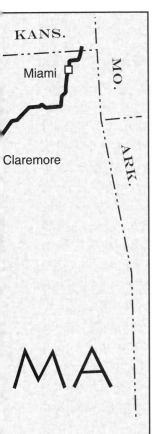

However, U.S. 66 was deliberately calculated to take traveling Americans through Cy Avery's stomping grounds. He reasoned correctly that such a highway would put Oklahoma "on the map" and cause lots of travel-related dollars to be spent all across the state.

This placement of the highway became somewhat fortuitous when the dust bowl years of the 1930s imposed such a hardship on Oklahomans that many of them fled the region for California. Then, all of the surrounding roads became tributaries, adding their flow to the Mother Road and inspiring the dark *The Grapes of Wrath* imagery, which the highway still evokes today.

One of the reasons Oklahoma needed to be put on the map, more so than some other states, has to do with its unique past. The area had, for many years, been designated as Indian Territory, and was home to tribes which had participated in the forced march, known as the Trail of Tears, to the region. It was only in 1907 that Oklahoma attained statehood; therefore, it had been a state for less than two decades at the time of the establishment of the interstate highway system in the '20s. By traveling through the state, however, Americans could see for themselves that Oklahoma was no longer a "territory," nor as primitive as that word implied. Route 66, then, would be Oklahoma's ticket to joining the twentieth century as a full partner.

If you've just traveled the old highway's short course through Kansas, you'll enter Oklahoma moving south on U.S. 69. Like the small section of Kansas you've left behind, this district of Oklahoma is mining country, and there's very little to differentiate it at first. The changes, however, will not be long in coming.

Oklahoma, as befits its unofficial status as the birthplace of Route 66, is very 66-friendly. By that I mean that you will have less difficulty in following the old route here than you will probably have elsewhere. Official state maps, distributed free by the Oklahoma Department of Transportation, have for years now clearly marked the path of Historic Route 66. Not only that, but one of the later alignments of old 66, as it existed at the time of bypassing by the turnpikes, has been designated as Oklahoma 66. That means you can follow the double sixes almost continuously across the state. Keep in mind, of course, that the alignment marked as State Highway 66 is one of many that the route followed over the years. As always, observation and exploration are your tickets to maximum enjoyment.

Less than five miles into Oklahoma, you'll come to the Route 66 community of:

QUAPAW

The village of Quapaw, about four miles from the Kansas state line, boasts a few buildings with murals painted on them, which one of the locals told me were painted in the 1970s. Keep alert as you cruise through town.

COMMERCE

Commerce is the boyhood home of baseball star Mickey Mantle, lending him the nickname "Commerce Comet." The main drag (old 66 bypass) has been re-named Mickey Mantle Boulevard. The house where he grew up is at 319 S. Quincy, and there is a metal-sided barn on the property full of dents where Mickey practiced his hitting. A few years ago, there was a plan to build a Mickey Mantle museum in town, but those plans have been abandoned. I spoke with someone involved in the project who told me a decision had been made that such a museum would need to be located in a larger community (no decision as to where yet). On June 12, 2010, a large bronze statue of the **Commerce Comet** was unveiled in front of Mickey Mantle Field on the south side of town.

Originally, Route 66 passed along the town's main business district on Commerce Street. Today, near the west end of Commerce Street, there is

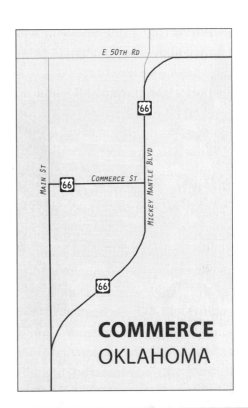

COMMERCE
OKLAHOMA

Mickey Mantle Field, Commerce, Oklahoma.

an old cottage-style gasoline station with a small collection of petroliana and such. Open only on weekends, it's at 101 S. Main.

MIAMI

Named for the Native American tribe, and pronounced *my-AM-uh*, this was at one time informally known as Jimtown, after four farmers named Jim in the area.

Near Commerce, Oklahoma.

The jewel of Miami is by all accounts the **Coleman Theatre**, at 103 N. Main. Originally designed in Italianate style, during construction it was converted to Spanish Mission Revival, resulting in a unique piece of architecture. Opening night was in April of 1929, just six months before the beginning of the Great Depression. The Coleman was on the Orpheum Vaudeville circuit, and saw the likes of Will Rogers, Tom Mix, the Three Stooges, and Sally Rand as performers. Today, free guided tours are available.

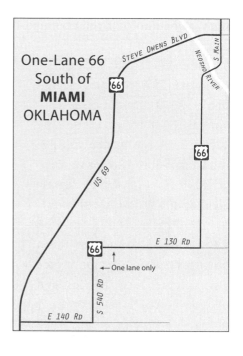

One-Lane 66
South of
MIAMI
OKLAHOMA

STEVE OWENS BLVD

NEOSHO RIVER

S MAIN

66

66

US 69

E 130 RD

66

←One lane only

S 540 RD

E 140 RD

MIAMI ATTRACTIONS

For regional history, visit the **Dobson Museum** at 110 A Street SW, which includes Native American artifacts, mining items, and other articles relating to the area's early settlement. There is also an extensive collection of Texaco-related materials.

On the grounds of the county courthouse is a scale replica of the **Statue of Liberty**. This is one of 200 erected nationwide by the Boy Scouts of America in 1950 to honor the 40th anniversary of the organization.

There is a **Marathon Oil Gasoline Station** at 331 S. Main that was built in 1929, and thought to be one of the oldest of its kind still standing.

A recent addition to Miami is **Route 66 Vintage Iron**, a motorcycle museum with what they tout as one of the largest collections of Steve McQueen-owned gear. 128 S. Main.

As of this writing, Miami has tentative plans to install a reproduction **Ozark Trail** milepost marker somewhere in town. The original was 21 feet in height, and stood in the middle of the intersection of Main and Central. You can see an original example of one of these markers further west near Stroud. In their heyday, these obelisk-style markers were

The Coleman opened its doors in 1929, at the threshold of the Great Depression. Miami, Oklahoma.

typically lighted, and bore the names of several nearby towns and the distances to them. Also planned is a reproduction of an early archway over the road, welcoming travelers to downtown Miami.

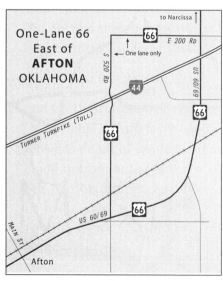 On the southern outskirts of Miami you can still find some portions of old 66 which are even older than the route itself (pre-1926). In the vicinity are some one-lane-wide sections of concrete roadway paved in the early '20s. It's said that money was tight, and there was only half the amount needed to do the job completely. Rather than cover half the mileage, the decision was made to pave the full distance, but at half the normal width. This meant—and of course it still means today—that driving it requires being very cautious of oncoming vehicles, particularly where visibility is short. Just move your passenger-side wheels off onto the ample shoulder when necessary. To locate this section, just continue straight (on Main Street) past the Steve Owens Boulevard intersection, then turn right when you can no longer continue straight ahead. The one-lane section of 66 will demonstrate very clearly that early highway alignments were constructed with a considerable number of 90-degree corners. The removal of such harsh turns by re-routing was a major thrust throughout the country during the 1930s.

NARCISSA-AFTON

Between Narcissa and Afton is another section of the one-lane 66. To access it, turn right at a street called E. 200 Road. However, once you've explored this you might want to backtrack a bit on the newer alignment, which passes the former site of the **Buffalo Ranch**. Buffalo Ranch was a good old-fashioned

Afton, Oklahoma.

Long-time sentinel in Afton, Oklahoma.

Laurel Kane's restored DX station serves as the de facto welcome center for the town of Afton, Oklahoma.

"tourist trap," featuring trained animals (technically American bison), plus the requisite curio shop, etc. The ranch itself is now gone, replaced by a modern truck stop/convenience store, although they do maintain a few bison in an adjacent field.

One of my favorite Mother Road artifacts is here in Afton—the sign for the Rest Haven Motel. I hope it's still there when you visit. A short distance away is the restored **Afton DX Station** and Packard showroom (at First and Locust). The DX station is now an informal visitor center for Mother Roaders. Across the highway from the DX there used to be the World's Largest Matchbook Collection. Unfortunately for all of us, that building burned in the summer of 2003—no irony intended.

FURTHER AFIELD

Not far from Afton is Monkey Island, a peninsula community jutting into the Grand Lake O' The Cherokees, and home to **Darryl Starbird's National Rod & Custom Car Hall of Fame Museum**. The collection features over 40 street rods and other custom-built automobiles, as well as plenty of photographs and other memorabilia. 55251 E. Highway 85A, at Highway 125.

Just east of Afton you can take a side trip south on U.S. 59, across a portion of the Grand Lake O' The Cherokees, to the community of **Grove**. Perhaps the most popular destination in town is **Har-Ber Village**, described as one of the largest antique displays in the country, which features a reconstructed turn-of-the-century village with over 100 buildings, a walking trail, herb garden, and other exhibits. 4404 W. 20th St.

The town of Grove is also host to the *Cherokee Queen I* and *II*, a pair of paddlewheel riverboats which offer tourist excursions on the lake. In Grove's **Polson Cemetery** is the gravesite of General Stand Watie—the last Civil War Confederate General to surrender, and a full-blooded Native American.

VINITA

One of the oldest settlements in Oklahoma and originally called Downingville, the town was later re-named for Vinnie Ream (1850–1914), the sculptress who

You'll enter Vinita on Illinois Avenue/U.S. 69. Just continue following 69, which will include a left turn onto Wilson Street. West of town, state highway 66 splits away—begin following 66.

fashioned the life-sized image of Abraham Lincoln in the nation's capitol. It is also the birthplace of "Dr. Phil" McGraw of advice/TV fame.

It was here in 1935 that Will Rogers had planned to attend the town's first-ever annual rodeo. He died, however, in a plane crash at Point Barrow, Alaska, just weeks beforehand. Nowadays, that rodeo is known as the **Will Rogers Memorial Rodeo**, and it is held each August.

Rogers somewhat facetiously called Vinita his "college town," having attended a secondary school here. In Vinita there is an old cottage-style gasoline station that has been converted to the local Greyhound bus station.

When the Lewis Motel in Vinita, Oklahoma, was demolished a few years ago, the sign was sold off and now stands on a ranch in California.

VINITA ATTRACTIONS

The town's self-guided **Historic Homes Tour** directs you to 35 turn-of-the-century houses built by the area's founding families. You can get a guide at the Eastern Trails Museum (below). General visitor information is available by calling 918-256-7133, where you can also get directions to the **Barker Gang Gravesite** and the **Cabin Creek Civil War Battle Site**.

On the highway west of Vinita, Oklahoma.

The **Eastern Trails Museum** has a re-created post office, general store, printing office, and doctor's office, as well as items representing Native American history. 215 W. Illinois.

Clanton's is an over-80-year-old café with lots of old photos lining the walls (319 E. Illinois). The **World's Largest Calf Fry Festival & Cook-Off** is held in Vinita each August, in which a full ton of the delicacies are annually consumed.

Vinita is also known to some as being the location of the largest McDonald's restaurant in the United States. It's in an unusual structure—formerly operating under the name Glass House—that actually spans the turnpike just outside of town.

West of Vinita, you'll need to ignore the turnoff for U.S. 69 and continue straight ahead. Then begin following Oklahoma State Highway 66.

WHITE OAK-CATALE

In this vicinity is an old tourist court called the Country Court Motel.

The first time I passed through, the red-and-white sign was barely visible over the tops of overgrown foliage.

White Oak, Oklahoma.

Just before you arrive at the town of Chelsea, on the left side of the highway, you can take a turn onto a very old alignment of 66 across the Pryor Creek Bridge. If you continue on this route, you'll pass through a few blocks of residences before being reunited with the more modern alignment, more or less in the central part of town, right beside what remains of the Chelsea Motel, with its wonderful old sign.

CHELSEA

This community dates from 1882. The town includes an example of an underground pedestrian tunnel built to facilitate crossing the then-busy highway. A few miles to the

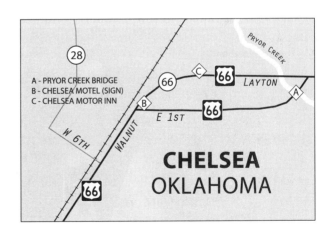

south and west of Chelsea is the site of the first oil well in Oklahoma, which was established in 1889. Will Rogers' sister lived here, whom he is said to have visited frequently.

Here in Chelsea is an original Sears Roebuck pre-cut house, purchased in Chicago in 1913 for $16 and delivered by railroad car. The **Hogue House** is the only known example west of the Mississippi that is still owned by descendants of the original purchaser. 1001 S. Olive Street, one block west of 66.

If it's getting late and you need a place to stay for the night, I can recommend the **Chelsea Motor Inn**, just a half-dozen lovingly-cared-for rooms beside a nineteenth century residence. 321 E. Layton (Route 66).

The modest Chelsea Motel had one of the nicest signs anywhere on Route 66. Chelsea, Oklahoma.

This old bridge is on the east edge of Chelsea, Oklahoma.

Chelsea, Oklahoma.

BUSHYHEAD-FOYIL

A Cherokee Indian chief lent his name to the community of Bushyhead.

> Modern Oklahoma 66 bypasses Foyil, so I recommend slowing down to take the old alignment through town along Andy Payne Boulevard.

Andy Payne, winner of the 1928 Bunion Derby—a cross-country footrace organized as a wildly extreme promotional stunt—was from the Foyil area. There is a **bronze statue** of Andy on an old alignment of 66 (Andy Payne Boulevard) at the far west edge of town.

Memorial to local hero Andy Payne, Foyil, Oklahoma.

Foyil's claim to fame today is that it is the home of Ed Galloway's collection of concrete Native-American-inspired structures in what is commonly called **Totem Pole Park**. This is truly

The Top Hat on the east side of town marks the turnoff to Totem Pole Park. Foyil, Oklahoma.

Ed Galloway's Totem Pole Park, just outside Foyil, Oklahoma, is folk art at its very best. *Left:* Fiddle House, Totem Pole Park, near Foyil, Oklahoma.

a landmark, and a great old-fashioned roadside attraction to boot. Get there by leaving State Highway 66 and turning onto Highway 28A at the Top Hat Dairy Bar, at the north edge of Foyil, and going about four miles east. The focal point of the collection is a 90-foot-tall totem pole made of brightly painted concrete. Ed Galloway created this collection of structures in the post-war years (the main totem pole in particular bears a date of 1948) as an expression of his own creative impulses.

SEQUOYAH

Established in 1871, the name of the settlement was changed to Beulah in 1909 after the postmaster's daughter. The name was changed back in 1913 to honor the famous Cherokee chief, also called George Guess, who developed the Cherokee alphabet. Remarkably, even the most advanced Native American peoples had not developed written forms of their languages as late as the nineteenth century. Sequoyah, son of a Cherokee mother and a British trader named Nathaniel Gist, became convinced that the white men's superior power and influence derived from their written language. He began developing a system of writing for the Cherokee people in the belief that this would help maintain their independence from the whites. He developed his syllabary, a system of 86 symbols denoting all of the syllables of the Cherokee language, in about 1821. The system was easy to learn and use, and by 1828 the Cherokee *Advocate* newspaper was being published.

CLAREMORE

This is the county seat of Rogers County, which was named for Will Rogers' father, Clem Rogers. Claremore was known in years gone by as a place for "taking the waters." There was a well in town

A visit to the Will Rogers Memorial is well worth your time. Claremore, Oklahoma.

The Round-Up Motel is no longer with us. Claremore, Oklahoma.

that produced a dark, malodorous substance called radium water (even though it contained no radium). This water was touted as being therapeutic for rheumatism and other ailments, and was a big selling point for staying at the **Hotel Will Rogers**, which was known for its baths. The hotel re-opened in 1997 after partial restoration.

As you enter Claremore from the east, there is an older alignment of Route 66 off to your right (J. M. Davis Boulevard) that is pretty easy to recognize. Along that stretch, on the left-hand side, is an old motel court now serving duty as an apartment complex called Adobe Village. It appears to be from the 1930s, and bears a resemblance to the Alamo Courts chain which used to be found scattered about in this part of the country.

CLAREMORE ATTRACTIONS

The most important thing not to miss when in Claremore is, of course, the **Will Rogers Memorial** at 1720 W. Will Rogers Boulevard. The museum, mausoleum, and grounds are beautifully done, and there is far too much included to even begin to list. Will's body was moved here in 1944, having been interred from 1935 to 1944 at Forest Lawn Cemetery in California. This was property which he had purchased with the intent of finally settling down permanently after the Hollywood career played itself out. Memorial services are held here each November 4th, his birthday.

Will's most famous quote is, "I never met a man I didn't like," but pithy statements were his stock-in-trade. There are thousands worth repeating, but he seemed particularly to be speaking to people like you and me when he wrote in 1930: "But if you want to have a good time, I don't care where you live, just load in your kids, and take some congenial friends, and just start out. You would be surprised what there is to see in this great Country within 200 miles of where any of us live. I don't care what State or what town."

The **J. M. Davis Arms & Historical Museum** is also a Claremore mainstay. Included in the thousands of firearms on display are weapons owned by the likes of Pretty Boy Floyd, Cole Younger, Pancho Villa, and other outlaw-types. This is the world's largest privately owned gun collection, with examples spanning six centuries of the gunsmith's craft. Besides the guns, there are trophy heads, swords, musical instruments, Native American artifacts, World War I posters, and even John Wayne movie posters. 330 N. J. M. Davis Blvd.

The **Lynn Riggs Memorial Museum**, at 121 N. Weenonah, includes the actual "surrey with the fringe on top" made famous in the musical *Oklahoma!*, which was based upon Riggs' play *Green Grow the Lilacs*. When the production premiered in the state in 1946, officials declared a state holiday.

On the campus of Rogers State University is Meyer Hall, which houses the **Oklahoma Military Academy Museum**. The academy operated at this location from 1919 to 1971, when its functions were taken over by Claremore Junior College. 1701 W. Will Rogers Blvd.

Several Claremore buildings are listed on the National Register of Historic Places, including the **Will Rogers Hotel**, the **Belvidere Mansion**, and **Meyer Hall** (above). The Belvidere Mansion is a restored, pre-statehood Victorian home offering tours by costumed docents at 121 N. Chickasaw. The Belvidere has a ballroom that occupies the entire third floor of the house.

The **Swan Brothers Dairy Farm**, operated by three generations of the Swan family since 1923, has a store and tours at 938 E. Fifth Street.

Claremore holds a **Bluegrass & Chili Festival** in September and a Will Rogers birthday celebration each November.

Belvidere Mansion, Claremore, Oklahoma.

FURTHER AFIELD

Northwest of Claremore via Highway 88 is the town of **Oologah**, Oklahoma. Here, overlooking Oologah Lake, is Will Rogers' boyhood home, known as **Dog Iron Ranch**, with house, barn, petting zoo, and vintage films and newsreels for your enjoyment. Rogers was born in this log-walled house in 1879. Today there are 400 acres and a herd of longhorn cattle. The town itself also has a bronze statue—called the *The Cherokee Kid*—of its favorite son on horseback, and much of the turn-of-the-century downtown has been restored. The **Bank of Oologah**, circa 1906, boastsauthentic period interior and furnishings. Today this bank is touted as having "closed during the Depression." I'm sure that at the time no one considered it much of a selling point (Maple and Cooweescoowee Streets). On the same corner is the **Oologah Historical Museum**, with Will Rogers photos and a complete doctor's office on display. Miniatures of the *The Cherokee Kid* statue in town are available in the museum's gift shop.

VERDIGRIS-CATOOSA

The Port of Catoosa is the nation's largest inland seaport, connecting Tulsa with the Mississippi River and the port of New Orleans. The **Arkansas River Historical Society Museum** will educate you on the construction of the project (5350 Cimarrow Rd.). You might also want to visit the **Catoosa Historical Society Museum,** at 207 N. Cherokee, for a taste of the

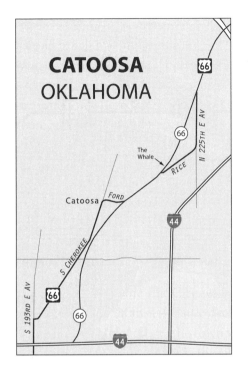

CATOOSA
OKLAHOMA

The Whale

Catoosa

city's heritage. Look for the Frisco caboose parked outside.

The **Cherokee Nation** maintains a tourism bureau at 777 W. Cherokee Street, where you can get information about a plethora of significant sites across the state.

The **D.W. Correll Museum** houses a collection of rare and antique automobiles, rocks, gems, and other items in three separate buildings. Among the rare cars is a steam-powered Locomobile dating from 1898 (19934 E. Pine).

Near Catoosa is what I refer to as the **Catoosa Whale**, an example of a small-scale mom-and-pop roadside attraction. Restored by volunteers in 2002, it is a large whale-shaped structure, painted blue, which sits in a small pond. In its heyday, visitors could enter the whale's mouth, and then either slide down a chute, which exits behind the whale's

Roadside picnic area, Catoosa, Oklahoma.

ear, or dive off a small platform at the tail and into the surrounding swimming hole. Adjacent is a wooden "ark" that used to house a roadside menagerie. Just across the highway from them both is the former Arrowood Trading Post.

 Leave Catoosa on Cherokee Street. You'll then veer left (south) onto S. 193rd East Avenue, then right onto Eleventh Street.

LYNN LANE

This community appears in my 1957 atlas east of Tulsa, a little to the southwest of the current I-44/U.S. 412 junction, just inside Tulsa County. It has been swallowed by the expanding Tulsa city limits, which now run all the way out to the county line. A reminder persists in the Lynn Lane Reservoir nearby.

TULSA

A city which owes much to the oil industry, Tulsa was also the home of Cyrus Avery, the man so instrumental not only in the establishment of Route 66, but more particularly in getting it routed through his home state and town. Perhaps his strongest case was the presence of the Eleventh Street Bridge, easily the best

> **Enter Tulsa on Eleventh Street, which runs for several miles to very near the town's center. A variation is to turn north at Mingo, and go west on Admiral Place, which was the original alignment. That routing takes the traveler into the downtown area, just as all highways used to do. You would do well to explore downtown in either case.**

A - MEADOW GOLD PAVILION
B - BLUE DOME STATION

TULSA OKLAHOMA

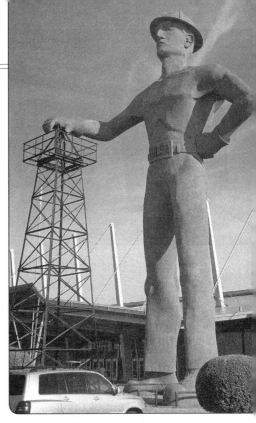

crossing of the Arkansas River at the time. At this writing, the bridge has become the center of a project to create a Route 66 tourist attraction, so plan to linger awhile.

Notorious outlaw Kate "Ma" Barker lived in Tulsa in 1930 and 1931. That was about the same time that Madison W. "Daddy" Cain bought a former garage at 423 N. Main and called it Cain's Dance Academy, later to become **Cain's Ballroom** and a thriving center for what later came to be called Western Swing.

In 1938, Tulsa gave birth to the **Society for the Preservation and Encouragement of Barbershop**

This giant oilworker presides over the Tulsa Fairgrounds.

Quartet Singing. Now headquartered in Kenosha, Wisconsin, as the Barbershop Harmony Society, the organization has thousands of chapters coast-to-coast and internationally.

Also in the 1930s, Meadow Gold Dairy, at that time a part of Beatrice Foods, erected a large rooftop sign on a single-story building on Route 66 (i.e. Eleventh Street) at Lewis Avenue. In 2004, with the building about to be demolished, the iconic **Meadow Gold** sign was saved and restored. It now sits proudly on top of a purpose-made brick base a few blocks to the west, at Quaker Avenue. The Meadow Gold neon was ceremonially re-lit in May 2009.

In June of 1921, Tulsa was the scene of a race riot which took the lives of more than 30 people and left the African-American district of town a burning ruin. Today, the **Greenwood Cultural Center** and the neighboring **Mabel B. Little Heritage House** recall those dark days in the heart of Black Wall Street through photographs and memorabilia, while celebrating the neighborhood's resiliency. 322 N. Greenwood Ave.

TULSA ATTRACTIONS

The **Philbrook Museum** combines a historical home, extensive art collections, and formal gardens. The Italianate home was built in 1927 by oil man Waite Phillips, and has been featured on the program *America's Castles*. Just a decade later, he donated the estate to the city of Tulsa. Today, the Philbrook is rated in the top 65 art museums in the country, and is surrounded by 23 acres of English gardens. 2727 S. Rockford Rd.

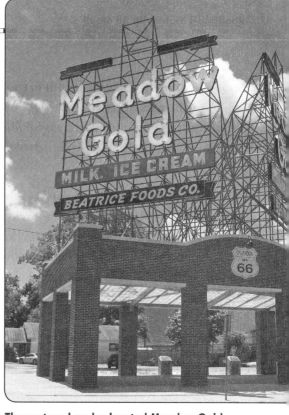

The restored and relocated Meadow Gold sign, Tulsa, Oklahoma.

The **Gilcrease Museum** houses one of the world's most extensive collections of Native American and Western art, and rests amid 475 acres of grounds with themed gardens. 1400 Gilcrease Museum Rd.

The **Willard Elsing Museum**, on the campus of Oral Roberts University, features a four-foot jade sculpture among its 60-year-old collection of gems, minerals, crystals, and other stones. Mr. Elsing at one time operated a rock and mineral shop on Route 66 at Joplin, Missouri. The university is at 7777 S. Lewis Avenue. Enter at

On Eleventh Street (Route 66), Tulsa, Oklahoma.

the giant **Praying Hands** sculpture, which is about 60 feet tall and weighs 30 tons—a rather arresting sight.

Lovers of Art Deco architecture have plenty to be thankful for here in Tulsa. A well-known example is the **Boston Avenue Methodist Church**, but there are also a number of deco office buildings in the downtown business district. Church tours are held every Sunday following the 11:00 AM service, or by appointment during the week (1301 S. Boston Avenue). You can also take a walking tour of Art Deco by picking up a brochure at the chamber of commerce office at 2 W. Second Street.

There is a **Frank Lloyd Wright** creation in a residential section of Tulsa. It's still a private residence, so no tours are available, but you can view two exterior facades by driving by. On a corner lot at 3700 S. Birmingham Avenue.

Mac's Antique Car Museum features dozens of vintage models from LaSalle, Packard, and more. Included is the 1948 Hudson used in the film *Driving Miss Daisy*. 1319 E. Fourth. Open weekend afternoons only.

The **Sunbelt Railroad Museum** includes restored 1920 passenger cars, memorabilia, video tapes, a reference library, and a working telegraph station. 1323 E. Fifth.

Lovers of miniatures will want to see the **Ida Dennie Willis Museum of Miniatures, Dolls, and Toys** at 628 N. Country Club Drive. The collection includes an ever-changing array of trains, planes, robots, and dolls, all housed in a 1910 Tudor mansion. One of many interesting exhibits is the Gates collection of ethnic and advertising dolls.

The **Tulsa Air and Space Museum & Planetarium** has lots

Tulsa, Oklahoma, west of the Arkansas River.

Tulsa, Oklahoma.

of aircraft on display, including an F-14 Tomcat (same as used in *Top Gun*) and a Lear 24D corporate jet. For those addicted to hands-on experiences, flight simulators are also on hand. 3624 N. 74th E. Avenue, on the grounds of the Tulsa International Airport.

The **Tulsa Historical Society Museum** is the official repository of the city's history, including official documents, vintage photographs, and other artifacts. Now located in a 1919 mansion at 2445 S. Peoria. There's a still-operating drive-in movie theater, the **Admiral Twin**, in the northeastern sector of town, at 7355 E. Easton. Starting out as a single screen in 1951 and called the Modern Aire, the name was changed a short time later when the second screen was added. The theater is featured as a hangout for characters in 1983's feature film *The Outsiders*, directed by Francis Ford Coppola.

At **Creek Council Oak Park**, a 170-year-old oak tree marks the spot where the Creek Indians

Tulsa, Oklahoma.

arrived in the 1830s after traversing the Trail of Tears, thus establishing the site which would later become Tulsey-town. At 18th Street and Cheyenne Avenue.

There's a 76-foot giant oil worker sculpture, known as the **Golden Driller**, standing outside of the International Petroleum Exhibition (IPE) Building at the Tulsa Fairgrounds. The IPE is said to contain the world's largest unobstructed interior volume. The roof is suspended by a system of booms and cables, which allows adequate room inside for oversized equipment shows. In fact, the original Golden Driller (he was upgraded in the 1970s) was put on display *inside* the IPE building for a while prior to his outdoor placement in 1966. 21st at Pittsburgh.

Also in Tulsa you'll find the **Center of the Universe**, a sort of acoustical mystery spot downtown. Stand in this spot, recite some words, and you'll hear your voice strongly reverberating back to you. The effect is quite striking. It's a circular feature on the Boston Avenue pedestrian walkway between First and Archer Streets. Just yards away are the Art Deco-inspired **Tulsa Union** railroad depot (now home to the **Oklahoma Jazz Hall of Fame**, 111 E. First) and a 72-foot sculpture titled *Artificial Cloud*, created in the early 1990s for the city's Mayfest celebration.

In downtown Tulsa, on a very early alignment of Route 66, stands the **Blue Dome**. A distinctively-shaped former gasoline station, the re-

stored Blue Dome is now the de facto centerpiece of a thriving new entertainment district. At the corner of S. Elgin and E. Second.

FURTHER AFIELD

About 47 miles north of Tulsa is the city of **Bartlesville**. The city's

Tulsa, Oklahoma.

historic district includes nearly 50 buildings from the oil-boom period of 1900 to 1920.

Bartlesville is also home to the **Inn at Price Towers**, a Frank Lloyd Wright structure from 1956, said to have been designed based on the structure of a tree. It's now a hotel and museum with 21 architecturally fascinating guest rooms, some of which are two-story suites. The Inn has its own restaurant and bar (Sixth and Dewey). The **Bartlesville Community Center** was designed by a student of Wright's (Wesley Peters) and features the world's largest *cloisonné* mural.

At 1107 SE Cherokee is the **Frank Phillips Home**, a 26-room neoclassical mansion completed in 1909. Phillips was founder of the Phillips Petroleum Company, the firm that saw fit to brand their gasoline with a highway shield emblazoned with the number 66. The **Phillips Petroleum Company Museum** is at 410 S. Keeler.

Frank Phillips' country home and guest ranch, named **Woolaroc**, is just outside Bartlesville. The ranch was designed as a sort of Old West preserve, and attracted the likes of presidents, tycoons, and other celebrities of the day as guests. The 3,700-acre compound, established in 1925, features a museum of western art, a collection of Phillips Petroleum memorabilia, a lodge house, picnic areas, nature trails, a petting barn, roaming buffalo, and the Phillips family mausoleum. Southwest of Bartlesville via State Highway 123.

The **Bartlesville Area History Museum** is on the fifth floor of the City Center, formerly the Hotel Maire and later the Burlingame. Of course, the museum has lots of things on exhibit, but at the core of it all is a collection of photographs taken by Frank Griggs, who moved to the area in 1908 and began recording daily life through about 200,000 photographic negatives. 401 S. Johnstone Ave.

Discovery 1 Park contains a replica of the first commercial oil well in Oklahoma, named the Nellie Johnstone No. 1. The park, formerly called Johnstone Park, is at 200 N. Cherokee. Bartlesville also holds a **Bi-Plane Expo** the first weekend each June.

Not far from Bartlesville is the town of **Dewey**, home to the **Tom Mix Museum**. Prior to his film career, Mix served as marshal in Dewey

(1911–12), and the third of his five wives was from here. Mix's film career came to include more than 300 films, some of which are available for viewing in the museum's small auditorium (721 N. Delaware). The **Dewey Hotel**, downtown at 801 N. Delaware, was built in 1900 and serves as a museum. A few miles east of Dewey on Durham Road is **Prairie Song, Indian Territory**, a replica nineteenth-century village of 20 or so hand-hewn log buildings.

 As you leave Tulsa, after crossing the river, keep an eye out for the 66 Motel sign on the western outskirts. The motel itself was razed and replaced with rental storage units, but the owners promised to reinstall the sign for the benefit of roadies like you and me.

RED FORK-OAKHURST

Follow Southwest Boulevard, which becomes Frankoma Road, en route to Sapulpa via the communities of Red Fork and Oakhurst. See reference map.

SAPULPA

The **Liberty Glass Company** was established here in the early 1900s by George F. Collins. The idea for the name seems to have

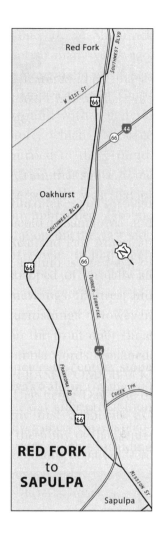

**RED FORK
to
SAPULPA**

Entering Sapulpa, Old Sapulpa Road and New Sapulpa Road merge to form N. Mission Street. Route 66 then turns west on Dewey Avenue through the downtown district. West of downtown, keep alert for the old alignment that crosses Rock Creek on a brick-paved bridge.

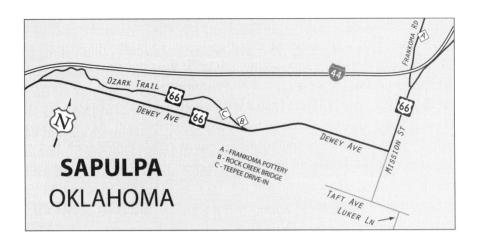

OZARK TRAIL

44

66

66

DEWEY AVE   66

C   B

SAPULPA

OKLAHOMA

A - FRANKOMA POTTERY
B - ROCK CREEK BRIDGE
C - TEEPEE DRIVE-IN

DEWEY AVE

66

FRANKOMA RD   A

MISSION ST

TAFT AVE

LUKER LN

come from the fact that 1886, the year Sapulpa was established, was the same year in which France made the United States a gift of the Statue of Liberty. Jack Rittenhouse makes mention of Liberty Glass at the time of his passing through in 1946.

Downtown Sapulpa includes a number of reproductions of antique advertising murals. These appear on the sides of several buildings along old Route 66. Be sure to explore Sapulpa thoroughly, because an older alignment at the far end of town takes you over a brick-paved iron truss bridge (Rock Creek Bridge)

Sapulpa, Oklahoma, embraces its Mother Road heritage.

Sapulpa, Oklahoma.

and past the Teepee Drive-In movie theater. This alignment will take you back in time for a bit and well away from the roar of traffic.

SAPULPA ATTRACTIONS

Sapulpa is fairly well known as the home of **Frankoma Pottery**, on an old alignment of 66 called Frankoma Road. Frankoma has been making earthenware using a local clay source since 1933. However, the company has struggled in recent years, ownership has changed hands, and the outlet store has been open less consistently. 9549 Frankoma Rd.

The **Frank family home** is now open for tours. The home was designed in the mid-1950s by Bruce Goff, and incorporates brickwork and tiling in the traditional Frankoma Pottery styles and colors. Tours, conducted by Frank daughters Joniece and Donna, are by prior arrangement only by calling 918-224-6566; the home is at 1300 Luker Lane.

Housed in a circa-1910 building that was formerly the home of the YWCA, the **Sapulpa Historical Museum** features an 1890s-era kitchen and schoolroom, a telephone exhibit, and items pertaining to the Frisco Railroad. 100 E. Lee Ave.

FURTHER AFIELD

Just east of Sapulpa—and a very short side trip—is the community of **Jenks**. Here you'll find the **Oklahoma Aquarium**, if sharks, piranha, and octopuses interest you, and also the **Karl and Beverly White National Fishing Tackle Museum**.

On an old alignment of 66, Sapulpa, Oklahoma.

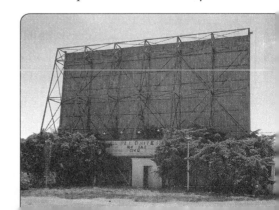

KELLYVILLE-BRISTOW

On my earlier trips through here, there was an old store west of Kellyville with a plywood Native American sign out front. The figure's arm was extended, as if pointing, and lettering on his outstretched arm promised: SOUVENIRS. Long closed, it was a treat for the Route 66 traveler to stumble upon. The sign has since been removed, however, and the remaining structures are nondescript. This is one of many disappearances reminding me to photograph, photograph, photograph.

According to the local chamber of commerce, Bristow's Sixth Avenue was at one time known as "Silk Stocking Row" due to the fact that there were more millionaires living here than any other place in Oklahoma.

BRISTOW ATTRACTIONS

The **Bristow Historical Museum** is located in the restored 1923 railroad depot and features rotating exhibits pertaining to the area's history, from the times of Indian Territory to the present. 1 Railroad Place.

Kellyville, Oklahoma.

While passing through Bristow, keep your eye out for a sign pointing to the **Wake Island Memorial** at Veteran's Memorial Drive in the western part of town. The city has commemorated those veterans who served in the battle for Wake Island in the Second World War, and there are some nice pedestrian-friendly walking paths in the vicinity.

Bristow, Oklahoma.

You can't see it, but along the stretch of road between Bristow and Stroud, there is an enormous underground storage cavity—a depleted gas field—which is used for storage of natural gas during periods of surplus. What you *can* see is that there are at least three cemeteries along Route 66 between Bristow and Depew, and then there are two more west of Depew, where 66 approaches the Turner Turnpike (I-44).

DEPEW

The village of Depew seems rather isolated. The Mother Road cut off the somewhat circuitous route through Depew early on. Take at least a few extra minutes to drive through town, though. You'll see evidence that this was once a much busier place.

Downtown Depew, Oklahoma.

Near Depew there used to be several small vending stands by the side of the road. Not used for that purpose in many years, they were later plastered with the placards of local political campaigns.

West of Depew and east of Stroud, be on the lookout for the Shoe Tree—a small tree with shoes tied to the branches.

STROUD

The town was established in 1892. Henry "BearCat" Starr and his gang

OZARK TRAIL MARKERS

The Ozark Trail marker near Stroud is one of several which once stood in the area. There is a similar one—a replica—in the town of Stratford, Oklahoma. That reproduction includes an inscription that is instructive for today's explorer:

OZARK TRAIL PYRAMID

By 1916, plans were underway to promote a network of roads through Oklahoma called the "Ozark Trail." The trails were planned by the Ozark Trail Association. Its mission was to promote a system of better roads connecting the surrounding states. These were the first roads to be classed as public supported highways. Early plans were "grandiose." Originally the Ozark Trail was to be a link from ocean to ocean. The route was to be marked with impressive pyramids and concrete mileage posts. These roads were intended to be "above high water, hardsurfaced, and later oiled." Routes increased rapidly as towns competed to be included on the Trail.

The Ozark Trail Pyramid was one of many marking the trail for travelers in the early 1920s. Oklahoma trails crossed the state, east to west and north to south. They have either become robbed two banks here in 1915. Starr was the nephew of the famed Belle Starr.

The focal point of Stroud is the **Rock Café**, which is built of stones that were unearthed during the construction of Route 66 in the area, and which features a nice sign that fans of neon will appreciate. A more recent addition to the café is **Mamie's Market**, a gift shop standing just next door. The Rock Café suffered a terrible fire in May 2008, and there were a lot of doubters who thought it was lost to us. However, through a lot of hard work and the sheer determination of the café's owner, Dawn Welch, "The Rock" reopened one year later, nearly to the day. Dawn, by the way,

U.S. Highways or follow the same course, such as U.S. 60, U.S. 62, OK 9, the famous "Route 66," and the current Turner Turnpike. This pyramid was one of several placed on the trail from Tulsa to Dallas. Chandler, Meeker, Shawnee, and Sulphur also had identical pyramids marking the trail along this particular route.

Work began on the Stratford Pyramid in December 1921. The buried base was six feet square, the next section was four feet square, the top tapered and stood [sic] twenty-two feet high. The original pyramid stood in the center of Main and Hyden Streets, which is only ½ block to the east. Due to traffic and safety reasons, this replica pyramid could not be in the original location. It was constructed as close to the original site as possible. "Ozark Trail" appeared on all four sides of the upper part of the pyramid and each side listed the mileage for the next towns along the route. In April 1923, the pyramid was wired and lighted. In the early 1940s, it was pushed over and buried where it stood. In the early 1970s, its pieces were exhumed, partially restored, and now stands [sic] on a private ranch near Stratford. One other "original" pyramid, which is presumed to be the Chandler pyramid, is located west of Stroud off Highway 66.

This replica was erected in the summer of 1997.

A stop at the Rock Café is a longstanding Route 66 tradition. Stroud, Oklahoma.

also happens to be a big part of the inspiration behind the character of Sally the Porsche in the 2006 movie *Cars*.

Also in Stroud is the **Skyliner Motel**, which has a good-looking neon sign. Look for it near the west end of town. If you keep your eyes open as you pass through town, you might spot the Mother Load Laundromat on one of the side streets.

STROUD ATTRACTIONS

The town **library** is an example of 1929 Art Deco architecture, and was originally built by Bell Telephone. Seventh St. and Third Ave.

This part of Oklahoma considers itself wine country, and there are indeed several wineries nearby if that's your thing. As an example, just a mile or so west of downtown Stroud is **StableRidge Vineyards and Winery**. Their tasting room is in a former Catholic church built in the years 1898–1902.

Stroud is home to the **International Brick & Rolling Pin Competition and Festival**. The competition pits a handful of cities named Stroud against one another in games of skill. The other Strouds are in Canada, Australia, and the U.K.

West of Stroud there is a left turn (at N. 3540 Road) you can take which follows the old Ozark Trail Highway. This early 66 alignment

features an **Ozark Trail monument** (a tall obelisk) at one of its intersections. This old path of the highway is more easily spotted when facing east, because the later Route 66 alignment curves to your left, and straight ahead is an obviously older alignment which will take you directly to the marker—that's the way I was first able to find it.

DAVENPORT

Watch for high water in this vicinity. The first time I took Route 66 through Oklahoma, I had to skip Davenport altogether due to the closure of several roads at the time. There is an old Texaco station in town that has an ever-changing array of vintage vehicles parked on the lot. There is also a land run mural painted on the side of the Farmers Bank building in the tiny downtown district.

Stroud, Oklahoma.

Be on the lookout for the Lincoln Motel as you reach the eastern outskirts of Chandler. Built in 1939, and very much a product of the 66 era, the Lincoln is still in business. Our friend Rittenhouse made mention of it way back in 1946.

Davenport, Oklahoma.

CHANDLER

Chandler, the seat of Lincoln County, was established with a land run in 1891, and calls itself the Pecan Capital of the World. The town of Cromwell, southeast of here in Seminole County, is reputed to be the site of the last Old-West-style gunfight. That was in 1924, and it took the life of Bill Tilghman, former U.S. Marshal at Dodge City and sheriff of Lincoln County, Oklahoma. Poor Bill—he was 70 years old and had been retired quite a few years when he was called upon that one last time. Tilghman is buried in the Oak Park Cemetery on the west side of Chandler.

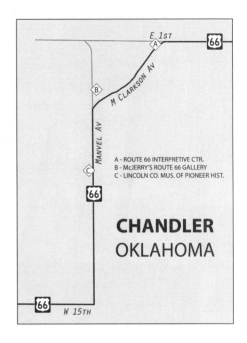

A - ROUTE 66 INTERPRETIVE CTR.
B - McJERRY'S ROUTE 66 GALLERY
C - LINCOLN CO. MUS. OF PIONEER HIST.

**CHANDLER
OKLAHOMA**

CHANDLER ATTRACTIONS

The **Route 66 Interpretive Center** opened in 2007 in what was once the National Guard Armory. It's located right where 66 takes a sweeping left turn, transitioning from east-west First Street to north-south Manvel Avenue. Aside from the Mother Road exhibits, the building also houses offices for the Oklahoma Route 66 Association and the local chamber of commerce.

The former National Guard Armory is now a Route 66 must-stop in Chandler, Oklahoma.

This old Phillips station is undergoing renovation. Chandler, Oklahoma.

While in Chandler, consider paying a visit to **Jerry McClanahan**'s art gallery at 306 Manvel Avenue in the north part of town. Jerry's Route 66 artwork is well-known, and he was honored with the prestigious Will Rogers Award in June 2010. Hours are irregular (after all, he's an artist), so call ahead (903-467-6384).

Further to the south on Manvel Avenue is an old cottage-style **Phillips 66** station. It has gradually been receiving restorative work. For example, it had been modified from its original form by the addition of two garage bays, probably during the 1950s, but those additions have now been removed.

The **Lincoln County Museum of Pioneer History** showcases Chandler's colorful early history, with an emphasis on their legendary sheriff, Bill Tilghman, and also hosts Miss Faye's Touring Historical Marionette Theater and rare films by cinematographer Benny Kent. 717-719 Manvel.

Between Chandler and Warwick there is a **Meramec Caverns barn**. However, you won't notice it heading west, as the painted side of it faces *eastbound* travelers in hopes of enticing them to stop at the cave many miles ahead of them in Missouri.

Chandler, Oklahoma.

East of Warwick, Oklahoma.

WARWICK

At the loosely-defined community of Warwick, you'll come upon the **Seaba Station Motorcycle Museum**. The Seaba has been restored by its newest owners to its circa-1920s state, and their passion for motorcycles is on full display. The building was formerly an engine-rebuilding shop and gasoline station. Take a look in back for the still-standing stone outhouse.

WELLSTON-LUTHER

Wellston was cut off from the main route in the 1930s, but there is a loop through town marked 66B, which follows the older, more circuitous alignment. At the junction of 66B on the east side of town is the site once occupied by Pioneer Camp, a tourist campground, and later the Pioneer Barbeque restaurant. Still visible is a pair of masonry bases which once supported an archway over the entrance to the camp.

Luther has a small downtown just south of the highway with several vacant storefronts.

West of Luther you can access a dead-end remnant of an older 66 alignment. There is a large sign at the entrance marked "Private

Business district of Luther, Oklahoma.

This old station is slowly decaying between Luther and Arcadia, Oklahoma.

Historical Site."

Further west of Luther and just east of Arcadia are the remains of a stone gasoline station (circa 1920s) reputed to have been the scene of a counterfeit ring. It's small, but it's also one of my favorite ruins on the route, one that I photograph again each and every time I pass through here. With each visit, I find that these ruins have deteriorated a bit more.

ARCADIA

There is a historical marker on the eastern outskirts of town designating the eastern boundary of the infamous 1889 Land Run.

ARCADIA ATTRACTIONS

Arcadia has a literary connection. **Washington Irving**, well-known as the author of the popular tale "Rip Van Winkle," camped here in 1832. He wrote about his travels in this area in *A Tour of the Prairies*, which was published in 1835. Look for the marker east of the Round Barn. Mr. Irving is considered by some to be the United States' earliest professional author, having written *A History of New York* in 1809 under the pseudonym Diedrich Knickerbocker. Like Shakespeare, Irving is credited with putting some phrases of his own invention into the vernacular. He is credited with the expression "almighty dollar," referring to "that great object of universal devotion throughout our land." He also is credited with the expression "happy hunting ground" to refer to the Native Americans' life in the hereafter. If that's not enough, then consider that his pen name of Knickerbocker has been synonymous with New York and New Yorkers since shortly after the publication of his *History* at the tender age of 26.

Arcadia is the home of the **Round Barn**, a world-famous Route

The Round Barn has stood in Arcadia, Oklahoma, for more than 100 years.

66 landmark. Constructed in 1898, the barn was restored several years ago and now houses a small gift shop. The interior walls are covered with photographs and other memorabilia having to do with unusual barns around the world. These include circular ones, octagonal, and other unconventional configurations. The upper level, above the gift shop, is available for rental for special events.

Also on the National Register is the **Tuton Drug Store** (now the Old Country Store).

Keep your sleuth eyes open in Arcadia for a very old alignment of

Roadside "rest area," Arcadia, Oklahoma.

One of the newer roadside attractions on the route is this 66-foot-tall lighted pop bottle. Arcadia, Oklahoma.

Route 66 which deviates from the main pavement for a short distance, and includes the home of author and publisher Jim Ross. Jim took his inspiration for the house's design from the ever-popular cottage-style Phillips 66 stations.

The western outskirts of Arcadia are dominated by the monumental **POPS**, a new Route 66 attraction (opened in 2007) that reaches out and grabs your attention like classic tourist traps of long ago. You certainly can't miss a 66-foot-tall illuminated pop bottle standing a few yards from the roadway. Inside, POPS has countless brands and flavors of soft drink to choose from, as well as a snack bar and internal combustion fuel for your iron horse. This decidedly over-the-top concept was brought to life by Rand Elliott, the same architect who designed the Oklahoma

---

ELMER McCURDY

For those of you interested in strange stories, this has to be one of the strangest. I have read four or five slightly different accounts of the Elmer McCurdy saga, and each one is as bizarre as the next.

In 1976, a film crew shooting an episode of *The Six Million Dollar Man* was on location at a Los Angeles-area fun house. One of the crew members moved what was thought to be a dummy hanging from the ceiling, but the "dummy's" arm fell off. Inside were what appeared to be the bones and joints of a real human being. That man was soon identified as Elmer McCurdy.

Elmer McCurdy was an outlaw who died in a shootout at the hands of authorities in 1911. His body was taken to a Pawhuska, Oklahoma mortuary, where the undertaker, not knowing how long he might need to hang onto the body before it was claimed, added arsenic to the usual embalming fluid and thereby mummified McCurdy's remains. Months passed, and the body still had not been claimed. By this time, McCurdy's corpse had be-

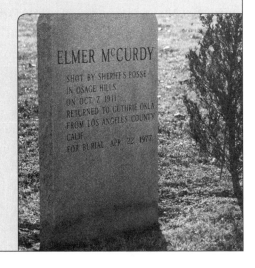

Route 66 Museum in Clinton, Oklahoma, in the 1990s.

FURTHER AFIELD

A real treat awaits you just a short trip north of old 66. Just a few miles east of downtown Edmond, take either 12th Street or U.S. 77 north for 20

come something of a local attraction, and people came by and paid a nickel apiece to look at it. Many years later, the funeral home had changed hands, the principals in the whole affair were deceased, and no one knew any more that the dried-up "dummy" in town was a real human body. A carnival passed through and offered to take the "dummy" off the current owner's hands for a small price. A deal was struck, and Elmer McCurdy entered show business posthumously.

No one knows for sure all the places McCurdy's mummified body might have been displayed in the intervening years up until he was discovered that day in the fun house in 1976. No relatives ever presented themselves to claim the body. Finally, a historical group arranged for McCurdy's body to be returned to Oklahoma for burial. The Warren Monument company of Guthrie furnished a tombstone bearing the inscription:

Elmer McCurdy
Shot by Sheriff's posse in Osage Hills on Oct 7, 1911
Returned to Guthrie, Oklahoma
from Los Angeles County, California
for burial, Apr 22, 1977

Elmer McCurdy was then laid to rest in Summit View Cemetery, Guthrie, Oklahoma. To ensure that the body would remain interred and not be trotted out again as a curiosity, the state medical examiner ordered that two cubic yards of concrete be poured over the coffin before the grave was closed.

miles or so to the very historic town of **Guthrie**, Oklahoma. On the outskirts of the town you'll see a still-working drive-in theater, the Beacon. In business since 1951, the **Beacon Drive-In** had an appearance in the movie *Twister*.

For some 20 years, beginning in 1890, Guthrie was the capital of Oklahoma (or Indian Territory, as it was known at the time). Virtually all of downtown was constructed during that period, and today Guthrie boasts the largest contiguous urban historical district on the National Register, consisting of 2,169 structures in 400 blocks on 1,400 acres, including 14 city blocks of Victoriana. The territory achieved statehood in 1907, and the capital was moved to Oklahoma City a few years later in 1910. The National Trust for Historic Preservation honored Guthrie as one of its "Dozen Distinctive Destinations" in 2004.

Tom Mix used to tend bar at the still-hopping Blue Bell Saloon. Just outside the Blue Bell, staged gunfights are held in the street for much of the year (Second at Harrison).

Cater-corner to the Blue Bell, at 301 W. Harrison, is the **State Capital Publishing Museum**. This turn-of-the-last-century publishing house still has lots of the original equipment in place, tons of samples of some of the print jobs over the years, such as textbooks and legal forms, and most of the original furnishings.

The **Scottish Rite Temple** is among the largest of its kind in the world, with an enormous number of stained-glass artworks. Guided tours are available. East of downtown at 900 E. Oklahoma Avenue.

The **Gaffney Building**, near Second and Oklahoma, houses both the Chamber of Commerce and the **Oklahoma Frontier Drug Store Museum**. The folks at the C of C will answer any questions you may have, and the drug store is well worth touring. Not only will you see all the tools of the trade from a circa-1890 pharmacy, but the attendant on duty when we were there was extremely knowledgeable, having been a practicing druggist himself for many years. In 2006, an apothecary garden was added in which medicinal plants are cultivated and studied.

Physically connected to one of the 1,946 public libraries endowed by the Carnegie Foundation in this country, the **Oklahoma Territorial**

Museum presents a history of Oklahoma during its earliest days, including the Land Run of 1889 and the subsequent influx of settlers. There is even some information about the infamous case of Elmer McCurdy. 406 E. Oklahoma Ave.

Back on Route 66 heading west out of Arcadia, past POPS, there is little Route 66 flavor evident between here and the town of Edmond; however, the stretch is rather rural in character and therefore relaxing.

EDMOND

Following Route 66 through Edmond means turning left (south) at Broadway. A right at that corner takes you into the smallish business district.

EDMOND ATTRACTIONS

Near the corner of Second and Boulevard stands the **1889 Territorial School**, the first public school established in Oklahoma Territory. It later housed a camera shop beginning in 1950, but in 2007 was rededicated in keeping with its historical past.

The **Edmond Historical Society Museum**, housed in an armory building constructed by the WPA in 1936, displays photos, documents, and artifacts relating to the town's development. There are also traveling exhibits, which change throughout the year. In the 1950s, this building

This little schoolhouse dates from pre-statehood days. Edmond, Oklahoma.

was used for the housing and training of dancing bears for the local circus (431 S. Boulevard).

The **Arcadian Inn**, now a bed-and-breakfast at 328 E. First Street, was originally a one-story private residence built in 1908. Twenty years later, the owner decided to convert it to two stories by lifting the original house and constructing a new first story and basement underneath. How's that for "doing things the hard way"?

Edmond is proud to be a supporter of **public art**. Stone and bronze sculptures, as well as a number of murals, can be seen throughout the city. A guide published by the city's convention and visitors bureau lists 115 such works of art, including a WPA-era etched glass mural inside the city hall, at 101 E. First Street.

If you like unusual architecture, you can check out the Hopewell Baptist Church, designed by Bruce Goff in the 1940s. It's been nicknamed the **TeePee Church**, since that's what it was built to resemble. It is conical in shape, about 80 feet tall, and was constructed using "tent poles," which are actually surplus oilfield pipes donated by an oil drilling company. It's located about eight miles west of downtown, at 5801 NW 178th (West Edmond Road). The building has been unused for several years, and a non-profit organization has been set up to preserve and restore this very unusual landmark.

Between Edmond and Oklahoma City is **Memorial Park Cemetery**, just east of U.S. 77 (Kelley) on the south side of Memorial Road (NE 136th). This is the burial place of Wiley Post. Although Post is more widely known these days as the friend of Will Rogers, who was piloting the plane in which they both perished in 1935, he was actually very accomplished in his own right. He first attained prominence in 1930 by winning the National Air Race Derby, a race from Los Angeles to Chicago (ring a bell?) in a plane named the Winnie Mae. He made the first successful solo flight around the world in 1933, and also designed the first pressurized flight suit. The aviator's likeness and biography are carved in a large stone over the burial plot.

OKLAHOMA CITY

Oklahoma City successfully ousted Guthrie as the state capital in 1910. For many years, the capitol building here was unusual for this country, in that it had no dome. A dome was indeed a part of the original design, but it was omitted for reasons of economy. In 2002, the citizens of Oklahoma saw fit to finally top their capitol with a dome, so the one you see today has not been there long. Oil was struck here in 1928, and before the boom was over, there were 24 oil wells pumping on the actual grounds of the Oklahoma state capitol.

> Between Edmond and Oklahoma City, leave U.S. 77/Broadway at Kelley Avenue and continue south. From there, you have a couple of choices, including a "beltway" route that skirted downtown but took in the village of Britton, where the Owl Courts tourist complex still stands. The primary route went all the way to the capitol before turning west.

Route 66 took many different paths through Oklahoma City over the years, and so you would do well to explore extensively if you can tolerate the traffic. The best-known route traced present-day Broadway out of Edmond (which becomes Kelley) straight toward the capitol, where it turned west on 23rd, north on May, and west again on NW 39th Street Expressway. Alternatively, a turn from Kelley onto Britton Avenue and then a left on Western Avenue takes you through the village of Britton along a more obscure "beltline" route, and passing the Owl Courts. Also, be sure to cruise Classen Avenue, where you'll see a great example of symbolic architecture when you pass the little triangular building with the giant milk bottle on top.

The first automatic parking meter was invented and installed in

The Owl Courts complex is undergoing renovation, Oklahoma City, Oklahoma.

Oklahoma City by brothers Carlton and Gerald Hale on July 16, 1935. Initially, the meters were placed on only one side of the downtown street. Within three days, the merchants from the other side of the street petitioned to have their side metered also. They liked the constant and rapid turnover that the meters engendered. Two years later, in 1937, Sylman Goldman introduced the shopping cart here on June 4th.

On July 22, 1933, Machine Gun Kelly kidnapped millionaire Charles Urscher from his home here at 327 NW 18th Street. Kelly was the gangster who coined the phrase "G-Man."

OKC ATTRACTIONS

Oklahoma City has known tragedy. The worst-ever act of terrorism on American soil—up to that time—occurred here on April 19, 1995 at the Alfred P. Murrah Federal Building. You can visit the **Oklahoma City National Memorial** at 620 N. Harvey Avenue.

At Reno and Robinson Streets, in the heart of Oklahoma City, is the **Myriad Botanical Gardens and Crystal Bridge Tropical Conservatory**. Truly an oasis, the gardens cover a 17-acre tract and include rolling hills surrounding a sunken lake. The focal point of the gardens is the seven-story, 224-foot-long Crystal Bridge Tropical Conservatory, a greenhouse providing habitat for an extensive collection of palms, orchids, cacti, and exotics from around the world.

The **National Cowboy & Western Heritage Museum** (formerly the National Cowboy Hall of Fame) is at 1700 NE 63rd Street. This is a large, first-rate complex including major exhibition galleries, a replica turn-of-the-century western town, and several heroic-sized works of sculpture, including a rendering of James Earle Fraser's world-famous *End of the Trail*, which won a gold medal at the 1915 Pan-Pacific International Exposition in San Francisco. Fraser also designed the Indian Head (or Buffalo) nickel, which began production in 1913. Also contained within the museum is the Hall of Fame of Western Film, which includes video clips and other memora-

Roadie ambience at Ann's Chicken, Oklahoma City, Oklahoma.

bilia associated with the likes of Gene Autry, Gary Cooper, Tom Mix, and Slim Pickens, among many others. There is also a research archive which includes photographs, papers, and personal effects of actor Walter Brennan and several other western notables.

Just down the street from the National Cowboy Museum (above) is the **County Line Barbeque** restaurant. In the 1930s, this place was a speakeasy known as the Kentucky Club, and was frequented by Pretty Boy Floyd. The building reportedly has features such as trap doors to facilitate escape in the event of a police raid.

The **Omniplex** is a collection of museums at 2100 NE 52nd. Included are the Hands-On Science Museum, the Kirkpatrick Planetarium, the Red Earth Indian Center, the Air Space Museum, and the International Photography Hall of Fame and Museum. With all of these attractions essentially under one roof, it's a near-overdose for the mind. The photography museum includes the world's largest Grand Canyon photomural, so you can get a preview of the big ditch before you reach Arizona.

At 1112 NW 23rd Street stands what is commonly referred to as the **Gold Dome**. It was built in 1958, using R. Buckminster Fuller's geodesic dome principles, and includes a gold-anodized aluminum roof. The

Dome originally housed a bank, but has recently been rehabilitated for retail and office space. Between Western Avenue and Classen Boulevard.

The **Paseo Arts District**, centered at NW 30th and Dewey, is a historically-rich neighborhood which has been taken over by the city's art community. Several artists have studios and galleries in this area, and the district hosts an annual art festival each Memorial Day weekend.

Bricktown is a former warehouse district, which has been turned into an entertainment hotspot with bars, restaurants, and music clubs. Recently added are some canals which are plied by water taxis. The loading area for the narrated taxi rides is across from the Bricktown Ballpark, home of the minor-league Oklahoma City RedHawks. The **American Banjo Museum** claims to have the largest collection of banjos in the world, and relocated to Bricktown in 2009 after having been in the town of Guthrie for years.

The **Oklahoma Country & Western Music Hall of Fame** at 3925 SE 29th consists of more than 10,000 square feet of items dedicated to country and western music performers.

The **45th Infantry Division Museum** is a highly-regarded military museum and has something of interest to everyone. Oklahoma's role in the Civil War and Indian Wars is represented here, but displays also include items from Hitler's bunker which were captured by the 45th in 1945. There are over 200 original "Willie and Joe" cartoons by artist Bill Mauldin, and outside are dozens of military vehicles, aircraft, and artillery. 2145 NE 36th.

On the grounds of the Will Rogers World Airport is the **Ninety-Nines Museum of Women Pilots**. Amelia Earhart is prominently represented here—as well as other early female aviators—and there are materials pertaining to women in the space program. 4300 Amelia Earhart Rd.

The **Oklahoma State Firefighters Museum** has helmets on display worn by Ben Franklin, John Hancock, and Paul Revere. Also on display is Oklahoma's first fire station (1864) as well as 100-year-old fire equipment actually used in Oklahoma communities. 2716 NE 50th St.

The **National Softball Hall of Fame and Museum** at 2801 NE 50th Street covers all variants of the game, including fast-, slow-, and modified-pitch versions. The museum is housed in the Amateur Softball Association (ASA) headquarters. The ASA stadium hosts national and world class competition in the sport.

The **Jim Thorpe Association and Oklahoma Sports Hall of Fame** honors excellence in athletics, with a variety of awards, scholarships, and honors that they bestow annually. 4040 N. Lincoln.

The **Henry Overholser Mansion** was built in 1903 by Henry Overholser at 405 NW 15th Street. This Victorian-style home contains 90 percent original family furnishings and is notable for its hand-painted, canvas-covered walls.

Built in 1928, the **Governor's Mansion** offers guided tours every Wednesday. The house is said to be haunted by the ghost of Oklahoma's Depression-era governor, William H. "Alfalfa Bill" Murray. On the grounds is a swimming pool shaped like the state's boundaries. 820 NE 23rd St.

The **Oklahoma History Center** has over 200,000 square

Oklahoma City, Oklahoma.

feet devoted to the state's heritage, organized by themes such as aviation, commerce, and geology, to name just a few. At the northeast corner of NE 23rd and Lincoln Boulevard, across from the governor's mansion.

The **Harn Homestead & 1889er Museum** is a complex of structures at 1721 N. Lincoln Boulevard, not far from the state capitol building. This homestead was one that was claimed in the Land Run of 1889, and includes a stone and cedar barn, three houses, and the former Stoney Point School, a one-room schoolhouse dating from 1897. The school was in regular use until 1947, and was moved here in 1988.

Evidence of the Mother Road spirit in Oklahoma City, Oklahoma.

Does pigeon racing tickle your fancy? The **World of Wings Pigeon Center** has dedicated itself to the heritage of the pigeon. A project of the American Homing Pigeon Institute, there is a small museum housed in a 1930s brick house on 10 acres. There are educational exhibits, pigeon lofts, and cultivated gardens. Pigeon races are held in the fall. White pigeons are available here for release at weddings and other special events. 2300 NE 63rd St.

At 2641 NW 10th is the **World Organization of China Painters Museum**. A large collection of hand-painted China accompanies a gift shop, a research library, and classrooms.

The **Classen High School Museum** (1901 N. Ellison) and the **Central High School Museum** (815 N. Robinson) are in competition to see who has the best school spirit. Classen has the country's largest high school alumni organization and boasts of Admiral William Crowe among its constituents. Central High's building (circa 1910) was designed by the architect of the state capitol and is on the National Register of Historic Places.

Enterprise Square is at 2501 E. Memorial Road, on the campus of Oklahoma Christian University. Your journey begins with a ride in the Heartbeat Rotunda, a glass elevator that takes you to the fourth floor and a multi-media, multi-screen extravaganza extolling the virtues of the capitalist, free-enterprise system. Sales agents include giants, robots, skeletons, and enormous cash registers containing dollar bills with singing presidents' heads on them. Truly a one-of-a-kind attraction. Be sure to spend some of that hard-earned cash in the gift shop by getting an "I Love

Capitalism" bumper sticker.

Evolved from an organization called the Oklahoma Hall of Fame, the **Gaylord-Pickens Oklahoma Heritage Museum** opened its high-tech doors in 2007, and has already received several accolades. The museum seeks to tell the story of Oklahoma through its most distinguished citizens, and you can search the database of more than 600 hall of fame inductees going all the way back to 1928. 1400 Classen Dr.

The **Oklahoma Museum of Telephone History** covers more than a century's worth of history in the form of vintage telephones and telephone company memorabilia. 111 Dean A. McGee Ave.

The **Oklahoma Railway Museum** is an open-air museum with a family-friendly vibe. You can even ride a train! 3400 NE Grand Blvd.

Oklahoma City still has an operating drive-in movie theater, the **Winchester Drive-In**, on the south side of town, away from the Mother Road. Built in 1968, it's at 6930 S. Western Avenue.

 You'll leave Oklahoma City headed west on 39th Street Expressway.

WARR ACRES-BETHANY

Warr Acres was named for a real estate developer named Warr. The town of Bethany was established in 1906 by members of the Nazarene Church. Today, both cities seem to be embedded in Greater Oklahoma City. The **Bethany Historical Society Museum** is located inside city hall at 6700 NW 36th.

Route 66 is a multilane, divided

This old bridge is at the edge of Lake Overholser, west of Bethany, Oklahoma.

thoroughfare in these parts. Just west of Bethany, it crosses a corner of Lake Overholser. Named for OKC mayor Ed Overholser, the lake at the time of Rittenhouse was a recreational area with speedboat rides. Prior to World War II, plans were being made to make Lake Overholser a layover center for seaplane excursions. This, of course, is a mode of travel which never really caught on well. Today, Alaskans use seaplanes very commonly, but they are short on roads up there.

A few years ago, I would have strongly encouraged you to take the old 66 alignment that crosses the vintage Lake Overholser Bridge and then hugs the lake's northern shoreline (N. Overholser Drive). It meets up with the later Route 66 alignment at Yukon. However, that stretch of road has undergone such build-up and modernization lately that there's little of the Route 66 flavor left, and so there isn't much to recommend it anymore. Don't feel bad if you skip it by staying on the later alignment.

YUKON

Singer Garth Brooks and actor Dale Robertson both hail from Yukon, and there is a sign at the edge of town proudly proclaiming Brooks its native son. The Garth Brooks Water Tower is at I-40 and Garth Brooks Boulevard.

One of my favorite motel signs on all of Route 66 once stood in front of the Yukon Motel. Unfortunately, a change of ownership at the motel led to the sign's untimely—and baffling—demise.

Yukon, Oklahoma.

YUKON ATTRACTIONS

You are in **Chisholm Trail** country now. Some sources say that Ninth Street through Yukon closely approximates the route of the Chisholm Trail. Other sources say that U.S. 81, which runs through El Reno further west, is more authentic. In truth, being a cattle trail, the Chisholm was of course never paved, and so the precise route varied considerably, subject to the vagaries of such things as water availability, prevailing weather, and individual whim. What we can be more certain of is that the trail ran from southern Texas, through central Oklahoma, and on to the cattle markets in Abilene, Kansas.

The trail was named for Jesse Chisholm, who was among the first to make regular use of the trail and to advocate its use by others. Yukon holds a Chisholm Trail festival each year, as do many of the towns and cities through which the trail once passed.

Yukon, Oklahoma's biggest landmark.

There's a park in Yukon (at 2200 S. Holly Avenue) that has a **Chisholm Trail monument** and also contains a "Bank Shot" setup. This is a sort of cross between basketball and miniature golf—it consists of bizarrely-shaped backboards on which to test your skill and patience in sinking your "free throws." I've never seen one of them anywhere else.

A major landmark here in Yukon is the **Yukon's Best** flour mural, which is prominently emblazoned on the side of a grain storage facility on the south side of the highway in town, right at the railroad tracks.

Yukon's Best Railroad Museum is a static display of a caboose and other rail cars across the boulevard from the Yukon's Best mural. Full tours of the contents of the rail cars are by prior arrangement only by calling 405-354-5079.

The **Yukon Historical Society Museum**, at 601 Oak Street, is housed in a 1910 school building and includes a doctor's office, Czech history room, and other local history.

About five miles north of town on 11th Street (Garth Brooks Boulevard) is **Express Clydesdales**. Rare black and white Clydesdale horses make their home here in a 1936 barn restored by Amish specialists from Indiana. There is also a gift shop and visitor center.

EL RENO

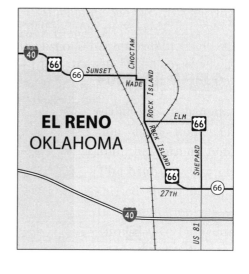

El Reno sits at the junction of two famous highways of very different kinds: U.S. 66 and the **Chisholm Trail** (roughly at U.S. 81), and is the seat of Canadian County. The town was reportedly named for a Civil War general, Jesse L. Reno, who was killed in action in 1862.

Look for the VFW post as you pass through town; there is a retired airplane displayed out front, which saw action in World War II. The sign for the Oasis Drive-In on the east side of town was refurbished in 2005 through the Route 66 Corridor Preservation Program.

Formerly in El Reno was the Big Eight Motel (originally the Beacon Motel), which had a large neon sign. The phrase "Amarillo's Finest" was added to the sign for the filming of the movie *Rain Man* at room 117. The owners left the odd addition there afterward, which caused bewilderment among some travelers. Since then, someone with no sensitivity for the things we roadies appreciate took down the vintage sign in favor of one which was duller than words could describe. Renamed the Deluxe Inn, the motel sported a simple plexi-faced box on a post, instead of what was once a unique example of the sign maker's art. Go figure. Since that time, the motel closed down altogether and was finally razed.

EL RENO ATTRACTIONS

The **Canadian County Historical Museum** has the old Rock Island depot as its core, but also has extensive grounds featuring a jail house, hotel, one-room school, an 1889 Land Run marker, and other items of historical and cultural interest, including the nation's first Red Cross canteen (300 S. Grand). Recently established is the **Heritage Trolley**, which originates at the CCHM and takes riders downtown to restaurants and shopping.

In El Reno is a **BPOE lodge** (Benevolent and Protective Order of Elks), at 415 S. Rock Island, which was part of an exhibit at the 1904 St. Louis World's Fair. The structure was pulled apart and transported here, where it was re-assembled. That 1904 fair was where the hamburger on a bun was introduced.

Every year, on the first Saturday of May, the town of El Reno grills a 750-pound **Onion Burger**, and you can get a free bite of the "Big One" as long as it lasts. El Reno is widely considered the home of the onion burger, with several small restaurants specializing in them, including Johnnie's, Sid's,

"Amarillo's Finest" was actually many miles away in El Reno, Oklahoma.

and Robert's.

There is an informa-
tion center for nearby **Fort
Reno** at 7107 W. Cheyenne
Street. What remains of the
fort itself we'll encounter in
a few miles as we head west
along the Mother Road.

El Reno, Oklahoma.

FURTHER AFIELD

Travel a little to the north of El
Reno via U.S. 81, and you'll be approximating the path of the Chisholm
Trail. The town of **Kingfisher** is proud of its Chisholm Trail heritage, but
a little less proud of its gridiron record. Between 1905 and 1919, Oklahoma U. beat the Kingfisher football team by scores of 55-0, 32-0, 51-0,
46-5, 66-0, 104-0, 40-0, 74-0, 67-0, 67-0, 96-0, 179-0, and 157-0. In 13
games, Kingfisher was outscored by a whopping 1,034 to 5.

Kingfisher was the birthplace of an outlaw named John King
Fisher. He was reputed to be a major-league rustler in the 1870s, and is
said to have admitted to killing seven men, "not counting Mexicans."

Another outlaw clan, the Daltons, grew up on a farm in the vicinity. Buried in the **Kingfisher Cemetery** are Adeline Lee Younger Dalton—mother of the Dalton boys and cousin of Cole Younger—and her
son, Emmett Dalton. Kingfisher is also where W. C. Coleman, of Coleman Lantern fame, first began selling lamps door-to-door in the 1890s.

Chisholm Trail museums are to be found both north (Kingfisher) and south (Duncan) of El Reno. There are still visible trail ruts at
Monument Hill near Duncan.

Back on 66, about four miles west of El Reno and just north
of the highway is **Fort Reno**. Although much of it remains, today it looks
like many a ghost town. Established in 1875, it was an important post for
keeping the Cheyenne and Arapaho tribes at bay during the territorial

struggles of the time, and later achieved a reputation for raising a large portion of the U.S. Army's horses during the pre-mechanized era. It was here that Black Jack, the riderless horse in President Kennedy's funeral procession, was raised. The cemetery here contains the grave of one Ben Clark, an accomplished scout and sometime Pony Express rider. During the Second World War, the fort functioned as a prisoner-of-war camp for German and Italian captives, some of whom are also laid to rest in the cemetery.

Though Route 66 was eventually straightened, for a time it veered north and passed through the town of Calumet. You can take this older course by turning north on U.S. 270. The description that immediately follows takes you along the older route through Geary. If you choose to take the later route straight ahead, you can pick up that thread at the town of Hydro.

CALUMET

Prior to the nineteenth century, "calumet" was the name given to what is now commonly called the "peace pipe." It is said to have come from the French *chalumeau*, meaning "reed."

Today, Calumet includes **Bethany Kars**, a family-run business specializing in 1964–87 Chevrolet El Caminos. Inventory browsing is by appointment only; call 405-615-3188.

GEARY

The **Canadian River Historical Society Museum**, at Broadway and Main, includes the area's first log jail, a train caboose, and a furnished 1901 home.

North of Geary, near the banks of the Canadian River, at the rather isolated Left Hand Spring Camp, is the grave of **Jesse Chisholm**, the man for whom the trail we crossed a little earlier was named. There are granite monuments marking Chisholm's grave and that of Chief Left Hand, an Arapaho Indian.

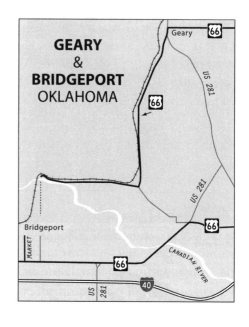

Heading south out of Geary, U.S. 281/OK 8 will return you to the "through" alignment of Route 66. If you're feeling adventurous, there is a partially-paved road that you can veer onto at the edge of town which parallels the railroad tracks. This was at one time the main highway. After about four miles or so, a right will take you toward Bridgeport and the old river crossing which gave the town its name. You can no longer make the crossing there, however. The other direction takes you back to a rendezvous with the newer 66 alignment, near the convergence of the Canadian, Blaine, and Caddo county lines.

Where U.S. 281 and OK 8 turn south and leave us is what is known as Hinton Junction. There is a ruin of a café there, which I'm told was also a bus station at one time. The sign over the door says "EAT."

BRIDGEPORT

Bridgeport was bypassed by Route 66, as the crossing of this branch of the Canadian River was moved further downstream. What remains of this town is quiet indeed. The last time I patrolled these streets there was a skunk doing the same thing, acting as if he owned the place.

FURTHER AFIELD

South of Bridgeport via U.S. 281 is the town of Hinton. The **Hinton**

Former café at the Hinton Junction, east of Hydro, Oklahoma.

Historical Museum & Parker House contains one of the state's largest collections of buggies and carriages, as well as nineteenth century farm machinery, bicycles, and several antique cars. One of the buggies is said to be "Oklahoma's Largest." 801 S. Broadway in Hinton.

Just outside Hinton is the **Red Rock Canyon State Park**, reputed to be the haven of horse rustlers and cattle thieves in days gone by. A covered-wagon migratory trail (California Road) once passed through the park, and today one of the many hiking trails will take you to where you can view some of the remaining wagon ruts from those days.

Both before and after Hydro you'll be passing over a stretch of the route which is truly classic. The roadway is segmented concrete, and it rises and falls with the gentle hills in this area. Even though the interstate is only yards away on your left, you get a true taste of what cross-country auto travel was like decades ago. Savor it, and remember it after you've returned home.

To the south of this Bridgeport-Hydro stretch of highway there are some features called **Steen's Buttes** or **Caddo Mounds**. They were reported by army explorers as early as 1840, and were subsequently used as landmarks for 49ers en route to California during the gold rush years. On some maps, one of the mounds is designated Dead Woman's Mound.

HYDRO

The highway passes just south of the town of Hydro. At a crossroads called Provine you'll see **Lucille's**, a fixture on Route 66 since 1941, when Lucille Hamons and her husband began operating a gas station and tourist court here. Lucille passed away in 2000, but not before earning the nickname "Mother of the Mother Road." For years she took time with each and every traveler who came through here, passing along stories of the road gleaned from her many years at its shoulder.

Hydro's **Nutopia Nuts 'N More** (formerly Johnson's Peanut Company) offers seasonal tours, and the gift shop is open all year. 206 W. Main St.

Lucille's famous station, near Hydro, Oklahoma.

WEATHERFORD

Weatherford is home to Southwestern Oklahoma State University, which holds an annual Jazz Festival each February.

WEATHERFORD ATTRACTIONS

Being the birthplace of an astronaut has its responsibilities. Approaching Weatherford from the east you'll pass the entrance to the **General Thomas P. Stafford Airport Museum**, at 3000 Logan Road, Bldg. 2. It features moon rocks, space suits, rocket boosters, and other memorabilia. You can even walk through a space shuttle fuel pod.

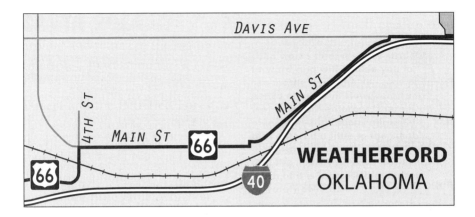

DAVIS AVE

4TH ST

MAIN ST

MAIN ST

66

66

40

WEATHERFORD
OKLAHOMA

Also on the east outskirts of town is a modern-day restaurant named **Lucille's Roadhouse**, honoring the memory of Lucille Hamons (see Hydro, above). They've gone to some lengths to conjure the general shape and form of the original Lucille's, and retro-style gasoline pumps at the entrance complete the effect.

Four generations have plied their trade at the **Cotter Blacksmith Shop** (sometimes called Owl Blacksmith) in the same building since 1910. There is turn-of-the-century equipment here, some of it still in use (208 W. Rainey). Newer to the scene is the **Heartland of America Museum**, which opened its doors in 2007. On display are a portable jail, a one-room school, and a diner that once stood on

At the turnoff for the General Thomas P. Stafford Airport Museum, Weatherford, Oklahoma.

Weatherford, Oklahoma.

Route 66, where Elvis Presley is said to have stopped at least three times. On the I-40 service road, between Exits 82 and 84, in the southeast section of town. On the western outskirts of town stands the **66 West Twin Drive-In Theater**.

To the south of Weatherford is **Fort Sill**, where numerous Native American chiefs were imprisoned, and where some of whom, notably Geronimo, are interred.

CLINTON

The town was named for Judge Clinton Irwin. For years, the U.S. 66 Highway Association, an early booster organization for the highway, was run here in Clinton by Jack and Ruth Cuthbert, who became known as "Mr. and Mrs. 66."

There are multiple 66 alignments through town. I suggest you sample all of them, each of which is attractive in its own way. The modern "bypass" route boasts the first-rate Oklahoma Route 66 Museum, which every true-blue 66-er needs to visit.

CLINTON ATTRACTIONS

On the east side of town is the **Mohawk Lodge Indian Store & Trading Post**, first established in 1892, and occupying this location since 1940. The original sales counter was brought over in the move and is still in use. The owners say it's as much a museum as it is a store.

McLain Rogers Park, on historic 66 (S. 10th), has a

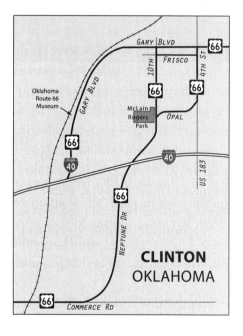

classic enamel and neon sign dating from 1936, and a WPA-constructed outdoor theater.

The Oklahoma Route 66 Museum in Clinton is a must-stop for every Mother Road adventurer.

The **Oklahoma Route 66 Museum** opened here in 1995 on a later bypass route around town. The building itself is uniquely Route 66-themed, and designed by the same architect who later gave us POPS in Arcadia. All of the museum's exhibits are very professionally done, portraying the highway's changing roles in society through the various decades of the twentieth century. More recently, a tiny restored **Valentine diner**, which once served Route 66 travelers in Texas, was placed on the museum grounds. The restoration work on the diner earned Virgil Smith the Cyrus Avery Preservation Award the following year. 2229 Gary Blvd.

Across the highway from the museum and diner is the **Trade Winds Motel**. This was one

Clinton, Oklahoma.

Clinton, Oklahoma.

of Elvis Presley's favorite places to stay, having overnighted in room 215 on many occasions. Elvis was a creature of habit, and Clinton evidently was just about a good day's drive out of Memphis for him. Room 215 is available by reservation.

FOSS-CANUTE

There is a ruin of an old roadside establishment here at Foss with red, peeling paint, called Kobel's Place. A little to the north on Highway 44, just past the railroad track, is the actual town. North of town via State Highway 44 is Foss State Park.

Further west, Canute is notable for its Catholic cemetery on the east side of town, which includes a stone grotto dating from around 1930. A church dating from 1926 is now the **Canute Heritage Center**. Also in Canute is the **Cotton Boll Motel**, which is now being used as a private residence. The vintage sign, however, remains.

ELK CITY

Originally called Crowe, the townspeople attempted to persuade Adolphus Busch to put a brewery here by renaming the town Busch. When that

The old Cotton Boll Motel is now a private residence, but the sign still stands tall. Canute, Oklahoma.

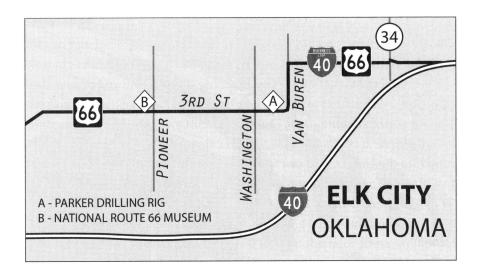

plan failed, the name Elk City was adopted, after the nearby Elk Creek. The Dodge City (Kansas) Cattle Trail is said to have passed through here in the nineteenth century; the town was established in 1901. According to Jack Rittenhouse, Elk City was the site of an early experiment in collective health care in the 1940s—the first HMO, perhaps? Also in the '40s (August 15, 1946, to be more precise), song composer extraordinaire Jimmy Webb was born right here in Elk City.

ELK CITY ATTRACTIONS

In 1998 Elk City introduced the **National Route 66 Museum** at 2717 W. Highway 66. This museum covers the route in all eight states through which it passed. Outside is a continually-expanding collection of buildings known as the **Old Town Museum Complex**, which includes both historical and painstakingly-reproduced buildings, railroad cars, and other features of interest. The family of museums now includes a transportation museum and a farm and ranch museum, and all of this is within the same city block. The 66 Museum itself is getting more impossible to miss all the time—the exterior now includes perhaps the most enormous Route 66 shield ever conceived. The large kachina figures outside once stood at the Queenan Trading Post, an old-school curio shop on Route

66 that closed long ago. 2717 W. Highway 66 (west of Pioneer Road).

A brief oil boom period in the area is recalled by a huge oil derrick, **Parker Drilling Rig No. 114**. It stands about 17 stories tall, right next to the old Casa Grande Hotel, which hosted a Route 66 conference way back in 1931. Today, the old hotel houses the **Anadarko Basin Natural History Museum**, on 66 (Third Street) between Madison and Main. A few blocks further west at the corner of Washington, in an expanse of lawn on the south side of the highway, is an **elk sculpture**.

National Route 66 Museum, Elk City, Oklahoma.

Part of the Old Town Museum Complex, Elk City, Oklahoma.

SAYRE

At Fourth and Elm there are what appear to be storm cellar entrances on either side of the main street (Route 66) as it passes through town. These actually lead to an underground pedestrian walkway, which allowed the once-busy thoroughfare to be crossed safely. They are, of course, no longer needed, but there are many other towns along the route whose citizens

would have appreciated this same innovation in the days when traffic was incessant.

SAYRE ATTRACTIONS

The **Beckham County Courthouse**, in the town square, made a cameo appearance in

Sayre, Oklahoma.

the film version of *The Grapes of Wrath*. The post office, at 201 N. Fourth, is decorated with a Depression-era mural depicting the Oklahoma Land Run. The **Owl Drug**, at Fourth and Main, has the state's largest antique soda fountain.

The **Short Grass Country Museum**, at 106 E. Poplar in the old Rock Island depot, features changing exhibits pertaining to early day life in Beckham County and western Oklahoma's shortgrass country in general.

Model railroaders should see the **RS&K Railroad Museum**, featuring hundreds of model trains, including working layouts, as well as railroad memorabilia. 411 N. Sixth.

FURTHER AFIELD

North of Sayre via U.S. 283 is the town of **Cheyenne,** where you can find the **Washita Battlefield National Historic Site** and the **Black Kettle Museum**. These sites center around a surprise cavalry attack on a Cheyenne village headed by

A venerable old sign in Sayre, Oklahoma.

Black Kettle in 1868. The U.S. troops of the 7th Cavalry were commanded at that time by Lieutenant Colonel George A. Custer. There is also a sculpture on the grounds of the nearby Roger Mills County Courthouse (in Cheyenne) commemorating the events.

The Sayre–Hext–Erick stretch of old 66 is an open book for you to read. As you drive this corridor you will see that there are two older, disused lanes of highway to your right. Those indicate the original alignment of 66 through here, right beside the railroad track. The pair of lanes you are driving on were added later, as eastbound lanes separated from the other lanes by a median, in the days when Route 66 was a major thoroughfare for this area. Later, as I-40 was completed to the south, traffic diminished significantly on 66 and two of its lanes were retired.

What remains of the small community of Hext is between old 66 and I-40 just north of Exit 14.

ERICK

The main street through town has been named Roger Miller Boulevard, in honor of Erick's favorite son, who in turn is most noted for his rendition of the song "King of the Road." The town now has a **Roger Miller Museum**, at the corner of Route 66 and Sheb Wooley Avenue, and holds

an annual Roger Miller Festival in his honor.

Also hailing from near Erick is performer **Sheb Wooley**. Sheb started out as a country music performer in the late 1940s, then went to Los Angeles and took acting lessons to pursue a film career. He got the break he was looking for when

East of Erick, Oklahoma.

he was cast in an Errol Flynn film in 1950. He became better known, though, for his extended role in the television series *Rawhide*.

Stop in at the **SandHills Curiosity Shop**, located in an old meat market at 201 S. Sheb Wooley. There are tons of memorabilia on display, and you'll experience live entertainment by the Mediocre Music Makers 'til the cows come home.

Open sporadically or by appointment, the **100th Meridian Museum** presents information relating to the oft-disputed boundary line between Oklahoma and the Republic of Texas. At one time, the area you are entering here was claimed by the Lone Star State. Sheb Wooley Avenue at Roger Miller Boulevard.

At 102 S. Sheb Wooley Boulevard is what the town of Erick likes to call the **Bonebrake Hardware Museum**. You can't go in; you just have to shade your eyes and peer into the windows. The story goes that the Bonebrake family, who owned and ran the hardware store, simply closed the door and walked away sometime in the 1960s, and everything is still just as they left it.

TEXOLA

This town was named for the fact that it rests nearly astride the Oklahoma-Texas border. The more obvious Texoma is already in use elsewhere in the state. Texola can rightly be called a ghost town, having only a tiny fraction of its residences and commercial buildings inhabited. There is a tiny jail (one cell, actually) just a block or so off of Route 66.

Texola is Oklahoma's quiet farewell to the Mother Road.

Seasoned road warrior in Texola, Oklahoma.

TEXAS

Texas, proud as it is to be the largest state in the contiguous 48 and prouder still of its heritage as a former independent republic, ranks next-to-last in the mileage it can claim along the path of

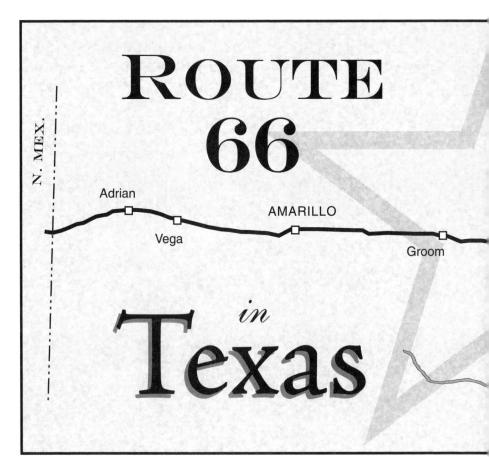

Route 66. That's because the Mother Road crosses the state through what is known as the Texas Panhandle. That panhandle, the northernmost extension of the state, is but an eroded stump compared to what might have been.

If you took time to stop at the 100th Meridian Museum back in Erick, then you know at least a part of the story. You know that if the Texas-Oklahoma border had been decided differently, the westbound Route 66 traveler of today would have entered the great state of Texas at what is now Erick, Oklahoma. What you might not know is that, if some other political decisions had gone a bit differently, that same traveler would not be leaving Texas until he'd passed through what is now Albuquerque, New Mexico, and crossed over the Rio Grande, some 400 miles to the west.

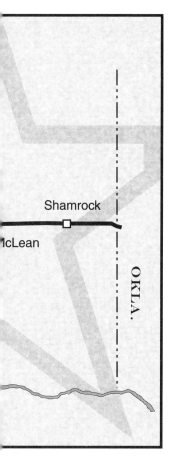

During Texas' early days of statehood (1845–49), it laid claim to territory almost 50 percent larger than its current boundaries, including portions of present-day Oklahoma, New Mexico, Kansas, Colorado, and Wyoming. Since some of this territory was contested by other factions within the U.S., emotions ran high on the subject. At the same time, the former Republic of Texas (1836–45) had incurred significant debts in its struggle for independence. Texas therefore ceded about one-third of its territory in exchange for $10,000,000 in an agreement known as the Compromise of 1850. Much of the territory given up in 1850 makes up the portion of present-day New Mexico east of the Rio Grande.

Texas, as someone once said, is a State of Mind. And, fittingly, there's very little to indicate that, just moments after leaving Texola, one has entered the Lone Star State. Your first signal, other than the official state line sign erected by the highway department, is the character of the pavement itself. This early stretch of Texas highway is made up of the classic segmented concrete, which imparts that rhythmic *thump, ka-thump, ka-thump* to your pneumatic-tire journey. You'll also note that the road tends to rise and fall with the general lay of the land. If you can succeed in ignoring the raging interstate just a few yards to your right, the rhythm of the road will provide you with that elusive taste of what long-distance highway travel was like decades ago.

Just west of the state line, and right about where old 66 sidles up to the edge of Interstate 40, some maps place the community of Benonine.

BENONINE

My 1957 atlas sees fit to depict Benonine just west of the Oklahoma-Texas state line, but you won't see much from the highway today.

SHAMROCK

Until just a few years ago, as one entered the outskirts of the town of Shamrock from the east, there was a sort of auto graveyard in a field along the north side of the old highway. Those autos have since been removed without a trace. On the left, or southern, side of the road, however, the careful observer may still detect subtle signs that there was once a drive-in movie theater in what is now a pasture filled with livestock, sundry junk, and what looks suspiciously like an old projection booth. There were a great many other ruins along

Shamrock, Texas.

U Drop Inn, Shamrock, Texas.

Route 66 in Shamrock not so many years ago. Among them was Lewis Camp, a tourist campground with a general store, which has since burned to the ground. A ruin that spoke to me personally was that of an unbranded gasoline station on the east side of town. It had been stripped of virtually all markings, fixtures, and furnishings. However, on the front door three simple words remained: PLEASE COME BACK. That being Day One of my first deliberate excursion on Route 66, I've never been able to get the irony of that sentiment out of my mind. I felt as though ghosts of people long departed were reaching out to me.

But life goes on in Shamrock, albeit at a different pace than in the Mother Road era. As befits a town with such a name, Shamrock puts its all into an annual Saint Patrick's Day celebration. Men grow beards in preparation for the big day—not only is there a prize for the best beard, there is even a price on the head of any adult male failing to sport one.

About midway through town is the junction with U.S. 83, a major north-south highway. Before the interstates came along, the crossing of U.S. Routes 66 and 83 in the center of town was a very happening place, and this intersection was, and still is, dominated by the U Drop Inn.

The **U Drop Inn**, known for a time as Nunn's Café, is an Art Deco masterpiece made all the more impressive by its placement on the Texas plain. The structure, dating from 1936, thrusts two steeple-like projections heavenward. The story goes that, when first constructed, there was a contest to come up with the name for the new enterprise, and that the winner was a youngster who suggested the name U Drop Inn and collected the cash prize. Fortunately for today's traveler, the U Drop Inn recently underwent a thorough restoration, right down to every last piece of neon tubing. Neon outlines many of the building's design features, which makes it quite an amazing sight at dusk and later. The local chamber of commerce now has its offices here. Viewers of the 2006 *Cars* movie might also recognize the U Drop as inspiration for part of Radiator Springs.

SHAMROCK ATTRACTIONS

The **Pioneer West Museum** is housed in the former Reynolds Hotel, which dates from the 1920s. The museum has 20 or so rooms filled with a variety of exhibits, from Plains Indian culture to NASA moon-mission articles. There are rooms outfitted as doctor and dentist offices, a general store, and a pioneer-era schoolroom (204 N. Madden St.). Next to the museum is a restored **Magnolia fuel station**.

There's a fragment of the true **Blarney Stone** on display at Elmore Park, 400 E. Second Street. The Blarney Stone itself is in County Cork, Ireland, and is reputed to confer eloquence on those who kiss it. Legend has it that the original Lord Blarney was rather accomplished in stretching the truth.

The town has recently taken an interest in its **water tower**, said to be the tallest of its type in the state. There is now a small "park" at the foot of the tower, which includes some information on its construction and general history.

FURTHER AFIELD

North of Shamrock on Highway 83, and just a few miles south of the town of **Canadian**, Texas, is a 50-foot-long **brontosaurus sculpture** crafted by one Gene Cockrell. The brontosaurus overlooks the highway from a small mesa, but the Cockrells' yard is home to lots more creations, including a formerly nude (now scantily clad) Dallas Cowboys football team cheer-leader. A local story goes that the nearby town of Shamrock once approached Mr. Cockrell about fabricating a 40-foot leprechaun to attach to their water tower, but the Shamrock elders balked at the asking price of several thousand dollars, and the deal was scuttled. No word on whether the leprechaun was to be clothed or not.

LELA

Lela these days is little more than the crossing of I-40 with Farm Road 1547. You might notice during your time in the Texas panhandle that people are rather neighborly around here. Make eye contact with passing drivers and you'll find them giving you "The Wave": the fingers on the hand atop the steering wheel will suddenly spring upward into a sort of peacock spread that means "howdy." Please learn to duplicate this maneuver so as not to appear out of place.

Just west of Lela, and on the way to McLean, you can see some trees in the median which are the remnants of the windbreaks referred to by Jack Rittenhouse as he came through here in 1946. It's clear from a look at the shape of these trees that there's a prevailing wind in these parts. It was near here on one of my own Texas 66 forays that I nearly ran over a five-foot snake trying to cross the road.

McLEAN

Upon entering the town of McLean, Route 66 splits into eastbound and westbound segments, separated by a city block, with two lanes running in

McLean, Texas.

each direction. McLean is home to the **Texas Route 66 Museum**, and the town has been quite tenacious in refusing to roll over and die. There are a number of re-born highway businesses, some of which have gone through multiple incarnations attempting to find favor—and a

McLean, Texas.

future—with today's motoring public. The Cowboy Café is such a place. McLean even has a couple of still-operating small motels, as well as a surprisingly good lunch place in the Red River Café. This is an excellent town in which to get out onto the sidewalk and do some exploring.

MCLEAN ATTRACTIONS

The **Texas Route 66 Museum** and the **Devil's Rope Museum** share an address on Kingsley Street, in the block between eastbound and westbound lanes of Route 66. The place is well worth a stop. You certainly can't help but be impressed with the enormous balls of barbed wire on display out front. This building formerly housed a brassiere factory which was known as Marie Foundations. The Route 66 Museum exhibits include a

This tiny station dates from the 1920s. McLean, Texas.

McLean, Texas.

mock 1950s-era diner and a large snake sculpture which once graced the property of the Regal Reptile Ranch in Alanreed, just several miles west of here. Although I'm not knowledgeable at all on the subject of barbed wire (devil's rope, that is), I have it on good authority that this museum houses one of the finest collections in the world, and believe me, there are people that take this stuff very seriously indeed—almost as seriously as you and I take old Route 66, for example.

The restored **Phillips 66 Station** is right on the highway (westbound) and is an irresistible photo opportunity. It's the classic, tiny, cottage-style variety of Phillips station of which we saw a larger example in Chandler, Oklahoma, earlier. This one was restored by the Texas Route 66 Association (circa 1991).

The **McLean-Alanreed Area Museum**, at 117 N. Main, houses panhandle history exhibits as well as artifacts relating to the prisoner-of-war camp located near here during the Second World War. If you're traveling east to west, you'll need to backtrack in order to get to the old POW camp site. Take I-40 Exit 146 and then go north on County Line Road about a mile or so to the historical marker. Part of the McLean/Gray County Airport is on the site of the camp.

Depression-era Texaco station, Alanreed, Texas.

ALANREED

Alanreed has been known by several names over the years, including Prairie Dog Town and Spring Tank. But Gouge Eye is by far the most colorful, and was obtained in connection with a barroom brawl. At one time there was a community to the north of Alanreed called Eldridge (or Elderidge). That town was established prior to Alanreed, and even had an established post office. However, when the railroad came through a few miles to the south, the lure of those steel rails and the promise of commerce made the citizens of Eldridge pack up their belongings (and their post office) and re-locate to the Alanreed townsite. You can still see a remnant of the community of Eldridge by going north on Highway 291. About five miles north of I-40, turn west on a dead end called County Road X. A short distance brings you to a small cemetery that once served the town. There are few marked graves there, and fewer still with actual names. One of the markers states that it is thought to be the grave of a 12-year-old girl who died from a rattlesnake bite.

While in Alanreed, be sure to travel along the older highway alignment that takes you right through the heart of the village of Alanreed (Third Avenue). There are some very old café ruins here, as well as a restored gas station, the **66 Super Service Station**. The station bears a plaque: "Built by Bradley Kiser 1930—then in downtown Alanreed." When one peers around Alanreed today, it's a little difficult to think of it as ever having what one would call a "downtown" district, but if you're at Mr. Kiser's old station, you're standing in the middle of it, what with the ruined Magnolia Café only a few yards away.

North of the "old" alignment, and right alongside the interstate, there is a newer bypass-style Route 66 alignment which now acts as a sort

At the site of the former Regal Reptile Ranch, Alanreed, Texas.

of frontage road. It was there that the Regal Reptile Ranch once lured families out of their iron chariots with the promise of a close-up look at rattlesnakes, Mexican beaded lizards, and other natural curiosities of the American Southwest. The Regal is now gone, a victim of time and the bulldozer. Several years ago, there were still a few ruined buildings and quite a bit of fencing with some of the original lettering visible.

On the west side of Alanreed there used to be some ruins of motel courts which have since been completely removed, leaving only an empty lot. I bring this up as a reminder to you that what you see today may be gone tomorrow, so keep your camera handy and use it—not only for the enrichment of your own experience, but perhaps for the sake of posterity as well.

FURTHER AFIELD

West of Alanreed, the Highway 2477 North exit will take you on a side trip to Lake McClellan, an old stopover with WPA-era structures, now designated the Lake McClellan National Grassland Park.

Also at the above exit, you can get turned around in order to visit the eastbound I-40 rest area. It's Route 66-themed, and the stylized architecture pays homage to the 66 Courts that used to stand in Groom until recently—in Mother Road years, that is.

You'll notice that once you've left Alanreed heading west, the Texas landscape begins to change as the lower plains of the eastern panhandle give way to the Caprock. The so-called Caprock is an elevated plateau from which the rest of Texas slopes noticeably downward toward the southeast and the Gulf of Mexico. As you climb, the landscape seems to open up to ever more impressive views of the surrounding country.

Also in this vicinity, you might initially be confused by some signs along the roadside first announcing Donley County, then Gray County, and then Donley again. It's not that the shape of those counties is so irregular; rather, the highway wanders back and forth across a political boundary which was designed by a man with a ruler in his hand. The highway's path, on the other hand, makes some allowances for the lay of the land. Once atop the Caprock, you are on the *Llano Estacado*, or Staked Plain. There are multiple theories on how the area got its name, but the one given the most credence comes from the days of Coronado. When his entourage began crossing the region, they drove stakes into the ground as a substitute for natural features (trees, boulders), which in this area are rare-to-nonexistent. This was done to prevent needlessly retracing steps. The Staked Plain begins roughly at the Caprock escarpment and continues to just east of the Pecos River Valley in New Mexico.

JERICHO

At Texas Highway 70 South, about the only remaining thing to be seen is a ruined motel court and a nearby cemetery. The cemetery has some

Jericho, Texas.

Long-disused tourist accommodations, Jericho, Texas.

unique features and is worth a look. The area around Jericho, however, earned an ugly reputation during the days of Route 66 travel as being something of a quagmire. There was an unpaved section, or gap in the pavement, which could be difficult to navigate under some conditions. Travelers were advised to take extra care in the vicinity of Jericho Gap, lest they become another ledger entry for the folks making a living towing stranded vehicles out of the mess.

BOYDSTON

Little is left of this community other than an interstate exit for Boydston Road. However, my 1957 road atlas portrays it on a par in size with other neighboring communities, such as Alanreed or Groom, and about two miles west of the Highway 70 North junction. There is still a tiny cemetery in this vicinity, about two miles south of I-40.

GROOM

Exit Interstate 40 at the first Groom exit, the one with the leaning water tower. I wish I had a nickel for every time I've heard someone describe this water tower as having "one leg shorter than the others." To the careful

Distinctive landmark at Groom, Texas.

observer, this is pure hokum. Look carefully and you'll note that there are five appendages—four legs and one central water conduit. The end of that water pipe was intended to be beneath the surface of the ground, so it is in fact longer than the four true legs, which is why the tower sits at such an angle. The legs are actually all the same length, just as they should be. The owners of the Britten Truck Stop that once operated here thought that the spectacle of the leaning tower made for a good gimmick; and besides, it would've been unnecessarily expensive to install the thing properly.

Make a left turn under the interstate here to enter the town of Groom. The road will soon take you to the right, and you'll be surrounded by the spirit of old Route 66. Groom has that lonely and delicious air about it of a town that was robbed of its life by the bypassing of the old highway. The road is very wide through town, and the traffic very light, so take your time. There are a pair of more or less identical motels in town that were called Golden Spread, but their signs have long since been removed and the premises converted to other uses. One of them

Groom, Texas.

has been transformed into a mini-warehouse rental facility. "Golden Spread" is an old term referring to the relatively rich resources to be found here in the high plains region of the country, including rich soil, mineral deposits, and plentiful subterranean water for irrigation.

My favorite Groom landmark used to be the remains of the 66 Courts, just across the road from the grain elevators. Now demolished, it was at one time a combination motel court and Magnolia gasoline station. For years there was an Edsel parked beneath the 66 Courts sign that made for a great photo opportunity, and there

The site of the former 66 Courts, Groom, Texas.

were several other retired road warriors scattered on the property. It was the 66 Courts which provided the inspiration for the vaguely Art Deco-flavored design of the eastbound I-40 rest area west of Alanreed.

GROOM ATTRACTIONS

A modern addition to the community of Groom is the **giant cross**, which can be seen from quite a distance. It's said to be the largest in the western hemisphere, at 190 feet tall. The complex includes sculptures depicting the various Stations of the Cross, and the whole affair is lit at night.

Groom is home to the **Blessed Mary Restaurant**, a non-profit entity where you pay what you want for your meal, with the proceeds going to charity.

CONWAY

If you're on I-40 as you approach Conway, make sure to exit at Highway 207. As you enter Conway, on your right there are some buildings surrounded by chain link fencing. Pressed up close to the highwayside is a building which acted as a sort of general store and café. There is faint, barely readable lettering on the side, part of which reads, "Eat." The opposite (west) side clearly says, "Buddy's Café."

Conway, Texas.

A little further on there is a crossroads with what was at one time a mom-and-pop-style gas station or convenience store. A right turn here quickly returns you to the interstate. Continue straight ahead (Highway 2161) so as not to join the mad rush any sooner than necessary.

Also at Conway is a more recent addition to

Mother Road lore: **Bug Ranch**. This is a spoof of the famous Cadillac Ranch art installation several miles ahead in Amarillo. It consists of a set of Volkswagen Beetles buried nose-first in the earth. Like Cadillac Ranch, Bug Ranch is not actually on Route 66; it's more properly described as being on I-40 (in this case, at Exit 96).

AMARILLO

As was the case with most cities of significant size, the path of Route 66 through Amarillo varied over the years. The easiest alignment to follow is one of the later incarnations, which more or less bypassed the core of the city via what is now Amarillo Boulevard. This version of the route takes a northerly detour around the city, and this alignment still retains

Nice-looking graphics at the Silver Spur Motel, Amarillo, Texas.

plenty of evidence of its having been a major thoroughfare in the pre-interstate era. Most of this part of Amarillo has been neither maintained or restored over the intervening years, and gives the traveler a genuine taste of the seedier side of the highway life-cycle. The majority of the motels that remain accommodate a longer-term clientele, and most of

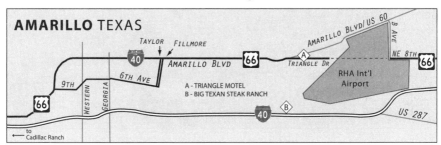

Amarillo, Texas.

the other buildings have been recycled many times over and enlisted in lines of work their original owners and designers neither envisioned nor intended.

An earlier alignment of the highway went directly through the heart of the city, during the years when that was common practice. A section of Sixth Street, roughly between Georgia and Western Streets, has recently seen some revitalization work in order to make the most of its Mother Road heritage. This has resulted in some modest gentrification of the neighborhood, with a collection of antique shops, cafés, and

Old English Motel, Amarillo, Texas.

boutiques now lining this stretch of the route.

Amarillo was first settled as a buffalo-hide tent camp in the 1880s and named for the nearby Amarillo Creek, which was in turn named for the yellowish soil and wildflowers that were prevalent in the area. Curiously, Amarillo is closer to four other state capitals (Santa Fe, Denver, Topeka, Oklahoma City) than it is to its own (Austin). This undoubtedly contributes to the region's independent-mindedness. The city is considered the Helium Capital of the World, producing about 90 percent of the world's supply of the unique element. There is a six-story structure at 1200 Streit—just off Amarillo Boulevard in the western part of town—which commemorates the centennial of the discovery of helium in the area. When it was first erected in 1968, articles were collected to create four time capsules, the last of which is not slated to be opened until AD 2968, 1,000 years (!) after its interment. Included in the capsule is a $10 passbook savings account at a local bank, which will then be worth at least one quadrillion dollars, assuming the bank—and money, for that matter—still exists.

Amarillo is one of the quirkiest towns on Route 66, if not the entire country. A disproportionate amount of that quirkiness seems to be attributable to one man, Stanley Marsh 3 (starting with that Arabic numeral in his name). He's the man behind something collectively referred to as the Dynamite Museum, a series of mock road signs scattered throughout

The world-famous _Cadillac Ranch_, Amarillo, Texas.

the city and proclaiming odd bits of philosophy, poetry, or just plain nonsense. Conceived by Mr. Marsh and erected by his merry band of part-time aspiring artists, they appear in front of small businesses, in residential neighborhoods, and in places that might aptly be described as no place in particular.

Stanley Marsh 3 is even better known for having commissioned *Cadillac Ranch* in 1974, which has since become a sort of Mecca for Route 66 pilgrims. Ironically, the construct, which was assembled by an art co-op calling themselves the Ant Farm, came along too late to be contemporary with Route 66 in the region. Instead, it was placed in a field beside I-40, the highway which had supplanted U.S. 66. That said, no trip through the Texas panhandle is complete without taking a walk out into that field to absorb some of the energy contained in those upended Cadillacs, which are said to be positioned at the same angle as the sides of the Great Pyramids of Egypt.

Another Marsh commission is *Floating Mesa*, a sort of topographic illusion about 11 miles out of town on Ranch Road 1061 (see Further Afield below).

AMARILLO ATTRACTIONS

In terms of its significance in Route 66 lore, the only thing in Amarillo that's in the same league with the Cadillac Ranch would be the Big Texan. After serving steaks to Mother Road travelers for many years, the **Big**

Texan Steak Ranch responded to the shift in American travel habits by relocating to the shoulder of Interstate 40 in 1968. There, they continue their long-standing tradition of

Big Texan Steak Ranch,
Amarillo, Texas.

serving a 72-ounce steak at no charge, provided the person ordering it can consume it (and all of its accoutrements) in less than 60 minutes. There is a sort of Hall of Fame on the premises where you can read the names of those patrons who have been successful in meeting that challenge over the years. As the sign outside says, "The Public Is Invited—Come One, Come All."

Included in the Big Texan restaurant and motel complex is a gift shop which has a display case featuring live rattlesnakes, a latter-day nod to the reptile ranch traditions of the glory days of 66. And just to make sure you notice the place, there is usually an enormous model of a beef steer on a small trailer parked out front. The steer features a painted-on saddle blanket emblazoned with "Big Texan Steak Ranch Motel." Located on the north side of Interstate 40, just west of the Lakeside exit.

Encroaching suburbia led to the relocation of **Cadillac Ranch**, a short distance to the west, in 1997. It now sits in a field between I-40 Exits 60 and 62 on the west side of town. For those of you who never visited it at its original location, it must seem improbable that such an installation would be literally picked up and moved after 20-odd years, but that's exactly what happened.

The **American Quarter Horse Association (AQHA) Heritage Center and Museum** is a world-class facility dedicated to the history and continued appreciation of the American Quarter Horse. The AQHA is the world's largest horse breed registry, and has had its headquarters (right next door to the museum) in the panhandle town of Amarillo since the 1940s. There is even a research library and archive for the serious enthusiast. 2601 I-40 East (Exit 72A).

Harrington House is a neoclassical mansion built in 1914, and later owned by one of Amarillo's most prominent and philanthropic families. The home contains the Harringtons' extensive collection of fine and decorative arts accumulated over decades of world travel. Tours are conducted Tuesdays and Thursdays by prior arrangement; call 806-374-5490 (1600 S. Polk St.). The Harrington is in the midst of a two-block section of Polk Street featuring some of the city's most prestigious older homes—the **Polk Street Historic District**.

A recycled gasoline station in Amarillo, Texas.

The **Carey-McDuff Gallery of Contemporary Art** is at 508 S. Bowie Street. "Lightnin'" McDuff prefers to work in metal, and there is a veritable menagerie of creatures made from scrap iron, old farm implements, and so forth. He is also the creator of the *Ozymandias* sculpture outside of town (see Further Afield).

If burgers are your thing, you'll want to pay a visit to the **Arnold Burger**. This is the place to come when you need something special, such as a 10-pound, 18-incher that will feed 15 people (that's wider than most large pizzas, my friend!). Or perhaps a jumbo burger that's shaped like the state of Texas is more your style (with up to four patties!). Either way, enjoy it at 1611 S. Washington Street.

If you like buildings that don't really want to look like buildings, check out **Beef Burger Barrel**. This barrel-shaped walk-up started life as an A&W Root Beer stand, and over the years has had several names, menus, owners, and even varied locations. Today it's at 3102 Plains Boulevard, at S. Virginia.

Railroad buffs might want to see the **Madame Queen**, one of only five "Texas Type" Baldwin locomotives. This one is the original prototype of the 2-10-4 configuration dating from 1930. It's now located at E. Second and S. Lincoln near downtown, after having spent more than 40 years at the Santa Fe depot. The name comes from a fictional character from the *Amos 'n' Andy* radio series.

FURTHER AFIELD

Northwest of town via Ranch Road 1061, about 10 miles past Amarillo Boulevard, is *Floating Mesa*. It's an art installation that creates an illusion of a natural feature, a mesa, which has been sliced horizontally so that its top hovers above the base with no visible means of support. For the best effect, start looking for it at around seven miles from the Amarillo Boulevard junction. As you get closer, you'll see it more clearly and the illusion is less effective.

Just south of Amarillo, near the town of **Canyon**, is the **Palo Duro Canyon**. The first time you lay eyes on it, you're guaranteed to be surprised and impressed. The bright red cliffs are stunning. Cut by the Prairie Dog Town Fork of the Red River, the Palo Duro Canyon runs for many miles and is hundreds of feet deep. The drive through it is around 16 miles, but also available are horseback excursions, hiking trails of varying levels of strenuousness, and even a scenic railroad. Twelve miles east of Canyon via Texas 217 and Park Road 5.

The city of Canyon is home to the **Panhandle-Plains Historical Museum**, housed in a WPA-era building and the largest history museum in Texas. It's truly first-rate, with sections dedicated to art, western heritage, petroleum, transportation, and paleontology. Included are several dinosaur fossils, a wood-bodied Model A Ford (serial no. 28), and a replica Pioneer Town. Canyon also was once the stomping ground of artist Georgia O'Keeffe, who was a member of the art department at the local college for a time.

West of Canyon, Texas, on U.S. 60 is a **giant cowboy** statue at the former Cowboy Café. "Tex Randall" was built in 1959 as promotion for Wheeler's Western Store, which has long been closed. Tex is said to measure 47 feet in height and seven tons in weight. His future as a panhandle landmark is uncertain, so much so that the Society for Commercial Archeology included him in their Falling By The Wayside List in 2009.

Commissioned by Stanley Marsh 3 and inspired by the timeless Shelley poem, the ***Ozymandias*** sculpture, a piece by Lightnin' McDuff, is several miles south of Amarillo on I-27 at Sundown Lane. True to its poetic inspiration, it's a pair of torso-less legs recalling the temporary nature of man's works. There's even a tongue-in-cheek (but very official-looking) historical marker at the site advising that this was the actual ruin which inspired Shelley's poem, and that the face of the statue was removed and placed in the Amarillo Natural History Museum—which is, of course, nonexistent.

If you're willing to drive a little further, the town of **Hereford** is about 45 miles southwest of Amarillo via U.S. 60. Hereford is home to the **National Cowgirl Hall of Fame**, which of course includes exhibits pertaining to female rodeo stars. The town still holds an annual women's rodeo. 515 Avenue B.

North-northeast of Amarillo, near the shore of Lake Meredith, is **Alibates Flint Quarries National Monument**. Here, thousands of years before the Egyptians constructed the Great Pyramids, ancient Americans were quarrying a distinctive type of flint from which they made tools and weapons, which were subsequently used in trade with their neighbors throughout much of North America. These quarries were used continuously from about 10,000 BC to AD 1800. Contained on the grounds are pueblo ruins and petroglyphs (rock art). Free guided walking tours (about 1.5 miles) are available.

BUSHLAND-WILDORADO

There is little to note in the neighboring communities of Bushland and Wildorado. Bushland took its name from one W. H. Bush, who owned the land on which the town site was founded. Wildorado is marked by some cattle feed lots on the eastern approach to town. There is also a vintage example of roadside signage from the Route 66 era: a neon creation for Jesse's Café still adorns the north side of the highway.

VEGA

Opinions differ as to the midpoint of Route 66—for every person who claims it's in Vega, there's another who says it's actually in Adrian, a few miles further west. What seems certain is that the halfway point of Route 66, as it wends its way from Lake Michigan to the Pacific Ocean, lies somewhere here in the Texas Panhandle.

Unraveling this disagreement is not as simple as it might appear on the surface. While you will see some rather exacting figures published for the total mileage of Route 66—2,448 being one of the most popular—that "precision" is more smoke than substance. The route itself, and the total mileage that comprised it, was always in a state of change and flux. While in one town the road might add some miles in order to bypass the

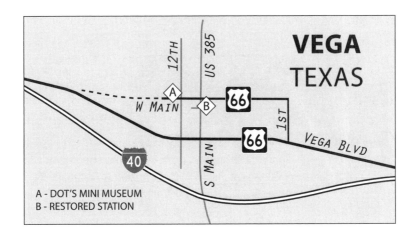

Vega, Texas.

downtown area, at the same time hundreds of miles away in another state the highway department would be rounding off some corners, replacing them with curves, and thereby shortening the overall length. Such changes occurred again and again, all along the route, and continued over the course of decades. In fact, even though U.S. 66 officially no longer exists, the roadway you drive today continues to undergo some of those same processes in its current role as a collection of secondary roads.

The town of Vega was established in 1900 by the Chicago, Rock Island, and Gulf Railroad, and is the Oldham County seat, a post it took over from the nearby town of Tascosa in 1915. South of the courthouse is a 1920s-era **Magnolia gasoline station,** which has been restored, partly through funding from the Route 66 Corridor Preservation Program.

Stretch your legs awhile in Vega by popping into **Dot's Mini Museum** at 105 N. Twelfth Street, near a dead-end segment of the route in the heart of town. Dot amassed an extensive collection of artifacts over a lifetime on Route 66. Dot herself is now deceased, but her family has chosen to continue making the collection available to the public.

Dot's Mini Museum, Vega, Texas.

FURTHER AFIELD

About 40 miles north of Vega on U.S. 385 is **Old Tascosa**, a western-style ghost town. In the 1870s, Tascosa was a lively place, and functioned as a supply depot for some large area ranches, such as the XIT and the LIT. It was the seat of Oldham County, was heralded as the Cowboy Capital of the Plains, and boasted its own newspaper, the Tascosa *Pioneer*. Such famous

East of Vega, Texas.

characters as Kit Carson and Billy the Kid were known to walk its streets. Billy the Kid was eventually killed by Pat Garrett, the sometime-sheriff of Oldham County (you can see Billy's grave later on, at Ft. Sumner, NM). Tascosa's decline came with fenced property and its being bypassed by the railroad in 1887. The county seat was moved south to Vega in 1915; at the time of the balloting, there were only 15 residents left in Tascosa. The last of those residents, Mrs. Mickey McCormick and her dog, finally departed around 1940.

It was about then that Cal Farley, champion wrestler and successful Amarillo businessman, entered the picture. He founded his Boys Ranch in 1939, with its center at the old Oldham County Courthouse (now the **Julian L. Bivins Museum**); the old townsite is now on the grounds of **Cal Farley's Boys Ranch**. Mr. Bivins donated the first acreage around the old town, which resulted in the establishment of this home for wayward and homeless boys. The compound has since expanded to include over 10,000 acres and cares for about 300–400 boys and girls annually. Visitors to the ranch are welcome daily. In September, the youngsters (4–18 years of age) participate in an annual Labor Day rodeo.

Before leaving Tascosa/Boys Ranch, be sure to visit the classic old west cemetery, aptly named **Boot Hill**, which is maintained by Boys Ranch residents.

 Getting back on Route 66, about seven miles or so west of Vega is the exit for Landergin. It was never really a town, but rather a railroad siding, a location given a name by railroaders for their own convenience. Landergin was the site of the "Run to the Heartland" celebration in 1996, the first of many national Route 66 celebrations to come. What with both Vega and Adrian laying claim to the Midpoint of the Route, Landergin made an ideal compromise, situated as it is between the two rivals for the title. George and Melba Rook, true Route 66 celebrities, used to run the store here and had a great Okie-style truck parked outside the premises.

Artist Bob Waldmire at work on a mural, Landergin, Texas.

That celebration was the scene of the first presentation of the John Steinbeck Award, Michael Wallis being the first such honoree. Not much has been happening at this place the last several years, however.

ADRIAN

Again we are—or continue to be—at the midpoint of Route 66. In the battle of one-upsmanship, the former Zella's Café in Adrian (circa 1928) is now known as the **Midpoint Café**, and has a slogan to match: "When You're Here, You're Halfway There." There is a small monument to that effect across the street from the café, and many travelers find it an irresistible

Adrian, Texas.

photo-op. The city of Adrian has even painted their water tower to proclaim it the midpoint of Route 66.

The Midpoint Café is a terrific place to stop in and sample some local hospitality. The staff will make you feel welcome, the food is great, and there is a gift shop where you can spend your money on terrific Route 66 stuff. If you like dessert, you'll love the "ugly crust" pies for which the Midpoint is justifiably well-known.

While in Adrian, keep on the lookout for the **Bent Door**. Years ago, someone used parts from an airport control tower in the construction of this roadside business. As in so many other cases, there has been talk for some years of returning the place to its former glory. I have seen a postcard of this place from the 1960s, at which time it was operating as Tommy's Café, with a yellow-and-red sign similar to the one in front of the Midpoint today.

In Adrian there has been an outbreak of the same fever so prevalent in Amarillo—various installations of the **Dynamite Museum** now abound here. Among them is my personal favorite: "Art is what you can get away with."

Near the halfway point of Route 66, Adrian, Texas.

GLENRIO

Glenrio can rightly be called a ghost town. Each time I have ventured here it has been deathly quiet, except for the barking of the junkyard dogs that commences a few moments after my arrival. Barking dogs, with no human owners in evidence, do not make for pleasant exploring. Today, Glenrio consists of a few ruinous buildings of unknown identity, and the equally-ruinous "Last Motel in Texas." If you pass by it and then look back from the west, you'll see that the sign once read, "First Motel in Texas" for the eastbound travelers arriving from New Mexico.

All in all, Glenrio is a somewhat spooky locale, which makes it all the more startling to learn that in the 1940s this was a thriving, bustling place. A current resident of Fort Worth tells me that he worked for the Texas Highway Department at Glenrio at an official welcome station in 1941–42. He witnessed firsthand the so-called "Okies" traveling westward with all of their earthly possessions tied to the roofs of their automobiles. At that time, they were headed for work at the shipyards and

Former gas station, Glenrio, Texas.

Last and First Motel in Texas, Glenrio, Texas.

defense plants of California.

Glenrio was founded in 1903, shortly after a railroad line was established in the vicinity. Many have observed that the name is formed from the English glen (for "valley") and the Spanish rio (for "river"), while the actual town site is located neither in a valley nor along a river.

According to a former resident of Glenrio, a film crew spent about three weeks in the town filming portions of *The Grapes of Wrath* in 1938. At that time, full-time residents of the town numbered about thirty.

Somewhere in the middle of Glenrio is the New Mexico border, but the *llano estacado* continues as far as the eye can see, having no respect for political boundaries.

NEW MEXICO

ew Mexico—Land of Enchantment. The name is fitting, in that the place, its people, and its traditions have a way of winning the hearts of all those who visit. Those of us fortunate enough to

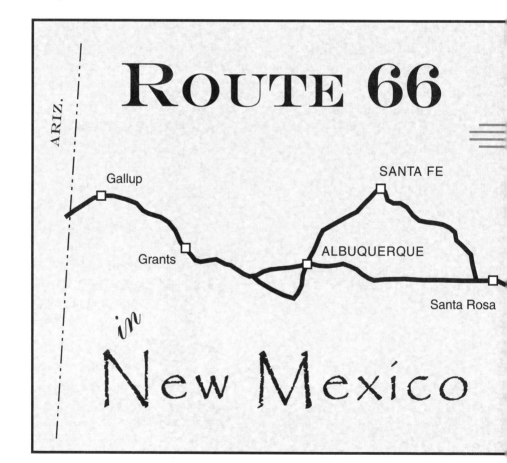

spend time in New Mexico invariably speak again and again of our experiences here, and perhaps even talk of making it our permanent home.

The land itself is beautiful, with its spreading plains, purple mountains, and colorful, overarching, cloud-filled skies. These features in themselves are alluring, but beyond that there is the profound sense of respect one feels for the centuries of history and tradition that permeate the land. Perhaps nowhere is there a more successful commingling of disparate cultures to form a unique whole than there is here in New Mexico. Tread softly, for you are on hallowed ground.

The *llano estacado* continues to the Pecos River Valley. This land was formerly a part of Texas, the part which was ceded to appease jealous rivals who worried over the enormous influence a full-sized Texas might wield as a state.

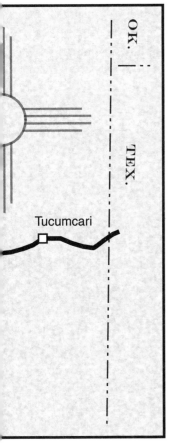

The land has seen and been inhabited by every walk of mankind: farmer, rancher, miner; Indian, Spaniard, Anglo; the base, the virtuous, and the merely foolish. All have left their marks, and those marks are here for you to see.

Here in the West, scars on the earth are slow to heal. New Mexico is a treasure chest of archaeological discoveries, some uncovered long ago, others waiting to be revealed. Here in New Mexico are the stone ruins of centuries-old civilizations and the still-visible wagon ruts of trade routes rendered obsolete by the iron horse. Also to be seen are the scars left by abandoned stretches of Route 66.

Unless you have a four-wheel-drive vehicle, or you are absolutely certain there has not been recent rain to make the dirt road hazardous, you should not attempt your entry into New Mexico by way of the spur of 66 that passes through Glenrio. You are safer to return to I-40 and cross the border that way. You'll see a sign advising you that you are entering Mountain Time, a very real-world indication that you are now starting a new chapter in your Route 66 adventure.

Part of that new chapter involves cuisine. In this part of the country, virtually every restaurant has a "Mexican" or "New Mexican" section of the menu. This can make for some strange bedfellows, such as the Chinese buffet that offers tacos, or the sandwich shop which has refried beans as a side order. And be prepared for the first time you are asked the Official State Question: "Red or Green?" The choice of either red or green chili sauce with your southwestern meal is such a profound—and yet ordinary—question in these parts that the state of New Mexico passed a bill in 1999 adding the question to the list of other officially-recognized items such as the state flower, state bird, and so forth. (Incidentally, if you have difficulty choosing, you may want to answer "Christmas," ensuring that you get some of each.)

ENDEE

The name of this community was most likely adopted from the name of the ND Ranch, which was established in the area in the 1880s. If you took the unpaved road out of Glenrio, you'll come upon Endee about five miles west. If you had to use the interstate, you can exit at NM 93 and turn south to visit Endee.

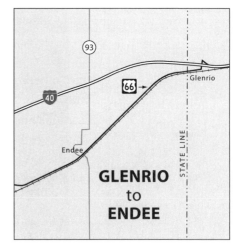

The old route from Endee to San Jon is also unpaved. Depending on conditions, you may need to go north and pick up I-40 for the ride into San Jon. If so, don't feel bad; my 1957 atlas shows Endee as having already been bypassed at that time

There aren't many motorists passing through Endee, New Mexico these days.

in favor of a newer alignment to the north, where today's I-40 roadbed is.

BARD

Although Bard usually shows up on older (1930s–40s) maps of the area, there is not much for today's traveler to see. I've been unable to find out much of anything about it in my own research. Try some exploring south of I-40 at Exit 361, which is about four or five miles east of San Jon.

SAN JON

There are still several abandoned motels on the old route through town, among them the Western Motel. On a recent trip through here, there was

San Jon, New Mexico.

an early '60s Plymouth sedan rusting in the parking lot of the Western.

You can eschew the interstate and take old 66 all the way into Tucumcari from San Jon (south frontage road).

TUCUMCARI

This is the town that changed my life by starting me on a quest to see all of Route 66—more on that in a moment.

Formerly called Six-Shooter Siding, there are at least two stories circulating as to how Tucum-cari (pronounced

Route 66 east of Tucumcari, New Mexico.

"two-come-carry") got its modern name—one romantic and one less so. Legend states that an Indian maiden named Kari was so grieved over the death of her lover, Tocom, at the hand of a rival, that she took her own life. Her father, upon discovering the tragedy, exclaimed, "Tocom! Kari!" A wonderful fable, with shades of Romeo and Juliet; but sober heads inform us that the name comes from a Comanche word, *tu-kamukaru*, meaning to lie in wait, as in an ambush.

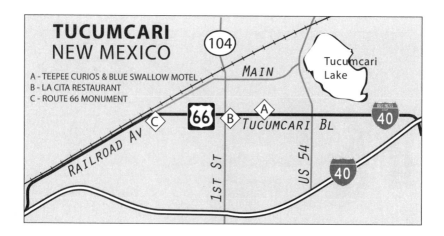

Speaking of sober heads, I lost mine permanently in 1992 on a trip through here on my way to Fort Worth, Texas, from Greeley, Colorado. My wife and I were on the stretch of I-40 west of Tucumcari, heading east, when we started seeing billboards shouting, "*TUCUMCARI TONITE!*" and, "*ON HISTORIC ROUTE 66!*" Since it was around nightfall, we decided on the spur of the moment to stay the night in Tucumcari, a long-standing tradition for Route 66-ers that we were unaware of at the time. Pulling off the interstate and prowling through Tucumcari absolutely floored me. We saw a souvenir stand in the shape of an Indian teepee, and then we came across a restaurant shaped like a Mexican sombrero. I thought: "I can't believe there are still places like this! This is amazing!" I've been coming back to Route 66 year after year ever since. And it *still* amazes me.

Tucumcari has lots of Route 66 spots that folks around the globe recognize. There's **Teepee Curios**, of course, which in the 1940s was actually a gasoline station. The sombrero-shaped Mexican restaurant we ate at that night was **La Cita**, and it has since been painted to make it even more dazzling to the eye. The real cornerstone of Tucumcari highway businesses, though, has got to be the **Blue Swallow Motel**. Built in the

Tucumcari, New Mexico.

One of the best-looking signs on all of Route 66 is in Tucumcari, New Mexico.

1940s from surplus WWII cabins, the motel was later presented as an engagement present to Lillian Redman, the proprietess for many years, by her husband-to-be, Floyd. That was in 1958. Lillian kept things going for many a year and only recently (in Mother Road terms) has it fallen into other capable hands.

The **Redwood Motel**, dating from around 1954, has been placed on the state register of historic properties—it has authentic redwood used in its construction. Another landmark is the **Trails West Lounge**, whose distinctive sign appears in the Route 66 upholstery fabric so ubiquitous in recent years, making the Trails West familiar even to those who haven't yet made it to Tucumcari.

Tucumcari truly has a wealth of vintage roadside

Longstanding roadside eatery in Tucumcari, New Mexico.

Tucumcari, New Mexico.

businesses, far beyond the short description in this book. You could spend hours just exploring, not only along the old route with its dozens of classic neon signs, but also downtown, where there is a still-running, Depression-era theater and a large railroad depot. As if Tucumcari didn't have enough going for it already, in recent years they've added several murals scattered through downtown, including a Mother Road-themed one on the side of Lowe's grocery.

South of town you'll see Tucumcari mountain, tattooed with a big letter "T." The **Tucumcari Mountain Cheese Factory** is a few blocks north of 66, at 823 E. Main Street. It is housed in an old Coca-Cola Bottling Plant building, which dates from 1951. Also in town is the **Mesalands Dinosaur Museum**, run by the Mesa Technical College. Notable is the fact that the dinosaur models on display are cast in bronze (rather than more fragile plaster or resin commonly used), and visitors are invited to touch. These bronze castings are made right here at the college by students and volunteers. The dinosaur museum is at 222 E. Laughlin. At 416 S. Adams

is the **Tucumcari Historical Museum**, which, of course, includes an exhibit on Route 66 through the area, and is housed in a 1903 schoolhouse.

On the west end of town, as you pass the

Tucumcari, New Mexico.

convention center, pause to admire the Route 66 **monument** by artist Thomas Coffin. The piece was installed in 1997 and incorporates a '50s-style automotive tail fin, a mock-adobe base, and, of course, the double sixes.

You'll have to drive superslab for awhile after entering the I-40 at the west end of Tucumcari, but be sure to leave it at Exit 321 for the run into Montoya.

MONTOYA-NEWKIRK

Route 66 crosses a fair number of other routes of significance over its course. For example, we crossed the Chisholm Trail back in Oklahoma, which was used primarily for the transport of cattle. Another cattle trail is at hand now. The **Goodnight-Loving Trail** crosses our path somewhere between the communities of Montoya and Newkirk. One of the best maps I've seen places it very close to Newkirk, and so the highway that stretches northward out of Newkirk, numbered 129, must be the closest thing we have to an actual road that follows that course. The Goodnight-Loving Trail passed through Fort Sumner to the south of us before going on to the markets in Denver and Cheyenne to the north.

CUERVO

Cuervo has been what can only be called a ghost town for many years. Although there are still some inhabitants, large tracts of the town are now deserted, with broken windows and gaping doors.

Street scene in the ghost town of Cuervo, New Mexico.

SANTA ROSA

New Mexico is generally an arid place, but Santa Rosa is the exception. Thanks to a collection of artesian springs in the area, it's a veritable garden spot, nicknamed the City of Natural Lakes. The most famous of the springs here is the **Blue Hole**, which attracts scuba divers from far and wide to ply their trade. The Blue Hole is more than 80 feet deep and 60 feet wide, with water temperatures hovering around 64 degrees Fahrenheit. It's on Blue Hole Road, just off of an early alignment of 66. Another favorite with scuba divers is **Perch Lake**, which has a twin-engine plane

In Santa Rosa, the I-40 Business Loop works fine; it's very straightforward and will enable you to see most everything you may have heard of in town. However, if you feel more adventurous, there is an older, non-continuous alignment that entered a little to the south along what is now Blue Hole Road and the nearby airport. However, much of it is inaccessible and/or privately owned.

Santa Rosa, New Mexico.

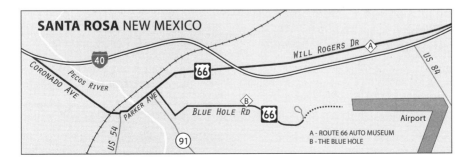

Santa Rosa, New Mexico.

submerged below for exploration. Perch Lake is about two miles south of town on State Highway 91.

If you're into classic cars and other automotive memorabilia, check out the **Route 66 Auto Museum**, at 2866 Will Rogers Drive, east of town. Look for the yellow car atop a pole.

The **Club Café**, long a fixture at Santa Rosa, has been closed for many years now. There were a great number of billboards along 66 (and I-40) in New Mexico with the Smiling Fat Man logo. Speaking of billboards, there may yet be some weathered concrete ones visible on the eastern side of town just west of the airport on an early 66 alignment. I don't know what they might once have advertised.

The Pecos, a river prominent in the lore of the American West, is crossed here at Santa Rosa. This is reportedly the place where Coronado made the crossing, too, in 1541. From the Pecos River crossing, the highway begins climbing toward the continental divide, more than 200 miles to the west. In the movie *The Grapes of Wrath*, there's a brief scene showing a steam-powered train crossing a long bridge over a river. That scene was shot right here, where the railway crosses the Pecos River, a little to the north of the automobile bridge.

FURTHER AFIELD

About 10 miles south of Santa Rosa via State Route 91 is **Puerto de Luna**, an abandoned Spanish settlement. Along the way the road follows the Pecos River Valley, and there is some very attractive canyon country.

About 45 miles southeast of Santa Rosa via U.S. 84 is **Fort Sumner**,

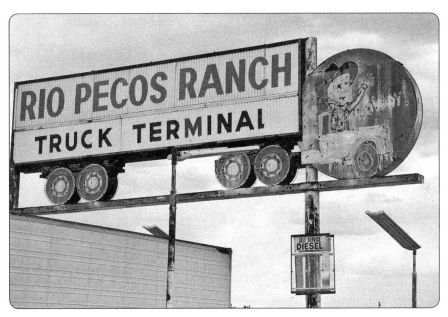

Abandoned roadside establishment in Santa Rosa, New Mexico.

both a military post and a town of the same name. It was here in 1881 that Billy the Kid was shot and killed by Pat Garrett, and his grave site is here at Fort Sumner—or at least we think that it is (more on that in a moment). Billy the Kid (or William Bonney) was a hired gun in the Lincoln County, New Mexico, range wars, and in that capacity killed a man for every year of his life—"not counting Indians and Mexicans"—by his own account.

Fort Sumner was constructed in 1862, and was a major stop on the Goodnight-Loving Trail, a cattle trail that ran from Texas to Wyoming. In 1869, the land the fort stood on was sold to Lucien B. Maxwell, who converted the officers' quarters to a private residence. That was where Billy was killed by Garrett years later. Judging from conditions in Fort Sumner today, if anyone could get their hands on Billy's corpse now, it would be torn into at least two pieces. An explanation is in order.

In downtown Fort Sumner is the **Billy the Kid Museum**, at 1435 E. Sumner Avenue. This museum originated in the 1950s, and it shows its age. There are disintegrating mannequins of Billy the Kid and Pat Garrett, a stuffed two-headed calf, old farm implements, and antique

typewriters—the flot-
sam and jetsam that a
down-to-earth museum
curator accumulates over
the decades. Outside is a
graveyard with markers
for Billy and two of his
cohorts, surrounded by
a chain link fence. Fas-
tened to the fence, how-
ever, and located so that
it appears in virtually every snapshot taken of the
grave site, is a small sign
that states: REPLICA.

Billy the Kid Museum in the town of Fort Sumner, New Mexico.

What goes on? According to the lady at the museum, the replica had to be created because the real grave is in such a very poor state. But where is that?

Drive about seven miles southeast of the town of Fort Sumner (U.S. 84 East to NM 212 South) to the **Old Fort Sumner Museum**, established in 1932. This museum also has Billy the Kid artifacts, such as Billy's letters to the governor asking for amnesty. Outside is what is billed as "The Real Grave of Billy the Kid." Like the replica in town, the grave site also includes a pair of companions. This grave is completely covered in a metal cage to prevent vandalism. It seems that the original headstone was stolen in 1950 (remember the lady at the replica grave saying the real one was in bad shape?) and not recovered until 26 years later. Then it was stolen again in 1981, and again recovered. Now they take no chances. The ground over the grave has even been encased in concrete, just to make sure there won't be any more funny business.

Adjacent to the real Billy the Kid grave and the Old Fort Sumner Museum is the **Fort Sumner State Monument**. This is the site of Navajo and Apache confinement at the hands of the U.S. military in the 1860s.

Back on the road: Leaving Santa Rosa, the old highway we love so much has pretty much been buried by the interstate. Several miles west of Santa Rosa, you'll come to a crossroads—not so much in the physical sense, as in the spiritual sense. What you do encounter physically is the junction where U.S. 84 splits off and goes to the north. That northerly route more or less follows the older Route 66 alignment, which for several years wandered up through Santa Fe. Straight ahead is the alignment born in the 1930s, when a straighter course was carved through the countryside, shaving significant miles and time from the passage through New Mexico. The two alternate paths will meet again in Albuquerque.

The narrative immediately following takes you along the older route through Santa Fe. If you choose to take the later route straight to Albuquerque, you can pick up the account for that segment below at the Flying C Ranch.

ROMEROVILLE

The town of Romeroville was named for Don Trinidad Romero, who entertained President Rutherford B. Hayes at his home, and whose father founded the Romero Mercantile Company, a firm which became one of the leading wholesalers of the region.

From Romeroville onward, Route 66 closely approximates the track of the **Santa Fe Trail**. The trail originated in central Missouri (at Old Franklin) and took a northerly tack through Kansas and Colorado. It was a very significant trade route for several decades of the nineteenth century, connecting the ancient city in newly-independent Mexico with the western United States.

FURTHER AFIELD

Las Vegas, New Mexico, founded in 1835, is a very special place indeed. Over the past four centuries, the area has been inhabited by native Americans, Spanish conquerors, Anglo settlers, desperadoes, robber barons, and dance-hall girls, all of whom have wielded their respective influences.

La Castaneda is the former Harvey House in Las Vegas, New Mexico.

Doc Holliday and his girlfriend, Kate Elder, moved here in 1879 and opened a saloon; they were followed a few months later by their friend Wyatt Earp. Butch Cassidy once worked in town as a bartender. Bob Ford, a Las Vegas saloon-keeper, was the man who later became known for killing Jesse James. In 1915, Tom Mix made several of his Westerns here. And film-making in the town didn't stop there. The town fire station appears in a scene from *Easy Rider*, where Jack Nicholson's character makes the decision to hit the road with Peter Fonda and Dennis Hopper. Scenes from *Charlie Siringo* and *Red Dawn* were also made here.

Las Vegas boasts more than 900 buildings (that's right, 900!) on the National Register of Historic Places. Two of the most notable are **La Castaneda Hotel**, an example of the Harvey House chain of fine railroad-era hotels, and **El Fidel Hotel**. Walking tour information is available at the local chamber office, at 727 Grand Avenue.

Sharing the same address with the chamber of commerce, the **City of Las Vegas Museum and Rough Rider Memorial Collection** commemorates Teddy Roosevelt's famous Rough Riders, who distinguished themselves in the Spanish-American War in Cuba. The collection also exhibits Native American artifacts and items pertaining to the local history of Las Vegas. The museum is housed in a WPA-era structure originally built as the city hall. When the Rough Riders were originally formed, the largest contingent from any one state or territory came from New Mexico; later, in 1899, Las Vegas hosted the group's first reunion. Over the years, many attendees of those reunions donated various mementos of the campaign, and so established the collection now held here at the museum.

The **Bridge Street Historic District** offers an impressive array of architectural styles, including Victorian, Italianate, and nineteenth century commercial.

A series of several *acequías*, or early irrigation channels, are preserved here in Las Vegas. There is also an operating drive-in theater north of town on Highway 518.

Five miles northwest of Las Vegas (via NM 65) stands **Montezuma Castle**, an opulent resort hotel from the 1880s on the grounds of the Armand Hammer United World College of the American West.

About 28 miles or so to the northeast of Las Vegas is **Fort Union National Monument**, a significant stop on the old Santa Fe Trail. Fort Union was the chief quartermaster depot for nearly 50 other western forts during the late 1800s, and its troops stood guard here to protect the settlers in the region and travelers on the Santa Fe Trail. The two major branches of the trail—the Mountain Branch and the Cimarron Cutoff—converged in this area. Just outside the fort is the largest network of visible Santa Fe Trail **wagon ruts** still remaining. Fort Union was also the intended objective of Confederate forces in the Battle of Glorieta Pass, which occurred west of here and is sometimes called the "Gettysburg of the West." There is a 1¼-mile tour trail which explores not only ruins of the fort, but also adobe villages nearby. There is also a visitor center with museum.

Some of the many ruins at Fort Union, northeast of Las Vegas, New Mexico.

Back on Route 66, go southwest out of Romeroville. The modern highway (I-25/U.S. 84) closely adheres to the path of the old Santa Fe Trail. Near a community called Rowe, you can exit the main highway and use State Highway 63 to enter the village of Pecos.

PECOS

This is a very old pueblo which once held over 2,000 residents. It was abandoned circa 1838, at which time the remaining inhabitants reportedly went to Jemez.

Just outside Pecos Pueblo is the **Pecos National Historical Park**, which includes the ruins of two Spanish colonial missions, as well as ancient pueblo features. Unlike most pueblo ruins, the kivas here are accessible to the public. The ruins are very scenic, and there is an easy self-guided trail sprinkled with interpretive plaques to explain all of the features. The park also now includes the Glorieta Battlefield a few miles to the north.

There is a Benedictine Monastery located on the northern edge of Pecos pueblo. Continue out of Pecos westward on NM 50 toward Glorieta.

Colonial-era mission at Pecos, New Mexico.

GLORIETA

Just prior to reaching the village of Glorieta, there is a highwayside historical marker. It was here, at a Santa Fe Trail stopover called Pigeon's Ranch, that the **Battle of Glorieta Pass** occurred in March of 1862 during the American Civil War. There is still one adobe structure remaining from the 18-room stage station complex. The battlefield is a National Historic Landmark.

Just after passing through the town of Glorieta, you will come through Glorieta Pass, the passage through the mountains which made this circuitous route to Santa Fe a necessity in the days of the old trail.

SANTA FE

Santa Fe is the oldest capital city in the U.S., having been designated as such in 1610, when the plaza was laid out and the Palace of the Governors was established. It is also the focal point of the famous Santa Fe Trail, a primarily trade-oriented route which was at its most important from about 1821 until 1880, when railroad transport effectively supplanted it.

Your entry into town is along the same path as the old trail, and the modern-day street is so named: Old Santa Fe Trail.

Route 66 through Santa Fe was short-lived, so there isn't a variety of routes to choose from, as you'll find with many of the larger cities. What makes Santa Fe difficult is that many of the downtown streets have been converted to one-way, so you can't drive the city the way you'd like—the way motorists traveled it in the early days of the highway. The current traffic patterns are more conducive to eastbound travel. The gist of it is this: Route 66 entered from the southeast along NM 466/ Old Pecos Trail, which then merges with Old Santa Fe Trail, which comes to an end at the central plaza. Route 66 then left town for Albuquerque, headed southwest along Cerillos Road. Take your time and explore Santa Fe, but make sure you heed the one-way signs.

A monument to mark the end of that trail was placed at the southeast corner of the central plaza by the Daughters of the American Revolution in 1911. It was not until a year later, in 1912, that New Mexico attained statehood. Today, **La Fonda Hotel** (circa 1920) occupies the site of the old inn that marked the end of the trail and served as a mass meeting place for those who had made the arduous journey. It is said that Billy the Kid washed dishes at the inn for a time.

Oddly, the Sangre de Christo Mountains near Santa Fe were the set for the filming of the "Oh What A Beautiful Morning" scene from the movie *Oklahoma!*

SANTA FE ATTRACTIONS

Museum Hill is a collection of museums including the Museum of Spanish Colonial Art, the Museum of International Folk Art, the Museum of Indian Arts and Culture, and the Wheelwright Museum of the American Indian. Also part of the family are five historical monuments across the state. Museum Hill can be reached by riding the M-Line city bus from Santa Fe's central plaza.

Georgia O'Keeffe, whose nearby museum is housed in a renovated adobe mission church, is one of only a very few widely disparate American artists with memorial museums, including Norman Rockwell, Frederic Remington, and Andy Warhol. 217 Johnson St.

Canyon Road, said to have originated as an Indian foot trail, is Santa Fe's gallery district, lined on both sides with upper-echelon art galleries, coffee houses, and so forth.

An interesting tale awaits at the **Santa Fe National Cemetery**. Among row upon row of thousands of simple, identical headstones on these hallowed grounds stands the lifelike statue of Private Dennis O'Leary. The statue depicts the young O'Leary in his army uniform, leaning against a tree. Legend states that he was a lonely and unhappy soldier stationed at Fort Wingate, and that he carved the likeness himself in his free time. According to the story, he wrote a suicide note describing the location of the statue and asking that it be placed over his grave. He then shot himself with his own pistol. Army records, however, list his death as having been a result of tuberculosis. When Fort Wingate was decommissioned in 1911, Private O'Leary and several others were re-interred here.

Ambiance at the El Rey Inn, Santa Fe, New Mexico.

You can take the **Santa Fe Southern Railway** on a day trip. The 36-mile, four-hour round trip runs from the historic depot (410 S. Guadalupe Street) to the nearby town of Lamy. The old Santa Fe depot, established in 1880, has been an inspiration to artists and photographers for generations.

The **Miraculous Staircase** is located in the Loretto Chapel, at 207 Old Santa Fe Trail. There is a very interesting story involving a "mysterious carpenter" who constructed the unusual staircase in the latter part of the 1870s. He appeared with a donkey and a toolbox, constructed the staircase over the course of several months, then abruptly vanished without pay or thanks. The staircase was innovative for its time, incorporating two full turns (720 degrees) and showing no obvious means of support. The Miraculous Staircase has been the subject of numerous articles over the years, as well as an episode of *Unsolved Mysteries*.

Also on Old Santa Fe Trail is the **Chapel of San Miguel por Barrio de Analco**, referred to as the oldest continuously occupied church. The chapel was constructed in 1626–28. Nearby, on DeVargas Street, is the **Oldest House**, which dates from approximately AD 1200.

The **Mission of San Miguel of Santa Fe** was constructed in 1610, and has on display a bell which was cast in Spain in 1356, and then brought here by oxcart in the early 1800s.

Established in the 1930s, the **El Rey Inn** is a terrific place to stay the night in Santa Fe. It's utterly unique, and it's right on old 66 (Cerillos Road at St. Michaels Drive) on your way out of town.

FURTHER AFIELD

Fans of Georgia O'Keeffe may want to be aware that about 45 miles or so north of Santa Fe, at **Abiquiu**, is the **Georgia O'Keeffe National Historic Site**. The 5,000-square-foot adobe structure here at Ghost Ranch was the artist's home and studio for more than 40 years.

Further north of Santa Fe, and certainly more than just a side trip, is the very historic and distinctly artsy district of **Taos**, Taos Pueblo, and Ranchos de Taos. The Church of San Francisco de Asis is one of the most painted and photographed buildings in the United States. Note that the Taos Pueblo charges a fee for admission, for parking, and for photography, and that the pueblo has no modern conveniences, such as electricity and plumbing.

Nearby is the **Kit Carson Home & Historical Museum**, where the famous frontiersman kept his residence from 1843–68. Kit Carson and his wife are both buried nearby. Or visit the home of Ernest L. Blumenschein, artist and co-founder of the original Taos Society of Artists.

Narrated trolley tours of Taos are available, as are walking tours of Taos Pueblo. The Taos area is also a hub for skiing in winter and river rafting in summer.

To the north of Taos, at **Arroyo Hondo**, is the **D. H. Lawrence Ranch & Memorial**. The Lawrences spent about two years here in the 1920s, and the surroundings are said to have been significant influences on a number of his books. When Mr. Lawrence died in 1930, his wife scattered his ashes here at the ranch. The ranch is nestled in the Sangre de Christo Mountains on 160 acres.

West of Santa Fe, Route 66 encounters yet another very old highway: the famous **El Camino Real**. This old road (circa 1581–1800) connected Mexico City with Santa Fe and continued to San Juan Pueblo to the north. The old trail is thought to have crossed today's I-25/old 66 near the La Cienega interchange. There is a monument near the community of Los Lunas (a little further in our journey).

DOMINGO

Here, the Santo Domingo Indian Trading Post was featured in *Life* magazine and visited by President John F. Kennedy in 1962. Unfortunately, the
trading post burned to the ground several years ago.

ALGODONES

Here, leave the superslab at Exit 248 (NM 313), which takes you through
the communities of Algodones, Angostura, the Pueblo de Santa Ana, and
El Llanito. The road is signed both El Camino Real and Pan-American
Central Highway through here. Just south of El Llanito is the town of
Bernalillo.

BERNALILLO

Behind the Sandoval County Courthouse sits a nineteenth-century **stone
jail** that once served the area. Also in town is **Silva's Saloon** (in the 900
block of S. Camino Del Pueblo), which opened the day after prohibition
ended in 1933, and has been run by the same family ever since. There is plenty of memorabilia displayed on the walls—over 70 years' worth—including
a hat collection.

The **Perea/
Baca House** was
the last stage stop
before Santa Fe on
El Camino Real.

Just a mile
or so northwest
of Bernalillo by
way of NM 44

Bernalillo, New
Mexico.

(co-numbered U.S. 550) is **Coronado State Monument**. The famous Spanish explorer is said to have stayed here during his 1541–42 expedition. Today, there is a park overlooking the Rio Grande, as well as a river walk and museum gallery. Parts of the village of Kuaua were excavated here as part of a WPA project in 1936, and there is a self-guided trail taking you through the ruins, which include a kiva and pre-Columbian mural. To get there, cross to the west side of the Rio Grande via 550/44, then turn right (north) on Kuaua Road.

FURTHER AFIELD

Bernalillo is also your launch pad for a terrific detour: the **Jemez Mountain Trail National Historic & Scenic Byway**. Take NM 44 northwest from Bernalillo to San Ysidro. From here, NM 4 is the Jemez Mountain Trail. The Scenic Byway designation means that the trail has scenic, historical, and cultural importance, and is one of only a handful in the state. It winds through 5,000 years of human history, millions of years of geologic time, and four climatic zones. The trail takes you to Jemez Pueblo, Jemez Springs, Jemez State Monument, Soda Dam, Battleship Rock, and Bandelier National Monument. **Jemez Pueblo** features a visitor's center which is a destination in itself. **Jemez Springs** is known for its mineral waters and bath houses (some of which are clothing-optional), and features a number of galleries for you to stop in and enjoy. **Jemez State Monument** is the prehistoric site of the Pueblo of Giusewa ("boiling waters"), which includes the ruins of the seventeenth-century Church of San Jose de los Jemez. Marvel at the walls of these ruins, some of which are eight feet thick. **Soda Dam** is a natural dam formed on the Jemez River from mineral deposits built up over thousands of years. The river emerges through a hole in the dam, forming a waterfall. Further north is **Battleship Rock**, which towers over you as you wend your way through rugged terrain formed by volcanic activity ages ago. **Bandelier National Monument** is one of the most-visited collections of Indian ruins in the nation. Miles of trails leave the visitor center and radiate outward to dozens of cliff dwellings. Nearby is **Los Alamos**, America's "Secret City" and birthplace of the nuclear age. It was here that the Manhattan Project was undertaken during World War II in order to develop the atomic bomb. You can learn more about it at the **Bradbury Science Museum**, located in downtown Los Alamos at 15th and Central.

South of Bernalillo, and just east of the old highway, is the Sandia Pueblo.

About halfway between Bernalillo and Alameda, but on the opposite side of the Rio Grande from you, is the community of Corrales. This community was named Sandoval (the same name as the county you are now in) at the time my 1957 atlas was printed. There is an old church there, the **Old San Ysidro Church**, which is a favorite subject for painters and photographers. Built in 1868, it now serves as a community center. Nearby is **Casa San Ysidro**, a restored Spanish colonial ranch house—also known as the Gutiérrez-Minge House—now operated by the Albuquerque Museum.

ALAMEDA

As you approach the northern outskirts of Albuquerque, you will pass through a community called Alameda. The highway will split, with one branch being 2nd Street and the other 4th. Take 4th Street, which is old 66, into Albuquerque. On the way, you'll encounter the city's Madonna of the Trail monument.

Side trip: A right at the Highway 528 junction in Alameda will take you across the river to the town of **Rio Rancho**. In Rio Rancho is the **J&R Vintage Auto Museum** (at the Stagecoach Stop RV Park) and the **Intel Museum** on Rio Rancho Drive (Highway 528). Also there are the grounds where the **Friends and Lovers Balloon Rally** is held each year.

See the description for Albuquerque below, following the Flying C to Tijeras narrative.

The loop of old Route 66 which passed through Santa Fe was a rather circuitous route necessitated by the challenging terrain and limited road-building budgets and equipment of the time. However, it was recognized very early on that a more direct, through route to Albuquerque from Santa Rosa should someday be achieved. In 1934, then-New Mexico Governor Clyde Tingley, a personal friend of President Roosevelt's, secured a number of New Deal projects for the state. Among those projects was the straightening of Route 66. That new alignment opened in 1937, running into Albuquerque along Central Avenue, and leaving the state capital high and dry. A further tale relates that preliminary steps in the bypassing of Santa Fe were taken by spiteful, outgoing Governor A. T. Hannett, who lost the re-election in 1926, just as the federal highway system was coming into being.

In taking the newer alignment, you proceed due west out of Santa Rosa and continue straight ahead (on I-40) past the U.S. 84 junction.

FLYING C RANCH

Iconic sign at the Flying C Ranch.

The Flying C is of course not a town in the traditional sense, but it certainly is pure Route 66. At Exit 234 you'll find what's left of a once-proud roadside complex that offered cross-country motorists food, fuel, lodging, and entertainment. In later years, they called themselves **Bowlin's Running Indian**, a name for which they invented a distinctive sign.

CLINES CORNERS

Clines Corners is just that—an intersection. Today there is an enormous gift shop that purveys such classics as rubber tomahawks, beaded belts, and cedar gewgaws of every description.

Further west, I-40's Exit 203 is the **Longhorn Ranch** interchange. The Longhorn Ranch has been characterized as the ritziest, glitziest tourist trap on the

Not much remains of the Longhorn Ranch tourist complex west of Clines Corners.

route. It was a full-blown compound including motel, gas station, museum, curio shop, restaurant, and bar. The whole operation was packaged in the guise of a Wild West movie set. Most of the structures are gone now.

BUFORD-MORIARTY

NM 333 takes you on the old route through this community. Buford shows up on some early maps of the area, but it has been taken over or

absorbed by modern-day Moriarty. Look for the Buford Courts as evidence of the former community of that name.

The sign at **El Comedor** in Moriarty was fortunate to be the target of neon restoration work recently. Described as a rotosphere, it consists of two

Moriarty, New Mexico.

halves of a ball rotating in different directions, with numerous Sputnik-style spikes protruding all around.

MORIARTY ATTRACTIONS

The **Moriarty Historical Society Museum** is located at 777 Old U.S. Route 66 SW, in the town's first fire station.

Moriarty Airport is home base for the **Albuquerque Soaring Club**. The group chose this area for its unbeatable thermal conditions that result in many flights in excess of 250 miles each year. The airport is also home to the U.S. Southwest Soaring Museum. At this point, we're within the "Albuquerque Box," a favorable wind pattern that has also made this area home to one of the largest ballooning communities in the world.

Moriarty calls itself the Pinto Bean Capital—there's a pinto bean festival held here in the fall. In November, the town plays host to an annual meeting of the Sherlock Holmes Society. This, in spite of the fact that there is no known connection between the town's name and that of Holmes' notorious rival.

 Stay on NM 333 as you leave Moriarty and head toward Edgewood.

EDGEWOOD

At Edgewood is the **Wild West Nature Park**, a 122-acre facility harboring non-releasable wildlife, including deer, coyotes, and mountain lions. The

park is a project of the New Mexico Wildlife Association, and most of the structures were built by members and volunteers of the state's Youth Conservation Corps.

Edgewood, New Mexico.

TIJERAS

Somewhere in the Tijeras Canyon area was Balanced Rock, a distinctive rock formation destroyed by the highway department in 1951. The reasoning was that the vibrations brought about by passing traffic posed the danger of toppling the formation; however, it's been widely reported that the job took considerably more explosives than anyone predicted, and so it may have endured for quite some time if left alone. At one time there was a painted sign on the rock directing the passing motorist to Queens Rest Camp, 6200 Central Avenue, six miles ahead in Albuquerque.

FURTHER AFIELD

A great side trip from Tijeras is the **Turquoise Trail** (NM 14), a beautiful scenic byway which runs northward towards Santa Fe. The route takes the traveler through turquoise mining country, complete with three revived ghost towns: Golden, Madrid, and Cerrillos. Madrid, established in 1914, was a ghost town for many years until, in the 1970s, it began to be re-settled by artists. A few miles further north is Cerillos, which fits the bill as the stereotypical Old West town—it had over 20 saloons at one time. These days, that western atmosphere is being exploited by the film industry, with *Shoot Out* (1972) and *Outrageous Fortune* (1987) being filmed in the area. Cerrillos is also home to the Casa Grande Trading Post, which also houses the Turquoise Mining Museum and a petting zoo.

Just off the Turquoise Trail via NM 536 is **Sandia Crest**, with an elevation of over 10,000 feet. The view is spectacular, and you can hike the numerous trails in the Sandia Mountain Wilderness, which treat you to one gorgeous view after another. You can either drive to the top of Sandia Peak, or take the 30-minute chair lift from the Sandia Peak ski area. The adventurous can take along (or rent) mountain bikes, and ride down from the observation area on a 15-mile trail. Alternatively, there is a popular tram ride that departs from Albuquerque, the longest of its kind at 2.7 miles, with spectacular views of the Land of Enchantment.

From NM 536 in the Sandia Crest area, you can follow Highway

165 north toward **Placitas**. About halfway to Placitas is the site of an ar-chaeological dig where evidence of very early man has been discovered. The **Sandia Man Cave**, a self-guided hiking tour, is the earliest known archaeological site in the southwest (20,000 B.C.).

Also on NM 536 is the town of **Sandia Park**. This is the home of **Tinkertown**, the creation of a man named Ross Ward. Tinkertown con-sists of 20-plus rooms full of worlds in miniature, such as an animated miniature western town, a tiny three-ring circus, and other dioramas, all surrounded by a collection of over 50,000 bottles. The motto at Tinker-town: "We did all this while you were watching TV."

Tinkertown is an old-fashioned, family-run attraction. Sandia Park, New Mexico.

ALBUQUERQUE

There is a huge array of vintage motels on Central Avenue along the eastern approach to the city, though more are being demolished year after year. Decades ago, the city must have appeared

> As explained elsewhere, there are essentially two Route 66 alignments in the Duke City: east-west Central Avenue, and north-south 4th Street. The latter only lasted until the mid-1930s when Santa Fe was removed from the route.

almost oasis-like to the traveler who had just come the 100-plus miles from Santa Rosa, the last stopover of any size. Central Avenue is the nation's longest main street, at 18 miles east to west. In the 3200 block of Central, keep your eyes peeled for Kelly's Brewery, a modern-day brewpub which is housed in a restored Streamline Moderne-style auto dealership dating from 1939.

Albuquerque is the hometown of the fictional Ethel Mertz (in fact, Vivian Vance actually lived here for a time herself). It is also home to the **New Mexico Route 66 Association**, which is headquartered at the **66 Diner**, a 1940s-era Streamline-style structure at 1405 Central. The 66 Diner burned in 1995, but fortunately for all of us it has been lovingly restored to its full glory.

Architecturally, the city is marked by fine examples of Pueblo Revival architecture, including several examples at the University of New Mexico campus (even the UNM campus is on Central). The city also boasts the **KiMo Theater**, at 423 Central Avenue NW. The KiMo was built circa 1927, and was designed by the same team of architects that conceived the one-of-a-kind Coleman Theater in Miami, Oklahoma: Carl and Robert

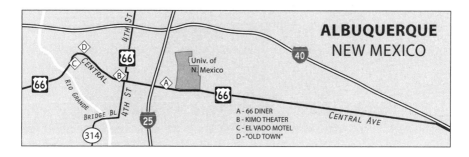

This restaurant occupies a former fire station. Albuquerque, New Mexico.

Downtown Albuquerque.

Boller. Its design, sometimes referred to as Pueblo Deco, was intended to reflect the three major cultural influences in the area: Indian, Hispanic, and Anglo. Details include painted murals and terra-cotta buffalo skull wall sconces. Some say that the KiMo is haunted by the ghost of a small boy who died there in 1951, when a hot water heater exploded. The old **Monte Vista Fire Station** (circa 1936), at 3201 Central Avenue NE, has been converted to a restaurant. **La Posada Hotel** was formerly a Hilton and one of Albuquerque's most prestigious hostelries. It was here that Conrad Hilton married Zsa Zsa Gabor on April 10, 1942. La Posada is one block north of Central on 2nd Street and includes a 1930s-era coffee shop.

You can take a **self-guided walking tour** of Pueblo Deco architecture, beginning at the KiMo Theater and also including the Maisel Building, Wright's Trading Post, the J. A. Skinner Building, and several others.

Check out Albuquerque's **Old Town**, where the city was first settled around 1706. The area is actually believed to have been inhabited

MADONNA OF THE TRAIL

In the 1920s, the National Society of the Daughters of the American Revolution (DAR) commissioned the design, casting, and placement of twelve monuments commemorating the spirit of the pioneer woman. All twelve monuments were placed alongside the National Old Trails highway between Washington, DC, and Los Angeles, California. Originally, the ambitious plan called for more than three thousand individual mile markers approximating the route of the National Road, the Santa Fe Trail, the National Old Trail, and others. Working with the National Old Trails Road Association, which at the time was headed by Judge Harry S. Truman of Independence, Missouri, the groups finally settled on the idea of one marker to be placed in each of the twelve states through which the route passed.

The monuments were dedicated at (from east to west): Bethesda, Maryland; Beallsville, Pennsylvania; Wheeling, West Virginia; Springfield, Ohio; Richmond, Indiana; Vandalia, Illinois; Lexington, Missouri; Council Grove, Kansas; Lamar, Colorado; Albuquerque, New Mexico; Springerville, Arizona; and Upland, California.

Madonna of the Trail monument, Fourth Street, Albuquerque, New Mexico.

prehistorically. The 300-year-old San Felipe de Neri Church stands on the corner of the plaza, and nearby is the 1912 Bottger Mansion, now a bed and breakfast, which once played host to Machine Gun Kelly and his gang. Free maps are available in Old Town for self-guided walking tours. There is also a tour company offering 76-minute motor tours of the city in an open-air trolley.

If you've entered town on the pre-1937 alignment from Santa Fe, you passed one of the **Madonna of the Trail** monuments at Fourth and Marble NW.

ALBUQUERQUE ATTRACTIONS

The 66 Diner in Albuquerque doubles as headquarters for the New Mexico Route 66 Association.

Petroglyph National Monument, with thousands of ancient examples of rock art on thousands of acres, is near the western edge of town on Unser Boulevard, north of I-40. Visitors can hike several trails of varying difficulty to view the rock art, which is strung out along some 17 miles of volcanic escarpment.

The **National Museum of Nuclear Science & History**, formerly known as the National Atomic Museum, has replicas of Fat Man and Little Boy on display, as well as films and other exhibits on atomic energy in both peace and war. The museum moved to a new facility in 2009, at 601 Eubank Boulevard SE.

The **Unser Racing Museum** celebrates four generations of a family that has become a household name in auto racing. There's even a section of wall from the Indianapolis Motor Speedway on hand. 1776 Montaño NW.

Pimentel & Sons have been crafting handmade custom guitars for more than 50 years. Each is made by one craftsman, and typically includes inlay made especially for the individual customer. The Pimentels say that the New Mexico air is like a kiln, and perfectly seasons the wood in 10 to 15 years. The shop and showroom are at 3316 Lafayette Drive NE.

The **American International Rattlesnake Museum**, at 202 San Felipe NW, has a sizable collection of captive-born rattlesnakes. The museum is the largest of its kind ever developed, and its specimens include the rare albino rattlesnake. A helpful sign reminds the visitor that it is "not a petting zoo."

The **Turquoise Museum**, at 2107 Central Avenue NW, is an immersive experience. You'll enter the exhibit area through a mock mine tunnel, just as though you were prospecting for the semi-precious stone yourself. There are even daily demonstrations on preparing the stone for use in jewelry. The museum even has a huge specimen on display that looks like the profile of George Washington.

The **Albuquerque Skateboard Museum** is housed in Skate City

Near the banks of the Rio Grande, Albuquerque, New Mexico.

Supply, at 1311 Eubank NE. Lots of models are on display, including the Skee Skate of the 1950s.

The **Telephone Museum of New Mexico** has three floors of telephone history on display—photographs, literature, and physical exhibits—dating back to 1876 and covering well over a century of telephone development. See the actual switchboard that was used to warn of the attack by Pancho Villa in 1916, or place a call to the Elvis novelty phone to hear how it rings. 110 Fourth St. NW.

Exhibits at the **New Mexico Museum of Natural History and Science** include full-scale dinosaur models, an Ice Age cave, a walk-through volcano, and a saltwater aquarium. 1801 Mountain Rd. NW.

The **Institute of Meteorites**, in Northrop Hall on the University of New Mexico campus, was established more than 30 years ago as an educational resource for the state. In its permanent collection is one of the largest stone specimens on record. Also on display, on long-term loan from the Field Museum in Chicago, is a spectacular 1,600-pound iron meteorite.

Ernie Pyle, the famous World War II news correspondent, once lived in Albuquerque at 900 Girard Avenue SE. His former residence has been converted to the **Ernie Pyle Memorial Branch Library**, which houses a small museum dedicated to the Pulitzer Prize winner who was killed in action in Okinawa.

The **Anderson-Abruzzo International Balloon Museum** is a scholarly presentation of the history of ballooning, with an emphasis on notable scientific and record-setting endeavors. For example, the collection includes the gondola from the first solo trans-Atlantic balloon flight in 1984. The museum is named for Albuquerque balloonists Ben Abruzzo and Maxie Anderson, who made the first non-stop gas balloon crossing of the Atlantic in 1978. Located at 9201 Balloon Museum NE.

The **Kodak Albuquerque International Balloon Fiesta** is held the first two weekends in October, and is considered one of the world's most-photographed events. Balloon entries have mimicked boats, bottles, houses, and animals ad infinitum.

Since 1988, Albuquerque has been home to the **National Fiery Foods & Barbecue Show** every March. This show is for both the trades and the public, and participants include retailers, wholesalers, growers, and just plain aficionados. There are product and cooking demonstrations—anything goes if it's even remotely chili-related.

On the western edge of Albuquerque is the Rio Grande (Spanish for "Large River"). It was here, on the east bank of the river and on the south side of old 66, that there was a sort of neighborhood bathing pool called Tingley Beach, which originated during the New Deal era and was named for City Commissioner (later State Governor) Clyde Tingley. Nowadays, Tingley Beach is a public park featuring fishing ponds very near the **El Vado Motel**. At this writing, and following a long and contentious struggle, the city has taken possession of the El Vado in order to prevent the loss of one of the most distinctive 1930s-era motels along all of Route 66. As you cross the Rio Grande, you are finally leaving the old territory of the Republic of Texas that you entered in western Oklahoma all those miles ago.

West of Albuquerque, the highway begins its climb up out of the Rio Grande Valley and onto the Colorado Plateau. The plateau continues until about halfway across Arizona. The hill on the horizon is **Nine Mile Hill**, so named because its summit is located that many miles from the town center of Albuquerque.

It should be noted here that the early alignment of the route, which entered Albuquerque from the north via Santa Fe, continued southward out of Duke City and passed through Isleta Pueblo, Los Lunas, and Correo. The later alignment heads due west toward Rio Puerco. To drive the *older* alignment, leave Central Avenue at Fourth Street and turn left (south). Then turn right (west) onto Bridge Boulevard, cross the Rio Grande, and follow the signs for NM 314 to Los Lunas. There, turn west on NM 6, which is Los Lunas' Main Street. The two alignments will come together again near the village of Mesita.

Vintage bridge over the Rio Puerco west of Albuquerque, New Mexico.

ISLETA PUEBLO

The mission church at Isleta Pueblo is a heavily buttressed structure built about 1613, making it one of the oldest in New Mexico. It was partially destroyed during the Pueblo Rebellion, and then restored after the 1692 re-conquest. Since that time it has been in constant use. Isleta is where Thomas Edison made the very first motion picture, a short piece called *Indian Day School*, using his newly-invented kinetoscope around 1898. These days, the pueblo engages in several commercial enterprises, including a casino and golf course.

LOS LUNAS

The **Luna-Otero Mansion** is an elegant former residence on the national register which is now a restaurant

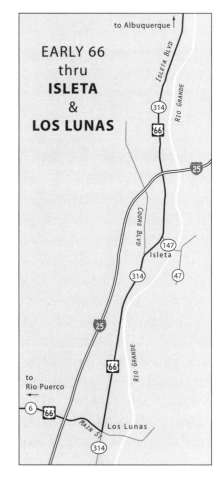

EARLY 66
thru
ISLETA
&
LOS LUNAS

to Albuquerque

ISLETA BLVD

RIO GRANDE

314

66

25

COORS BLVD

147
Isleta

314

47

25

66

RIO GRANDE

to
Rio Puerco

6   66

MAIN ST

Los Lunas

314

and bar at 110 Main Street. Blues/rock and roll musical legend **Bo Diddley** lived in Los Lunas for most of the 1970s. The **Santa Fe Railroad depot** was constructed in 1879, making it one of the very oldest in the state.

The **Los Lunas Museum of Heritage and Arts** is dedicated to local history and art, and is housed in the Agustin Archuleta house under the town's water tower. 251 Main St. SE.

West of Los Lunas via NM 6 is Mystery Mountain, at the base of which is **Mystery Rock**. The rock itself, actually a large boulder estimated at more than 80 tons in weight, is also known as Ten Commandments Rock and the Los Lunas Decalogue Stone. The rock carries an inscription, said to be a variation of the Ten Commandments, in a Paleo-Hebrew form of writing. Its origin is a matter of some dispute and contention.

FURTHER AFIELD

Just south of Los Lunas is the town of **Belen**. In Belen is a **Harvey House**, at 104 N. First, that has been turned into a museum operated by the Valencia County Historical Society (VCHS). The building is shared by the Belen Model Railroad Club, which is constructing a scale model of the historic Belen railyards. A walking/driving tour of the city, sponsored by the VCHS, includes such features as the Central Hotel, which figured prominently in the 1970 film *Bunny O'Hare*.

At 422 Dalies is a Sears Roebuck **mail-order house** built from a kit in 1909. It's still a private residence, but the owners occasionally hold open houses. The **Chavez Estate**, now a bed and breakfast at 1207 S. Main, includes a museum of Tibo Chavez memorabilia.

CORREO-MESITA

Correo is a Spanish word meaning "mail." The community was earlier known as Suwanee. At Mesita, use NM 124 to follow old Route 66. A little to the west is Owl Rock, an outcropping very close to the side of the road which has been pictured in many a postcard over the years.

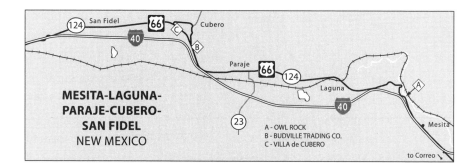

LAGUNA

Laguna is the site of a very photogenic church up on a hill—the **Saint Joseph of the Lake Mission Church**. This is where Kirk Douglas' character hurriedly picked up a priest in the movie *Ace in the Hole*, aka *The Big Carnival*.

Owl Rock, west of Mesita, New Mexico.

PARAJE

Route 66 once passed the old, long-abandoned Paraje Trading Post here. However, it has since been demolished.

FURTHER AFIELD

From here, a side trip to **Acoma Pueblo** is possible, about 13 miles or so to the south. Acoma Pueblo, or

Mission church at Laguna, New Mexico.

"Sky City," has been called the oldest continually-inhabited pueblo in America. These days, only about 50 individuals live here full time, but many more gather on traditional feast and festival days. Guided tours are available, which take visitors to the pueblo atop Enchanted Mesa (about 350 feet up). There is a mission church there, the Mission de San Esteban Rey, which is the setting for Willa Cather's book *Death Comes to the Archbishop*. The church was constructed in 1629, and all of the materials were carried to the mesa top by the builders. This includes the roof beams, which have been traced to Mount Taylor, some 30 miles distant. Until a road was built to the top of the mesa in the 1950s, the only access was by way of a steep stone staircase.

BUDVILLE

The **Budville Trading Company** still stands: a former gas station, garage, and general store, dating from about 1935. The tiny community was named for H. N. "Bud" Rice, who started a business hereabouts in 1928.

CUBERO

Cubero proper was an early victim of bypassing sometime in the 1930s. Afterward, the **Villa de Cubero** appeared—a cluster of enterprises at the new highway junction—including a

Budville, New Mexico.

Tourist court, Cubero, New Mexico.

tourist court, café, etc. The Villa de Cubero Tourist Courts found itself host to a number of notable events: the filming of *Desert Song* took place here; Lucy came and stayed here after leaving Desi; and Papa Hemingway came to stay awhile and wrote *The Old Man and the Sea* while a guest here.

SAN FIDEL-McCARTY'S

At McCarty's is a 1933 Spanish Colonial Church, built as a **half-sized replica** of the church at Acoma.

About five miles west of McCarty's is the interchange for NM 117. South of here is the eastern access to **El Malpais National Monument**. El Malpais, or "badland," is the largest contiguous lava flow in the U.S. at about 400,000 acres. Features include Sandstone Bluffs Overlook, Big Tubes, and Chain of Craters. Also here is La Ventana, one of the Southwest's largest free-standing natural arches. El Malpais can also be accessed

McCarty's, New Mexico.

via NM 53 south of Grants. The city of Grants has an El Malpais information center at 620 E. Santa Fe Avenue. Wear rugged footgear if you go, as the lava is very hard and sharp.

GRANTS

First settled in 1872, the local Native Americans refer to Grants as "Place of Friendly Smoke" as a result of a peace pact reached here between Kit Carson and Chief Manuelito. In 1887, Native Americans robbed a Santa Fe train of about $100,000 which was never recovered.

The Grants Motel and its distinctive sign have been demolished since this photograph was taken. Grants, New Mexico.

Some think it may be buried somewhere in the area. In more modern times (1950), uranium was discovered nearby at a place called Haystack Mountain.

It was outside Grants in 1958 that Liz Taylor's then-husband, Michael Todd, met his death in a plane crash.

Route 66, the main drag through Grants, is called Santa Fe Avenue, and is lined with a number of vintage motels and other structures. However, one of my personal favorites, the Grants Motel, was demolished several years ago.

GRANTS ATTRACTIONS

On Iron Street at the corner of Santa Fe Avenue is the **New Mexico Mining Museum**. Said to be "one of the few" uranium mining museums in the world, it

West Theater, Grants, New Mexico.

includes a simulated underground mine allowing visitors to explore underground tunnels and get a taste of the mining experience. The **Northwest New Mexico Visitor Center** is located in Grants just south of I-40 at Exit 85.

FURTHER AFIELD

Some 40-odd miles southwest of Grants, via NM 53, is **El Morro National Monument**. Also known as Inscription Rock, the main feature is a 200-foot sandstone cliff rising from the valley floor and bearing inscriptions

Uranium Café, Grants, New Mexico.

dating back centuries. The rock sits along an ancient east-west trail that
has been frequented by travelers since prehistory. The earliest "European" inscription belongs to Juan Oñate, the first colonial governor of New
Mexico, who made his mark in 1605. But there are petroglyphs which
are, of course, a great deal older. A half-mile trail takes the visitor on a
tour of the inscriptions, and a longer trail takes one to the top of the mesa
where there is a pueblo ruin. Interesting, isn't it, that once graffiti gets old
enough, it's considered a cultural treasure?

Also on NM 53, and on the way to El Morro, is the **Bandera Volcano and Perpetual Ice Caves**. It's said that Zuni guides brought Coronado here, and that the place has been a destination ever since. A study in
contrast, this privately-held attraction includes the 500-foot extinct volcano with hiking trail, as well as nearby caves which glisten with ice the
year 'round. Trails begin at the historic **Ice Cave Trading Post**.

MILAN-ANACONDA-BLUEWATER-PREWITT

Heading west out of Grants, you pass through country which in the time of Rittenhouse was a major carrot-producing area covering thousands of acres between here and Bluewater. Route 66 (or the modern-day NM 122) passes between the towns of Anaconda and Bluewater, which are on opposite sides of both 66 and I-40.

This well-weathered mural adorns the side of an old trading post near Prewitt, New Mexico.

Between Bluewater and Prewitt is the Route 66 Swap Meet. There is a wall covered with license plates facing the interstate. Nearby are the ruinous remains of a trading post covered in hand-painted murals.

As for Prewitt, I once saw a matchbook cover for sale on e-Bay that advertised Justin's Western Shop & Fountain "on Highway 66" in Prewitt. It looked as though it was printed in the 1940s. The telephone number, believe it or not, said "phone Prewitt No. 2."

Prewitt, New Mexico.

Near Prewitt, New Mexico.

THOREAU

Originally named Mitchell, but later re-named for the author, Henry David Thoreau, this town is home to the Zuni Mountain Kachina Company and also to the Frontier Trophy Buckle Company, manufacturer of over-sized belt buckles for rodeo champions.

FURTHER AFIELD

North of Thoreau is the town of **Crownpoint**, which is famous for its monthly Navajo rug auctions, held at the local elementary school. Crownpoint is also a potential launching pad for an excursion to **Chaco Culture National Historic Park**, although this is not the preferred approach (it is more advisable to access Chaco from the north). Chaco Canyon is one of the key sites in the Four Corners region exemplifying prehistoric culture in America. There are dozens of impressive sites here, two of the major ones being Pueblo Bonito and Chetro Ketl. The area was settled as early as the ninth century, and the culture reached its apex around around AD 1150. Archaeologists have determined that these people had established a network of roads connecting them not only with the other villages in this canyon, but with a broader community extending for many miles. The complexity of architecture, community, and social organization is astonishing. Chaco Canyon is quite isolated—plan on bringing plenty of food and drink if you go.

CONTINENTAL DIVIDE

Around five miles west of Thoreau is a small service community named after the backbone of the North American continent. There is a sign here explaining that rainwater which falls west of this dividing line flows westward to the Pacific, while that which falls to the east flows toward the Atlantic via the Gulf of Mexico. This was formerly home to Top O' the World, a dance hall, bar, tourist court, and boarding house.

The **Continental Divide National Scenic Trail** crosses Route 66 here as it wends its way along the divide from the Mexican border in the south all the way to the Canadian border north of Glacier National Park, a distance of more than 3,000 miles.

About 15 miles or so west of Continental Divide is the turnoff for **Fort Wingate** to the south (State Highway 400). Fort Wingate was established in 1862, at a site near San Rafael (south of Grants), as a base for Colonel Kit Carson's campaigns against the Navajos, when he rounded up thousands and marched them 300 miles to Fort Sumner in what has become known as the "Long Walk." The fort was moved to its present site in 1868, the same year Carson died. He is buried near Taos.

About four miles west of the Fort Wingate turnoff is the turnoff for **Kit Carson Cave**, which is a few miles north of old 66 via NM 566.

GALLUP

Old Route 66 through Gallup is unmistakable, paralleling as it does the

Gallup, New Mexico.

railroad tracks, which are only yards away.

The jewel of Gallup is the **El Rancho Hotel and Motel**. Boasting the "Charm of Yesterday and the Convenience of Tomorrow," the El Rancho is truly one-of-a-kind. The lobby décor is extraordinary, and the guest rooms are all named after Hollywood personalities who used to stay here in the glory days of filmmaking, when Gallup was a sort of Hollywood Southwest: Clark Gable, John Wayne, Claudette Colbert, and dozens of others are enshrined here. Photographs of stars line the walls. There is also a restaurant, lounge, and gift shop on premises.

Downtown Gallup invites pedestrian exploration in an area of several blocks, including old Route 66 and Coal Street (formerly part of 66), which is one block to the south. Check out the former Rex Hotel, the McKinley County Courthouse, and the El Morro Theater, which underwent extensive renovations and reopened in 2006.

GALLUP ATTRACTIONS

The **Gallup Cultural Center** is located in the restored Santa Fe railroad depot at 201 E. Highway 66. A project of the Southwest Indian Foundation, the center hosts a variety of events, and includes a gallery, cinema, museum, bookstore, gift shop, and café. The **McKinley County Courthouse** contains what is believed to be the largest WPA-sponsored mural still in existence. 201 W. Hill Ave. The Gallup Historical Society operates the **Rex Museum**, which specializes in railroad and mining history of the area, at 300 W. Highway 66.

The **Navajo Code Talkers' Room** is housed in the chamber of commerce building at 103 W. Highway 66. Here you can learn the fascinating story of how American strategists during World War II were stumped at finding a way to beat the Japanese code-breakers. Because the Navajo language is so different and complex that it cannot be learned without extensive training, and because virtually all Navajo speakers in the 1940s were living in remote areas of the American Southwest, it was determined that this might be a way to develop an unbreakable code for transferring military secrets without fear of enemy interception. When put to

Gallup, New Mexico.

CODE TALKERS

The Navajo language proved an important strategic advantage to the American forces in the Pacific during World War II. The U.S. Marine Corps employed some 400 Navajo speakers to transmit messages that would be indecipherable to the Japanese. This was mainly because the Navajo language is one of extreme complexity, has no alphabet, is unwritten, is spoken only in the American Southwest, and, at the outbreak of World War II, was understood by no more than thirty or so non-Navajos—none of them Japanese. For decades following the war, the U.S. military kept this part of history largely under wraps in case they might have a need for this capability again. Finally, in 1992 the information was made public and the hundreds of code-talkers so vital to the war effort were recognized and honored for their unique contributions. In 2002, MGM Studios released a feature film on the subject, *Windtalkers*.

El Morro Theater, downtown Gallup, New Mexico.

the test, the Navajo Code Talkers convinced the U.S. military of their effectiveness and confounded the enemy, thus helping to win the war in the Pacific.

Red Rock State Park, just east of town, is home to the Intertribal Indian Ceremonial gathering in August and the Red Rock Balloon Rally in December. More than 30 tribes from throughout North America participate in the Intertribal gathering, which has been held since 1922, and is the largest gathering of its kind, attracting some 50,000 visitors. Near the entrance to the park is **Mr. Wilson's Red Rock Trading Post**, a National Historical Landmark. The park's red cliffs have been the setting for many movie productions over the years, including *Sea of Grass*, starring Spencer Tracy and Katharine Hepburn in 1946.

FURTHER AFIELD

Gallup sits at the junction of U.S. Routes 66 and the former 666. The highway, which carried the apocalyptic designation (now known as 491), heads north out of Gallup toward the **Four Corners** region of the country. About 80 miles or so north of Gallup lies the town of Shiprock. It was named for the very distinctive remains of an extinct volcano situated a few miles

Gallup, New Mexico.

Gallup, New Mexico.

outside of town and resembling a many-masted sailing ship. From Shiprock, access to a huge wealth of ancient ruins throughout the Four Corners region is possible. These spectacular Anasazi sites include Salmon Ruins, Aztec National Monument, Chaco Canyon, Mesa Verde National Park, Hovenweep National Monument, Canyon de Chelly, and many lesser-known archaeological treasures. There is also the Four Corners Monument itself, right at the juncture of New Mexico, Arizona, Utah, and Colorado, where one can actually stand in four states at once. And straddling the Arizona-Utah border is Monument Valley, with an array of interesting geological features many of us recognize immediately from having seen John Ford Westerns.

The route (NM 118) will dead-end at Defiance. You'll need to cross to the south side of I-40 for a few miles.

DEFIANCE-MANUELITO

West of Manuelito, and just before the Arizona state line, the old highway passes the site used for the filming of *The Big Carnival* (aka *Ace in the Hole*) in 1950. The caves are in the cliffs on the north side of the highway. Many years ago, there was a sign near the border as one headed east advertising "Cliff Dwellings" one-half mile east of the state line.

ARIZONA

Quietly, New Mexico gives way to Arizona as you continue to motor west. The character of the land here is harsher than any you've seen earlier in your journey. There certainly are green

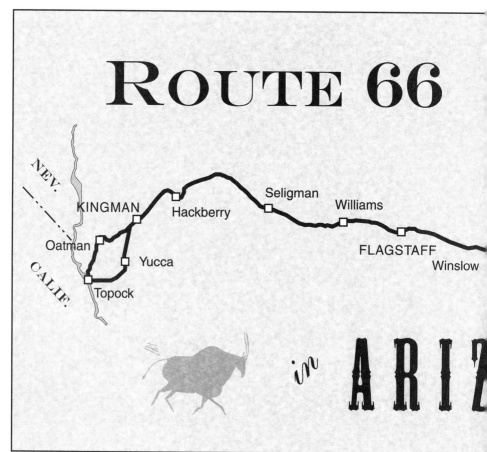

and inviting places in Arizona, but at this moment you could be forgiven for not believing it.

And yet, there are many who are profoundly drawn to this place. I first glimpsed it myself many years ago in what is called the Arizona Strip, that northwestern portion of the state which is cut off from the rest by the Grand Canyon. There, far from the bright lights of any metropolis, I lay on the ground one evening and saw more stars in the sky than I had ever thought possible—I could swear they overlapped.

Water, that most precious of commodities, is in short supply. You could say that water in this area is an acute condition, rather than a chronic one—you will see a great many dry stream beds which gush to life on only a few occasions during the year. The lack of a reliable supply of water through much of this territory has shaped Arizona's history and destiny. Early inhabitants, such as the Anasazi, were likely forced to move elsewhere when weather patterns made their already-marginal existence untenable; far more recently, the path of the railroads was dictated in part by the same limitations.

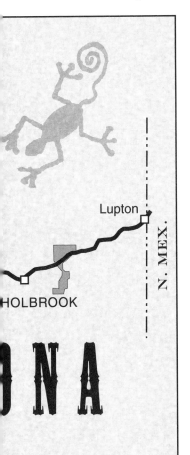

In this minimalist landscape, the austere is beautiful, and the beautiful sublime. This land is a canvas bearing the strokes of Mother Nature the artist, for whom a millennium is no more than a moment. Red rock country, a painted desert, and the scar from a meteoric collision all await you in a place where trees turn to stone and volcanic eruptions shape the countryside.

Just across the New Mexico-Arizona border you'll encounter the community of:

Lupton, Arizona.

LUPTON

From Route 66, Lupton looks to be mostly a sort of "strip" comprised of trading posts offering tourist-oriented souvenirs. The most notable thing about them is their garish appearance, including bright primary colors and replicas of teepees. At least one of them features a wooden Native American chief standing outside. The Yellowhorse Trading Post even has animal figures arrayed on the cliffs above. This area is an excellent place to pick up that bullwhip or rubber tomahawk you've been wanting.

About 25 miles or so to the north of here via Highway 12 is **Window Rock**, a natural feature consisting of an aperture carved in a large sandstone formation by the forces of wind, dust, and water. There is a viewing area at the Window Rock Tribal Park on Highway 12. The nearby community of Window Rock has been the official capital of the Navajo nation since 1938. There is a museum nearby on Highway 264.

Traveling Route 66 in Lupton, you quickly cross to the south side of I-40 for the run toward Sanders. Here you'll see **Ortega's Indian**

Galeria, which is housed in a geodesic-domed building. There's a similar structure, also a trading post, which you'll see later at Meteor City.

HOUCK-SANDERS

At Houck is something called Fort Courage, built as a replica of the fort used in the 1960s television series *F Troop*. Nearby is an old coffee house in a sort of Googie-wannabe style. If you're still driving on I-40 when you reach Exit 346, leave the interstate here and follow the north frontage road, assuming it's dry. You'll run out of pavement, but not to worry. This old 66 alignment takes you past the Querino Trading Post, as well as the ruins of the **Old Querino Trading Post**. These ruins have been rapidly deteriorating, so by the time you read this there may be very little left, but this slow-moving branch road is good for the soul anyway.

At mile marker 339 is the village of Sanders. Look for the **66 Diner**, which is housed in a building manufactured by the renowned Valentine.

CHAMBERS-NAVAJO

Rejoin the interstate at the I-40/U.S. 191 junction, and continue west.

The former Painted Desert Trading Post, east of Holbrook, Arizona.

FURTHER AFIELD

About 37 miles north of Chambers via U.S. 191 is the village of Ganado and the **Hubbell Trading Post National Historic Site**. Established in the 1870s, this is the oldest continuously-operating Navajo trading post, now run by the National Park Service. John Hubbell's grave overlooks the site from nearby Hubbell Hill.

Thirty-six miles further north from Hubbell's Trading Post is **Canyon de Chelly National Monument**, which contains probably the most-photographed ruin in the United States: the White House ruin. The ruin is reached by an arduous trail, about 2½ miles round trip, which may leave you breathless on the ascent, but is well worth the effort. The trail goes past an active farmstead and across a small stream before reaching the bottom of the canyon, where the ruin is built into the canyon wall. This is the only ruin in the park which is accessible without a guide.

Back on Route 66, you'll want to make a point of leaving the superslab at Exit 320 for a trip into the past. There is a much older alignment of 66 that will take you to the ruins of the old **Painted Desert Trading Post**. After exiting the interstate, go north a short distance to a crossroads. Turn left, and you are on an early stretch of the route. Go slowly, as the road is rough. Your patience will be rewarded as you approach the white walls of the old trading post on a graceful curve in the road. Just beyond the ruin is a mostly-dry river bed (the Dead Wash) which contains the wrecks of several old cars pressed

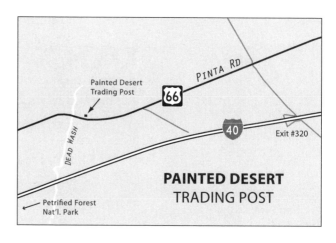

PAINTED DESERT
TRADING POST

up against the sandy bank in an elbow in the river. You'll need to turn around and return to the main road the same way you came in, and continue on I-40 westbound.

No longer accessible from what remains of old 66, the **Painted Desert** and the **Petrified Forest**, a pair of natural attractions straddling the highway, must be reached from I-40. However, in this vicinity you can use the I-40 overpasses to look at the adjoining terrain and pick out where the Highway 66 pavement used to run. The paving was pretty thoroughly removed in this area, but out here scars are slow to heal, and you can often spot differences in the color and character of the soil and vegetation signaling where the old roadbed was. Keep alert and you'll see what I mean.

The **Petrified Forest National Park** is about 26 miles east of Holbrook. It was established in 1906 during the Theodore Roosevelt administration, and designated a national park in 1962. This area was once a dense and humid forest eons ago, and conditions were such that fallen trees became transformed into mineralized versions of themselves. The agate and quartz which comprise these fossils still exhibit the visible characteristics of wood, such as grain and growth rings. The park includes natural formations, such as undisturbed fallen trees, as well as some man-made structures, such as Agate House, a pueblo which was fashioned from the rare material. Other features include the Puerco Indian Ruin, a 100-room pueblo dating from about A.D. 1300, and Newspaper Rock, which is covered in petroglyphs.

The **Painted Desert** is just north of the highway and connects with the Petrified Forest to the south. Plenty of photo opportunities are provided by the colorful mineral deposits, which give the area its name. These are particularly impressive with early-morning or pre-dusk light. The **Painted Desert Inn**, at Kachina Point, was built in the 1920s and then restored in the '30s by the Civilian Conservation Corps. Later, it became a part of the Harvey House chain.

Both the Petrified Forest and the Painted Desert are bona fide Route 66-era attractions, so be sure to take advantage of the opportunity to experience them.

HOLBROOK

Take the I-40 Business Loop exit into Holbrook (Navajo Boulevard), which follows the course of old 66, including a turn to the west on Hopi Drive.

Holbrook is well known to 66 travelers as the home of the **Wigwam Village Motel**. There were at one time seven such villages, all built between 1933 and 1950, with the original one in Horse Cave, Kentucky. The sister set of units near San Bernardino was the last to be built. Each village consists of several individual room units designed to resemble Native American teepees. Furthermore, all units of each village originally had pay-per-listen radios, the receipts of which were forwarded to the originator of the concept, Frank Bedford,

as a sort of royalty fee. The Wigwam Village is at 811 W. Hopi Drive.

HOLBROOK ATTRACTIONS

The old **Navajo County Courthouse**, built in 1898, now houses a museum and visitor center, and includes an original Old West jail. The jail has preserved some old inmate artwork on the walls. You can also pick up a copy of Holbrook's self-guided walking tour of various points of interest at the museum. Included is the **Blevins House**, where an Old West shootout occurred in 1887. The courthouse stands at the corner of Navajo Boulevard and E. Arizona Street.

The **Rainbow Rock Shop** has a collection of dinosaur sculptures outside to catch your attention; however, be advised that signs are posted insisting that you pay the owners a fee for any photographs you take of their enterprise.

Geronimo's, west of Holbrook, Arizona.

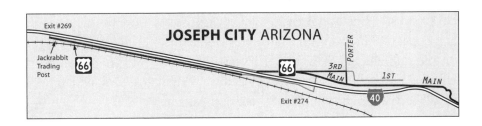

If you haven't had your fill of petrified wood yet—or if you skipped the Petrified Forest completely—you might want to exit at Geronimo (Exit 280), where the trading post has what they boast is the **World's Largest Petrified Log** on display.

JOSEPH CITY

This community was originally established by Mormons circa 1876—America's centennial year, and exactly 50 years before the establishment of U.S. 66 and the rest of the federal highway system.

West of the town proper is the famous **Jackrabbit Trading Post**. The billboard proclaiming, "*HERE IT IS*" has to be one of the best-known sights along the route. I for one find myself transported backward in time whenever I see it. Aside from the billboard, the Jackrabbit is also famous for its slogan: "If you haven't been to the Jackrabbit, you haven't been in the Southwest." Lots of travelers over the years have had their photographs taken sitting astride the giant jackrabbit figure on the premises. To get to the Jackrabbit, you can either cross to the south side of I-40 at Exit 274 and then turn west, or you can take the interstate west to Exit 269 and then double back on the south frontage road.

Exit #269

JOSEPH CITY ARIZONA

PORTER

Jackrabbit Trading Post

66

66

3RD

MAIN

1ST

MAIN

Exit #274

40

ROADSIDE MARKETING AT THE JACKRABBIT

A nticipation. That's something that comes to mind when I think of the Jackrabbit Trading Post. Sure, the big billboard exclaiming, "Here It Is!" is unique and impressive and known the world over. But the marketing strategy for the Jackrabbit was all about anticipation. And when it's done right, anticipation is one of the hardest things to resist.

In addition to the renowned billboard pictured, the Jackrabbit posted smaller signs up and down the highway, giving progress reports from both directions. When you were 87 miles away, you'd see a simple sign with a jackrabbit silhouette stating: "87 miles."

Several miles later, there'd be exactly the same graphic, but with the enticing figure: "69 miles."

As you, the Route 66 motorist, approached ever closer, the signs would appear more and more frequently: 26 miles...18...14...11....

No wonder, then, that by the time the family had arrived, everyone in the car—including dear old dad—was *desperate* to pull over and find out for themselves just what all the fuss was about. And we still do pull over, even today.

MANILA-HIBBARD-HOBSON

Manila shows up plainly as a town directly on Route 66 in my 1957 road atlas, as does Hibbard. Hobson by that time had already been bypassed, and appeared just south of the route. Hobson is still down there, right on the railroad tracks, as befits a very old alignment. The memory of Hibbard persists thanks to the I-40 exit sign—Exit 264 is called Hibbard Road. Today, the community at this exit is called Havre.

Here It Is: the most famous billboard on all of Route 66, Joseph City, Arizona.

If you have a rugged vehicle and are feeling adventurous, take the Hibbard Road exit, go to the north side of the interstate, and follow the road west. You will lose the pavement for most of the way, but you will be passing through what was once a well-traveled piece of backcountry. At the Highway 87 junction, cross to the south side of I-40 for the run into Winslow.

WINSLOW

As you enter Winslow, the highway splits into eastbound and westbound portions at a rest stop/picnic area. As always, when the highway splits like this through any town, I recommend that you double back after you've passed through town in order to see what's on the other side.

Winslow received mention in the Eagles' song "Take It Easy" many years ago, and the town has latched onto this bit of trivia for all it's worth. Go check out the "corner in Winslow, Arizona" yourself (Kinsley and Second Streets), where you'll see a sign quoting the famous line, a bronze statue, and a mural that includes a "girl in a flatbed Ford."

WINSLOW ATTRACTIONS

The **Old Trails Museum**, at 212 Kinsley, houses a collection of Winslow historical artifacts and Route 66 memorabilia in a former bank building that includes many of its original features.

Winslow's **First Street Pathway** runs a half-dozen blocks or so,

and links two of the town's most historic landmarks: La Posada Hotel and the Hubbell Trading Post. **La Posada**, a former Harvey House property, is at 303 E. Second Street. This masterpiece was created in 1928 by top-tier architect Mary Colter, today widely

Abandoned drive-in theater, Winslow, Arizona.

regarded as having been far ahead of her time. Offering a modest number of guest rooms in a space larger than Hearst Castle, this Spanish hacienda-style jewel was restored in the late 1990s, and features a museum, gardens, and meeting spaces.

The pathway above was only the first phase in a multi-phased project to revitalize the downtown area, collectively referred to as **Renaissance on 66**. In phase two, five blocks of Second and Third Streets have had new streetlamps installed, Route 66 banners hung, and brick inlays added to the crosswalks and intersections.

The **Hubbell Trading Post** is part of an extensive network of stores once operated by the Hubbell family in the Southwest. This one was established in 1924, before Route 66 became a reality. The building has recently been renovated in order to house historical exhibits, as well as a new visitor center and offices for the local chamber of commerce (523 W. Second). Ask here about the status of the Brigham City project (below).

North of town is an ongoing project to restore **Brigham City**, where a Mormon colony settled in 1876. They dispersed some years later, due in part to the inconsistency of the water supply. Now, ruined walls and foundations are being rebuilt so that the early history of the area can be appreciated by future generations.

Winslow's **Remembrance Garden** is a memorial to the lives lost in the September 11th terrorist attacks. On display are some beams from the World Trade Center wreckage. At the corner of E. Third and Transcon.

FURTHER AFIELD

Just outside Winslow on AZ 87 is **Homolovi Ruins State Park**. This is a 4,000-acre preserve with more than 300 archaeological sites and numerous petroglyphs. Homolovi is a Hopi word meaning "place of the little hills." The four major pueblo sites here are thought to have been occupied from A.D. 1200 to 1425. The park is an active archaeological site, with archaeologists working here Monday through Friday in June and July, revealing agricultural features and pit houses.

As you leave Winslow heading west, keep an eye out for the ruins of the **Tonto Drive-In** movie theater. The screen, projection booth, ticket booth, and marquee sign were all still standing the first time I passed through.

LEUPP CORNERS-DENNISON

According to my trusty 1957 atlas, Leupp Corners was a small community at the Route 66 junction with a gravel road going north to the town of Leupp. That road (or the closest thing to it) is marked today as State Highway 99.

Faded billboard for the Meteor City Trading Post.

METEOR CITY

At Exit 239 is Meteor City, a geodesic-dome-style trading post by the side of the highway. There is actually a partially paved road which heads south and eventually wanders over toward the crater to the southwest, but this is not the official approach and is not recommended.

RIMMY JIMS

Rimmy Jim was the moniker of the man who originally ran the **Meteor Crater** concession. The crater itself is about six miles south of I-44, at Exit 233. Upon impact, the meteorite was traveling at 45,000 mph, creating a crater 570 feet deep, one mile across, and three miles in circumference. You'll find here a gift shop, snack bar, interpretive exhibits, and observation platforms. You can hike around the crater via guided tour, but you

Meteor City, Arizona.

cannot enter it. Since the object causing the crater originated in outer space, there is also a sort of Astronaut Hall of Fame on the premises. A segment of 1984's *Starman* was filmed at the crater.

Nearby, on a disused stretch of old 66, is the **Meteor Crater Observatory**, the stone ruin of a primitive observation tower used in the old days.

The former observation tower near Meteor Crater, Arizona.

TWO GUNS

You may or may not be able to gain access to Two Guns (Exit 230), due to the fact that it rests on private property. It has gone through cycles where it has been posted against trespassing, and periods where visitors have been at least permitted, if not encouraged. Two Guns was a town only in the loosest sense; it was actually a made-

Two Guns, Arizona.

to-order tourist trap, with several cages of captive animals, such as coyotes and mountain lions, to lure the motorist off the highway. This is the stuff of which lasting memories are made for young boys traveling with mom and dad.

FURTHER AFIELD

If you go south from Exit 225, between Two Guns and Twin Arrows, you can find the **Raymond Wildlife Area**, which supports a herd of bison maintained by the Arizona Game and Fish Department.

TWIN ARROWS

Twin Arrows is an abandoned tourist complex featuring a café, trading post, and fuel station, and distinguished by a pair of enormous arrows sticking out

Twin Arrows, Arizona.

of the ground. I've been hoping for years that someone will make a go of it here, but so far those hopes have not been answered. I just love those larger-than-life arrows embedded in the earth. This is the type of feature which so distinguishes the old highway's attractions from today's cookie-cutter copies. Exit 219, south side of the interstate.

WINONA

This is the place made somewhat famous for its reference in Bobby Troup's classic song, wherein he exhorts: "Don't forget Winona."

> From Winona, you have a choice to make regarding your approach to Flagstaff. See the accompanying reference map.

There's not a great deal to see in Winona, other than the big, gleaming, vintage trestle bridge that used to carry the highway. From Winona, you can take an early alignment to Flagstaff by using Townsend-Winona Road, then turning south at Highway 89. To use the later alignment, return to the interstate and exit at Walnut Canyon Road/Historic 66 (Exit 204).

COSNINO

Once the Townsend-Winona Road loop mentioned above was bypassed, Route 66 took a slightly more direct path toward Flagstaff, which passed through the village of Cosnino, near today's Exit 207.

FLAGSTAFF

Nestled at the feet of the San Francisco Peaks, Flagstaff enjoys nearly the same elevation as Denver, and so has a considerable skiing season in the winter months. The same slopes in summer make for excellent hiking, affording views which sometimes extend into neighboring Utah to the north. There is a Flagstaff anecdote which says that Cecil B. DeMille almost made Flagstaff the center of filmdom instead of Hollywood. However, the day he arrived from the east there was snow falling, and so he decided to stay on the train and continue to California and sunnier climes. The rest, as they say, is history.

Entering Flagstaff from the east, prior to arriving downtown, you'll see a vintage roadhouse known as the **Museum Club**. Built in 1931 to house a taxidermy collection and other artifacts, it was originally called the Dean Eldridge Museum. Later it evolved into a honky-tonk nicknamed the Zoo because of all the animal trophies on display. Over the years, it has seen the likes of some top-tier performers. There are a few stories of ghost hauntings here, with one of the former owners having committed suicide in front of the fireplace. Look for the guitar-shaped

Venerable neon in Flagstaff, Arizona.

neon sign out front. 3404 E. Route 66.

In downtown Flagstaff you'll find a lot of vibrancy, mixed together with a lot of vintage architecture and still-working neon. The **Hotel Monte Vista** first opened its doors on January 1, 1927, and has played host to the likes of Jane Russell, Spencer Tracy, Humphrey Bogart, Theodore Roosevelt, and many, many others of similar celebrity. It's said that Zane Grey did some of his writing here at the hotel. The adjoining bar has a terrific neon marquee that says simply: "*COCKTAILS.*"

Route 66 runs right alongside the railroad tracks through Flagstaff, and so you'll see the old Santa Fe depot as well, which has recently been turned into a visitor center with gift shop. There is a colorful commercial strip along here which includes the Grand Canyon Café, Joe's, and Wigwam Curios (now closed).

FLAGSTAFF ATTRACTIONS

Walnut Canyon National Monument, established in 1915, is home to the ruins of a small Sinagua community. The thirteenth-century community is comprised of some 300 rooms. There is a steep, self-guided walking trail which meanders through the canyon past numerous cliff dwellings. I-40 Exit 204, east side of town.

The world-famous **Lowell Observatory**, established in 1894, is at 1400 W. Mars Hill Road. It was here that astronomers in 1930 discovered Pluto, and the telescope used at that time is still on display. Also here is the original 24-inch refractor used in the 1890s. Guided tours and lectures are available.

Riordan Mansion State Historic Park features the 40-room Riordan Mansion, built in 1904 in the Arts-and-Crafts style. The architect, Charles Whittlesey, also designed the Grand Canyon's El Tovar Lodge. This house was built for two close-knit families—the Riordan brothers married two sisters from another prominent family and both couples lived and raised their own families here. The house features log-slab siding, volcanic stone archways, and hand-split wood shingles. Interior appointments include handmade furniture and stained-glass windows. A truly unique feature of the house is the set of photographic windows in the Rendezvous Room. A prominent photographer, John K. Hillers, was commis-

sioned by the owners, and his photographic transparencies were fused to panes of translucent glass, so that the photos are illuminated by the incoming sunlight. These windows were painstakingly restored in the 1990s using Hillers' original glass negatives found

at the Smithsonian Institution. 409 W. Riordan Rd.

The Arizona Historical Society's **Pioneer Museum** is located north of town at 2340 N. Fort Valley Road in what used to serve as a hospital for the indigent from 1908 until 1938. Also on the grounds are a barn and root cellar that were utilized by the hospital, and a cabin which was moved to the site in 1967 from elsewhere in Flagstaff. From November to February each year, the museum presents **Playthings of the Past**, an exhibit of toys from the 1880s through the 1960s. Each June, there is a **Wool Festival** featuring sheep, goat, and llama shearings, as well as wool spinning, dyeing, and weaving demonstrations.

Here at Flagstaff, Route 66 crosses paths with the **Arizona Trail**, a hiking path spanning the state from the Utah state line in the north all the way to the Mexican border in the south. Conceived by a Flagstaff schoolteacher, the 820-mile trail earned designation in 2009 as a National Scenic Trail after decades of effort. You can get information about the trail at city hall, 211 W. Aspen Avenue.

FURTHER AFIELD

About 15 miles north of Flagstaff (take U.S. 89) is **Sunset Crater Volcano National Monument**. This cinder cone was formed around A.D. 1064, and was active intermittently for the next 200 years or so. The Lava Flow Nature Trail begins at the visitor center and offers a 45-minute walk, which traverses some of the lava flows and affords some nice views. For the stout of heart, the Lenox Crater Cinder Cone Trail is steep and strenuous.

From Sunset Crater, a paved road crosses the lava flow and connects with **Wupatki National Monument**. Established in 1924 by Calvin Coolidge, a president known for working four hours per day at most, Wupatki is composed of several ruins on 35,000 acres thought to have been inhabited by ancestors of the Hopi. Most impressive is the Tall House, a 100-room complex with nearby amphitheater and ball court. Self-guided walking trails take the visitor through each of the ruins.

To the south of Flagstaff (30 miles) is **Sedona**. A sort of New Age sanctuary, Sedona is famous for its red rock scenery, which changes in appearance throughout the course of each day. The nearby **Red Rock-Secret Mountain Wilderness** is a red-hued, canyon- and pinnacle-filled landscape with cliffs, ruins, and rock art. Sedona also hosts an **International Film Festival** every March.

Beyond Sedona, but still on ALT 89, is the old mining community of **Jerome**. This mining town, perched on the side of Cleopatra Hill, was just about gone until it was resurrected as a sort of art colony. Today, the town bustles with guests browsing the assortment of galleries, shops, and historic buildings. While in Jerome, check out the old **Douglas Mansion** at Jerome State Historic Park. The museum traces the history of Jerome, and the Douglas family in particular, through photos, minerals, and artifacts. Just walking the streets of Jerome is an enjoyable experience.

Very close to Jerome is **Tuzigoot National Monument**. Here you can tour a pueblo once inhabited by the Sinagua people, which rests on the summit of a ridge some 120 feet above the surrounding valley.

Southeast of Jerome and Sedona near I-17 are **Montezuma Castle National Monument** and **Montezuma Well**. Named by early explorers who assumed it was Aztecan in origin, the castle structure is about 90 percent intact, and is at the end of a paved trail, which makes for an easy stroll. The well is about 11 miles away, and consists of a spring at the bottom of a canyon-like depression. The sides of the canyon are filled with small pueblo ruins.

Farther south on ALT 89 from Jerome is the city of **Prescott** (pronounced "press kit"). Prescott is worthy as a destination in itself. There is a beautiful historic downtown district ideal for walking around. Prescott has more Victorian-era buildings than any other community in Arizona. The **Sharlot Hall Museum** alone has 12 buildings on three acres evoking the flavor of territorial Arizona. Included are the old Territorial Governor's Mansion, Fort Misery Cabin, and the Bashford House, considered a premier example of Western high Victorian style. 415 W. Gurley. Prescott also is home to the country's oldest rodeo, which has been held consistently since 1888. And, if you appreciate Western art, don't miss the **Phippen Museum,** named for the founder of the Cowboy Artists of America.

Back on Route 66, heading west out of Flagstaff, the road will eventually force you back onto the interstate. Leave the interstate again at Exit 185.

BELLEMONT

The name Bellemont means, literally, "pretty mountain." Here at Exit 185 are some fragments of old 66 occurring on both sides of today's I-40, both paved and unpaved, and in both directions from the exit. I recommend you explore the area, and make good use of the tips you learned in the "How to Find Route 66" chapter in the front portion of this book.

PARKS

This tiny town at Exit 178 (formerly called Maine) was severely damaged by the construction of the interstate. It includes the **Parks in the Pines General Store**, established in 1921, years before the highway was designated Route 66.

From Parks, I recommend you stay away from I-40 for a while by taking Parks Road/Old 66 westward. It becomes Wagon Wheel Road, and will lead you to **Deer Farm** near the I-40 Interchange 171. Deer Farm is a petting zoo that includes several varieties of deer, plus some more recent acquisitions.

Jump back onto I-40 near the Deer Farm for the run into Williams. Then use Exit 165, which will take you into town along Grand Canyon Avenue (old 66).

OLD 66 WEST OF **PARKS** ARIZONA

WILLIAMS

Williams was the last town to be bypassed by the construction of the interstate in 1984. It therefore had the last active stretch of Route 66 and the last stoplight on I-40.

Highway 66 through Williams is divided into east- and westbound portions, so don't forget to turn around when you reach the end of town so you can drive it in the other direction.

The town is named for Bill Williams, a prominent fur trapper, and widely held to be the first white man in the area. There is a mountain south of town also bearing his name, as well as the Bill Williams Trail, also to the south of town.

Williams has a very nice stretch of vintage 66 running through town, lined with small motels and other tourist-related businesses. Williams, though small, was very well-developed for the motoring public, due in large part to its proximity to the Grand Canyon. Williams is the traditional jumping-off point for **Grand Canyon National Park**, which lies about 60 miles or so to the north. You should explore the town extensively.

WILLIAMS ATTRACTIONS

The renovated **Frey Marcos Hotel** was formerly a Harvey House and acts as both museum and depot for the **Grand Canyon Railway**, per-

haps the most tradition-rich way of going to the canyon. The railway was established in 1901, and from then until 1927, more than half of all canyon visitors came by train. Today, you can get a taste of the old west by taking the train from Williams. The Grand Canyon Depot,

There's plenty of Mother Road spirit in Williams, Arizona.

Vintage neon in Williams, Arizona.

at the end of the run at the canyon's south rim, is one of only three remaining log-constructed depots in the U.S., and is on the National Register. It was built in 1909 of rustic logs in order to complement the adjoining ponderosa pine forest. At the Grand Canyon, facilities are plentiful, including a laundromat, post office, general store, and bank. The 1905 **El Tovar Hotel** is nearby. Activities include hiking, camping, mule rides to the bottom of the canyon, helicopter tours, and white-water rafting.

Notable businesses in Williams include the **Turquoise Teepee** and **Rod's Steak House**, a fixture on the route since 1945. The **City of Willams and Forest Service Visitor Center** has brochures to guide you on a historic walking tour of the city. 200 W. Railroad Ave.

If you like unusual accommodations, be sure to check into the **Canyon Motel & RV Park** east of town. Besides the standard motel rooms and campsites, you can choose from a small collection of cabooses and other railcars. 1900 E. Rodeo Road, near I-40 Exit 165.

Williams, Arizona.

Williams, Arizona.

At the west end of town, you'll need to rejoin I-40 at Interchange 161. Between here and Ash Fork there are some Mother Road fragments back in the woods, suitable for hiking or mountain biking. They get a pretty thorough treatment in Jerry McClanahan's *EZ66 Guide*. For this narrative, we're going to stay with I-40 until Exit 146 (Ash Fork).

ASH FORK

This is the self-proclaimed Flagstone Capital of the World. As we've seen in a number of other towns, Route 66 splits itself into eastbound and westbound portions, separated by a city block. Make sure to turn around and check out the eastbound portion before you move on. You'll need to enter I-40 at the west edge of town, but not for long—see below.

Important: Be sure to exit at Crookton Road (Exit 139), between Ash Fork and Seligman. This is the way to go in order to cruise the longest unbroken section of old 66 remaining—Seligman to Topock.

From now on, and all the way to the California border, you will remain on old Route 66 and not have to use any interstate highway at all. Yay! See the accompanying reference map to help you see what we're doing. This stretch was so completely bypassed by I-40 that it is today as unspoiled as any section of the road anywhere, all the way to the Colorado River.

SELIGMAN

Seligman is home to the Delga-dillo brothers, Angel and Juan. Angel used to run the barber shop in Seligman, and Juan (now deceased) operated the **Snow Cap Drive-In**. Juan's son

As you know, earlier alignments of Route 66 tended to cling close to the railroad tracks in town. So don't fail to explore Railroad Avenue, which is a block or so away from the official I-40 Business Loop (Chino Street). Both streets are genuine Route 66.

now continues the tradition at the drive-in. Open or closed, be sure to get out of your car and do some exploring on the grounds of the Snow Cap. It is chock-full of interesting artifacts, humorous signs, and other surprising touches. A little ways past the Snow Cap is Angel's **Route 66 Gift Shop and Visitor Center** where, if you're lucky, Angel can share a few stories and you can stock up on Mother Road merchandise. The Copper

Snow Cap Drive-In, Seligman, Arizona.

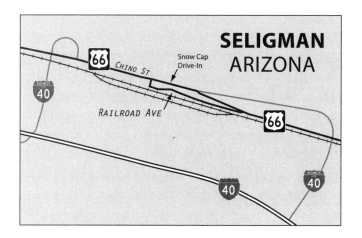

Seligman,
Arizona.

Cart is also a great vintage restaurant, and has a big one-of-a-kind sign out front.

Long-vacated motel, Seligman, Arizona.

One block north of Route 66 is the **Cottage Hotel**, a current restoration project of the Seligman Historical Society. Their goal is to have it converted into a full-time museum and visitor center by 2012 (Arizona's—and the hotel's—centennial year).

AUDLEY-PICA-YAMPAI

This is a series of small communities strung out along Route 66 when the predecessor to the alignment you are now driving was still current. They are all just to the south and west of the modern-day road.

GRAND CANYON CAVERNS

Here's a good old-fashioned roadside attraction. Called Coconino Caverns on some old maps—and later, Dinosaur Caverns—**the Grand Canyon Caverns** themselves are accessed by an elevator which takes you 21 stories underground. Aside from the normal cave formations, attractions below include a mummified bobcat. Outside, you'll see dinosaur replicas lining the walkway to the front door. This complex has everything: motel rooms, a restaurant, gift shop, and even an airstrip. The newest attraction, completed in 2010, is a motel suite down in the cavern itself, more than 200 feet below the surface of the ground.

 As you approach Peach Springs from the east, keep your eye

The sight of this dinosaur outside the entrance to the Grand Canyon Caverns has caused motorists to make unscheduled stops for many a year.

out on the north horizon. There is a point at which you can see all the way to the south rim of the Grand Canyon, which makes its closest approach to the highway along here.

It is possible to take Highway 18 from this vicinity (just east of Peach Springs) to a relatively untrammeled part of the Grand Canyon called **Hualapai Hilltop**. From there, there is a rather demanding trail that you can take down into the canyon to the remote village of Supai.

PEACH SPRINGS

The Hualapai tribal headquarters are located here in Peach Springs. On the west side of town is Indian Rte. 1, which goes north to Grand Canyon West Airport and the **Grand Canyon Skywalk**. The road is only partly paved. If you want to take in the Skywalk, it's best to make inquiries at the Havasupai Lodge in town to determine your best option.

Primitive Route 66 positioning system, Truxton, Arizona.

TRUXTON

The **Frontier Motel and Restaurant** still operates here. Out front is a pair of street signs. One says Will Rogers Highway; the other says Historic Route 66. Also be on the lookout for a wrecked car west of town serving as a milepost marker for various Route 66 destinations.

CROZIER

Although the town of Crozier appears plainly on the path of Highway 66 in my 1957 atlas, Rittenhouse already reports it as "bypassed" in 1946. It's near here that you'll run across **Keepers of the Wild**, a non-profit sanctuary for rescued exotic animals.

VALENTINE

A scene from the movie *Easy Rider* was filmed here, on the south side of

Valentine, Arizona.

the highway, just west of the Indian Agency. Peter Fonda fixes a flat in the background, while a cowboy shoes a horse in the foreground to demonstrate that some things don't really change.

HACKBERRY

General Store, Hackberry, Arizona.

The **Hackberry General Store** is a must-stop. The current operators are attempting to return the place to something close to its original state. For years, this location was Bob Waldmire's International Bioregional Old Route 66 Visitor Center. Spend some time walking around here, since there's plenty to see.

LOGASVILLE

According to local residents, back in the 1950s there once was a town called Logasville, located in what is now the eastern part of Kingman. It is said to have occupied the wedge-shaped area between Bank Street and Route 66, just north of present-day I-40. This community does not appear on my 1957 atlas, however, and it was at some point annexed by the city of Kingman.

KINGMAN

This settlement was named for Lewis Kingman, a civil engineer with the Santa Fe Railroad, in 1880. Today, there's no mistaking Kingman thanks to the huge beige-colored tower that's been painted with these words: "Welcome to Kingman, the Heart of Historic Route 66."

Kingman is the hometown of well-known character actor Andy Devine, who grew up at the Beale Hotel, which his parents used to run. Each September the city holds Andy Devine Days in his honor. Clark Gable and Carole Lombard got married at the local Methodist Church here in Kingman, and then raced down Route 66 to honeymoon in nearby Oatman. In the downtown area, one block from the route, there is a nice neon sign at the Kingman Club.

Follow Andy Devine Avenue all the way through town—not I-40 Business Loop, which veers away onto Beale Street near the beginning of the downtown area. There's a small park near the western edge of town that includes a retired steam locomotive from the Santa Fe line. It's there that you'll need to bear left in order to take the old Route 66 alignment into the hills toward Oatman.

KINGMAN ATTRACTIONS

The **Powerhouse Visitors' Center** houses a Route 66 museum, including a theater showing short films and an extensive gift shop. You can also pick up a walking tour map to historic sites in the city. 120 W. Andy Devine, across from Locomotive Park.

The **Bonelli House** is a two-story mansion built in 1915, on the site of an earlier dwelling that had burned down. Therefore, this structure was built of locally-quarried tufa stone, a material valued for its fire resistance and its insulating, cool-in-the-summer characteristics (430 E. Spring St.). The home is maintained by the **Mohave Museum of History and Arts**, located at 400 W. Beale, which also includes items relating to favorite son Andy Devine.

The **Kingman Army Air Field Museum** is at 4540 Flightline Drive, adjacent to the modern-day airport. The base in Kingman was one of a handful of sites assigned to dispose of thousands of warplanes at the close of World War II.

The Quality Inn here in Kingman (over at the interstate) has a couple of its rooms named in honor of George Maharis and Martin Milner, stars of the early 1960s television series entitled *Route 66*. There is even a memorabilia display in the lobby area. Although very little of the television series was actually filmed on Highway 66, it is in retrospect a very interesting series, with early guest appearances by such later notables as Alan Alda, Robert Duvall, Joey Heatherton, and Burt Reynolds.

Powerhouse Museum, Kingman, Arizona.

FURTHER AFIELD

South of Kingman is **Hualapai Mountain Park**. Established in the 1930s, the park has several cabins constructed by the Civilian Conservation Corps. The scenery is beautiful, and there are several trails for hiking, as well as a campground.

North of Kingman is the near-ghost town of **Chloride**, Arizona, founded in 1862. To reach Chloride, take U.S. 93 North. A sign will direct you to turn right on a county road to the small, now-quiet town of Chloride.

Also north of Kingman via U.S. 93 are **Lake Mead**, the **Boulder Dam**, and **Las Vegas**. Opinions on Las Vegas, Nevada, are generally of two kinds: love it or hate it. I count myself among the few who don't feel strongly one way or the other. I don't care for the casino scene, but what I do like about Las Vegas is its location. My wife and I have used it as a convenient launching pad for a number of other destinations. Easy day trips out of Las Vegas include Death Valley, Lake Mead/Boulder Dam, Zion National Park, the ghost town of Rhyolite, and—of course—Route 66.

The other redeeming feature to Route 66 fans, at least as I see it,

ROUTE 66 TV SERIES

In the fall of 1960, the CBS television network launched a weekly series called *Route 66*. On the show, two young men (portrayed by Martin Milner and George Maharis) traveled around the country in a Corvette and became involved in the lives of the people they met in each episode.

Although only a small number of the hundred-plus episodes were actually filmed on Route 66, the series is notable for a number of reasons. The early 1960s were a transitional period in America, and the series took on themes that were unconventional—even daring—for the time. The two protagonists came into contact with a runaway heiress, a dying blues singer, and a heroin addict, to name just a few. They tackled issues such as gang violence, racism, labor unions, and mental illness at a time when most television shows stayed on safer ground.

Also notable about the program were the logistical challenges involved. The series was shot on location throughout the country (even in Canada) and required a crew of 50 to 60 people, along with two tractor-trailers full of equipment. It was probably the largest mobile filming operation in television history up to that time.

Guest stars on the show included some fading film stars such as Joan Crawford, but more interesting in retrospect is the roster of up-and-coming talent featured, including such now-familiar names as Rod Steiger, Suzanne Pleshette, and Robert Redford.

is that if you think the Mother Road has some wild and kitschy signs and architecture, then Las Vegas has to be the record-holder. In Las Vegas there are casinos and other businesses which mimic Hawaiian islands, pirate ships, castles, pyramids, miniature cities of the world, and much,

much more, most of it open 24 hours per day and brightly lit all through the night. If Las Vegas should fall into disuse over the next generation or two as Route 66 has, then it will make for some fine exploration one day for the ruin-hunters among us.

For those of you who want to taste a little of Las Vegas, here are a few suggestions, including a few attractions you may not have heard of:

The older part of Las Vegas—the downtown district known as **Glitter Gulch**—was semi-enclosed several years ago and has received other infusions of cash to improve its image and desirability. This is where you'll find such venerable fixtures as the Golden Nugget and the Four Queens. The Strip, where the majority of Las Vegas development takes place these days, dates from much later, when Bugsy Siegel built his Flamingo Hotel out there in the 1950s and began promoting the **Vegas Strip** heavily.

There is a **Liberace Museum** at 1775 E. Tropicana. Not only that, but there is a Liberace Play-Alike Competition held at Carlucci's Piano Bar each year on Liberace's birthday, May 16th. Judging of the contest is based on technique, material selection, performance style, and (of course!) costume.

The **Gun Store** is at 2900 E. Tropicana. For varying fees, you can shoot an impressive array of handguns, including a real tommy gun.

The **National Canvention & Breweriana Show** [sic] is held each March and includes exhibition and sale of beer-related memorabilia.

The **Vegas Ventriloquist Festival** in June includes workshops on improving technique, building your own dummy, developing your own brand of comedy routine, and more.

Returning to Route 66: Soon after leaving Kingman on old 66 near the chamber of commerce, the scenery and terrain begin changing. Be mindful of the conditions out here; there are lots of dusty, gravelly switchbacks and plenty of low places in the road where flash flooding can occur.

McCONNICO

According to my 1957 atlas, roughly at McConnico there was a fork in the road that still remains today. The older stretch of road went on to Oatman from here, but that alignment had already been bypassed. By 1957, official Route 66 went southward through Griffin and on to Yucca, Haviland, Powell, and Topock. That, of course, is the same alignment which was later upgraded to become Interstate 40. The narrative in this book covers the preferred route through Oatman. Begin by crossing over to the west side of I-40 at Interchange 44, and then make a left turn onto Oatman Highway/ County Road 10.

    About 15 miles or so after crossing the interstate at McConnico, you encounter the Cool Springs success story. Not long ago it was little more than a pile of rubble, but **Cool Springs**

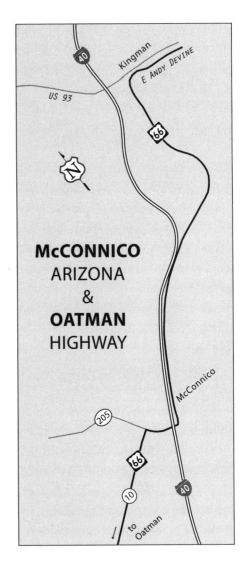

McCONNICO
ARIZONA
&
OATMAN
HIGHWAY

Camp has recently made a comeback, thanks to caring owners. The structure was temporarily rebuilt in the early 1990s so that it could be destroyed in a scene for the film *Universal Soldier*. This time around, however, it's a keeper. About a mile or so past Cool Springs is what remains of **Ed's Camp**. After that, get ready for numerous switchbacks in the old highway.

Ruins of Cool Springs Camp, which has since been restored. West of McConnico, Arizona.

GOLDROAD

Sitgreaves Pass, just east of Goldroad, was a very hard climb for vehicles in days gone by. Some cars and drivers had a very difficult time of it, and so there were wreckers in the area solely to haul hapless motorists over these crests. Some vehicles could make it in reverse, if not forward. The reason for this was two-fold: one, reverse is a substantially lower gear than first; and two, moving in reverse could overcome the shortcomings of early gravity-fed fuel delivery systems.

For a while, the old **Gold Road Mine** had shut down production and was conducting public tours of the mine instead. As of this writing, however, mining has resumed and tours have been discontinued. Of course, fluctuations in the price of gold could make mining impractical again. Only time will tell.

Cactus Joe's has more than its share of ambiance. Oatman, Arizona.

OATMAN

Mining was big business in this area through the 1930s and right up until the onset of World War II. The town was named after Olive Oatman, who was abducted as a young girl by the Mojave Indians and lived with them for several years.

Oatman, Arizona.

You can't really get lost in Oatman, as there's really just one road through it: old Route 66. This is a true Old West mining town, which went through a ghost town phase, and is now clinging to life as a tourist town. There are wooden plank sidewalks in Oatman, and the town's most celebrated inhabitants are the burros, descendants of forebears that were brought here in gold-mining days as beasts of burden. There are feed dispensers scattered around town so that you can indulge them. Get out of your car and do some walking around here.

The old **Oatman Hotel** is where Clark Gable and Carole Lombard came for their honeymoon in 1939. You can view their suite (room 15) and lots more of the place just by wandering upstairs. The bar downstairs has walls which are covered in dollar bills. If you find room, you can leave one of your own.

In the early 1960s, portions of *How the West Was Won* were filmed in Oatman and its environs. Each July, Oatman holds an annual **Egg-Frying Contest**. Entrants use every solar-based gizmo imaginable to try and fry an egg in 15 minutes or less. I've been told that the town's population sometimes increases tenfold for this event.

Oatman, Arizona.

GOLDEN SHORES-TOPOCK

Neither of these communities qualifies as much of a town. Golden Shores is really no more than a housing subdivision that sprouted where the Oatman-Topock highway merges with Highway 95. Topock comes from the Mojave word meaning "water crossing," which is certainly appropriate.

There is an arching bridge (circa 1916) here which crosses the Colorado River, but it carries no vehicle traffic, only a pipeline. Today's Route 66 adventurer is forced to make the crossing on the I-40 bridge.

FURTHER AFIELD

Consider a side trip down Highway 95 to **Lake Havasu City**. It was here that the London Bridge, purchased from the City of London by entrepreneur Robert P. McCulloch, was rebuilt in 1971 after being painstakingly dismantled and all parts carefully labeled. McCulloch thought he was buying London's Tower Bridge, which is much more picturesque, but after learning of his mistake, he decided to go through with the deal anyway.

Route 66 has now passed through seven states on its journey west, and is now poised at the crossing of the Colorado River. The promised land of California awaits on the opposite shore.

CALIFORNIA

After traversing the Illinois prairie, the Missouri Ozark country, the Indian Territory of Oklahoma, the Panhandle of Texas, the old Spanish colony of New Mexico, and then the harsh landscape

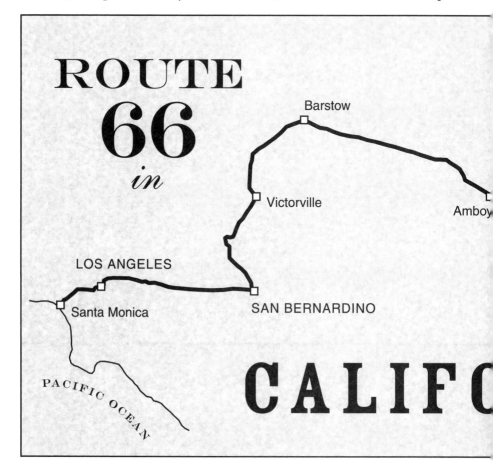

of Arizona, Route 66 finally arrives at the doorstep of California.

California, the land of milk and honey; land where dreams live, where fortunes are built, and where the soul longs to be. Surely this is where the end of the rainbow must lie. But Nature can be a cruel provider. The Colorado River, threshold to the Golden State, is a welcome sight to the traveler who has arrived after crossing the desert of western Arizona, but the fabled land on the other side looks no more inviting than that which has tested him for more than a hundred miles already.

How cruel must it have seemed to the fleeing Okies of the Depression that even in California the land appeared barren and forsaken. Greeting them here at the border was no Xanadu, but rather the Needles for which the nearby town is named, and many more miles of Mojave Desert yet to be crossed. The river is not an end to the desert, only a reference point.

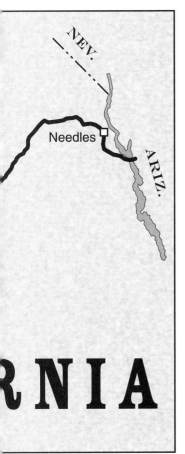

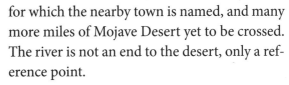 The actual crossing point of Route 66 over the Colorado River changed a number of times over the years. Unfortunately for Mother Road devotees such as you and me, the older bridges which used to carry the highway are either gone or inaccessible to traffic. You will be forced to use the I-40 bridge to

make the crossing into California. Leave I-40 at Exit 148/Five Mile Road. Turn left at the end of the ramp to cross to the west side and merge with U.S. 95 heading north.

NEEDLES

Route 66 passes through town primarily on Broadway, but as you've learned to suspect, earlier in its life it took a path alongside the railroad tracks—in this case, Front Street.

Established in 1883 as a stop on the railroad, Needles is known for being one of the hottest places in the United States. Temperatures frequently exceed 100 degrees Fahrenheit. Named for the rocky outcroppings across the river in Arizona, Needles was once the home of *Peanuts* cartoonist Charles Schulz, who often used Needles and the surrounding desert as the setting for Snoopy's cousin Spike. The river bath scene in *The Grapes of Wrath* was filmed here at Needles back in the 1930s.

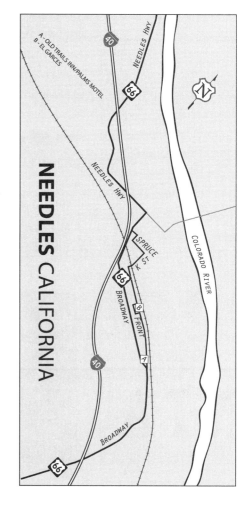

As you enter Needles from the east, there is an old wagon beside the road that is said to be the same 20-mule-team wagon used in the old *Death Valley Days* television show, which starred Ronald Reagan. Just across from it is the **Old Trails Inn**, which has also been known as the Palms Motel.

On Front Street, an older alignment of Route 66

This authentic wagon welcomes the westbound traveler to Needles, California.

through Needles, sits **El Garces**. This Santa Fe depot and hotel was built shortly after an earlier structure was destroyed by fire in 1906, and was designed with distinctive columns and balconies, which are unusual for this part of the country. Across the street from El Garces is the **Needles Regional Museum**, at 929 Front Street, which includes exhibits pertaining to Route 66.

Keep an eye out for the **66 Motel**, which has a neon sign in good condition. As you pass through the town of Needles, there are still a number of buildings to see which are from the Route 66 era.

Leave Needles on Broadway, then National Trails Highway. When it comes to a "T," turn left and join I-40 at Interchange 139.

One of the countless roadside businesses named for the highway. Needles, California.

HOMER-GOFFS-FENNER

> Exit I-40 with U.S. 95 (Exit 133) in order to experience less interstate and more Route 66. In about six miles, and just prior to crossing the railroad tracks, turn west on Goffs Road.

The loop that includes Homer, Goffs, and Fenner was cut off from Route 66 at an early date. The later alignment took a more direct path from Needles to Essex. You won't see much evidence of Homer, other than the fact that you may have noticed passing Homer-Klinefelter Road while on 95.

Goffs is situated right at the edge of the Mojave National Preserve. The crown jewel is a **schoolhouse** dating from 1914, which was meticulously restored in 1998–99 by the Mojave Desert Heritage & Cultural Association. The association maintains what must be the largest collection of Mojave Desert historical materials anywhere. Aside from the materials and exhibits displayed within the schoolhouse, there are dozens of artifacts, including vehicles, mining equipment, and a tiny portable courthouse, all on display outside in a self-guided tour format. In 2008, a new library was dedicated, the Dennis G. Casebier Memorial Library, which is a replica of the Goffs Santa Fe Railway Depot that graced the town from 1902 to 1956. Operating hours at the complex are limited, but you can call ahead at 760-733-4482.

Fenner is nothing more than a small set of travelers' services—fuel and snacks—at the place where Goffs Road crosses I-40. Continue past I-40 on Goffs Road toward Essex.

ESSEX

It was here in the Mojave Desert near Essex that U.S. troops under General Patton trained for desert conditions in preparation for the anticipated confrontation with General Erwin Rommel's (the Desert Fox) troops in North Africa. There is a public well (now dry) which offered free drinks of water to Route 66 travelers generations ago.

FURTHER AFIELD

Northwest of Essex is **Mitchell Caverns**, in Providence Mountains State Recreation Area, offering 90-minute guided tours. Caving is a refreshing activity here in the desert, with underground temperatures tending to remain in the 60s throughout the year. This state park sits in the midst of Mojave National Preserve, an area twice the size of Yosemite, at the confluence of three desert regions: the Mojave, Sonoran, and Great Basin deserts. Features include rock art, abandoned mines and ranches, and over 300 known species of wildlife.

CADIZ SUMMIT

There are remains of a small tourist complex here, with the ruined buildings now festooned with graffiti.

CHAMBLESS

In the vicinity of Chambless you'll see the rusting metal framework of what appears to have been a roadside billboard. Also, the remains of a huge restaurant sign with a roadrunner logo are baking in the desert nearby.

West of Chambless there is a berm, or small bank, along the north edge of the highway, which for several miles is covered with graffiti. Individuals have placed small stones and other detritus in such ways as to spell out words, make outlines, or otherwise communicate with future passersby. Among the symbols are peace signs, various initials, a Route 66 shield, and many more, which are difficult to either describe or to comprehend. One can easily become entranced by looking at this artwork for mile after mile through the side window.

AMBOY

For many years, the property owners here tried to capitalize on the isolated highwayside atmosphere here in Amboy. I saw some magazine ads extolling the virtues of the place for location filming, commercials, and so forth. I agree; in fact, I think this would make an excellent setting for an episode of *The Twilight Zone*. The **Roy's Motel & Café** complex definitely has that certain something. The large, circa-1959

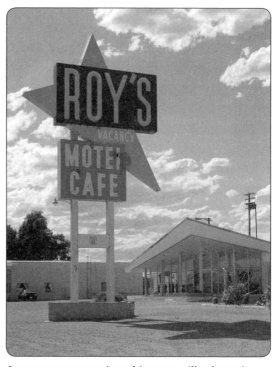

A new owner promises this town will rebound: Amboy, California.

sign is one of the most iconic on all of Route 66.

In 2005, the whole town was bought by a new owner—lock, stock, and barrel. The goal is to once again have Amboy humming with tourists stopping for fuel and other traveler's needs. Stop in and see how things are progressing.

FURTHER AFIELD

Amboy Crater is just a mile or two south of the highway. There is a turnoff to the dormant volcano (N. Amboy Road) just west of Amboy proper. The crater itself is accessible via a 3½-mile

Roy's Motel, Amboy, California.

Take some time to explore Amboy, California.

trail from the parking area.

For the truly adventurous, south of Amboy near Twentynine Palms is **Joshua Tree National Monument** (JTNM). Featured are a number of hiking trails, including one about four miles in length leading to the largest group of palms. A shorter trail (less than two miles) takes you to an oasis at Fortynine Palms Canyon. There is also a restored ranch within the confines of JTNM on which park rangers offer guided tours.

North of Amboy, at the town of **Baker** (near Death Valley), is a 135-foot-tall **thermometer**. Around here, having respect for the temperatures can mean the difference between survival and the alternative.

BAGDAD

Here's the inspiration for the name of the film *Bagdad Café*, which was actually shot a little further down the highway at Newberry Springs. Once upon a time, there actually was a Bagdad Café here, with a changing cast of road-weary travelers making up the clientele. Satellite photos show evidence that there were some sort of structures here in the past, but nowadays you'll be hard-pressed to see much of anything from the vantage point of your car.

SIBERIA

It seems an odd name for a community in the Mojave Desert, but it's somewhat in keeping with the community of Klondike nearby (a short distance off of 66). I suppose one name inspired the other. Today, only a few foundations remain in Siberia.

LUDLOW

This town was established circa 1882 by the Ludlow Mining Company. Most of the Mother Road-era part of town is now privately owned by the railroad and is slowly wasting away. Be sure to take a look at the classic Ludlow Mercantile Company building, which was constructed in

This is what's left of a once-thriving business district in Ludlow, California.

1908. Also nearby are a number of other ruins, including the old Ludlow Café. Ludlow hasn't completely died off, however, thanks to an I-40 interchange.

The road less traveled, Ludlow, California.

At Ludlow, cross to the north side of the interstate to avoid superslab driving. Cross the interstate again (to the south side) at Lavic Road. My 1957 map of the region shows no community by that name, only the Lavic Dry Lake to the south. Just a little further west is another extinct volcanic crater—in case you missed the one near Amboy. Pisgah Crater is just south of Route 66 via Pisgah Crater Road.

NEWBERRY SPRINGS

At Newberry Springs, pull over for awhile at an old Whiting Brothers station, now named Dry Creek Station. There are some wonderful old pumps standing in front, and the desert setting is perfect. The **Bagdad**

Café is here also (formerly named the Sidewinder). As mentioned earlier, this is where the 1980s movie of the same name was filmed.

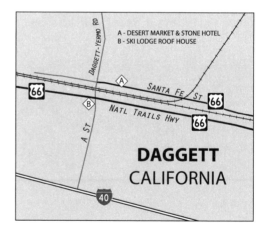 The highway will cross to the north side of I-40. At about where Barstow-Daggett Airport is on your right, old 66 picks up on the opposite side of the railroad track. You can either turn right at Hidden Springs Road to take that early alignment into town, or you can do as I do, which is continue straight into town and then, as part of my routine exploration, turn east on Santa Fe Street to see that section that formed the early eastern approach to Daggett.

Just before reaching town, to the north of the highway, is what is called a Solar Concentrator. This is one of the latest high-tech methods for converting solar light and heat into useful energy.

DAGGETT

> Don't miss out on the older alignment of Route 66, Santa Fe Street, north of the railroad tracks.

In Daggett stands the **Stone Hotel**, frequented in its day by the likes of Tom Mix, Death Valley Scotty, and John Muir. The hotel was constructed in the 1880s (some sources say even earlier), and has walls which are some two feet thick. As of this writing, it is undergoing rehabilitation. Also in town is the **Desert Market**, built in 1908, which in its day was the place local miners came to exchange their findings for legal tender.

A - DESERT MARKET & STONE HOTEL
B - SKI LODGE ROOF HOUSE

SANTA FE ST

NATL TRAILS HWY

DAGGETT
CALIFORNIA

There is a building at the corner of Route 66 and Daggett-Yermo Road (or A Street) with an unusual shape to its roof. This is locally known

as the "Ski Lodge Roof House," and originally opened as a visitor information center in 1926, the same year our beloved highway was designated number sixty-six.

Daggett, California.

The **Daggett Museum** is at 33703 Second Street, and includes a collection of railroad china and Navajo code-talkers memorabilia.

FURTHER AFIELD

North of Daggett (use Daggett-Yermo Road), near the small town of **Yermo**, is the **Ghost Town of Calico**. Calico was a silver-mining town and also a source of borax, a mineral known to mankind since ancient times that is used to make pottery glaze, fertilizers, and detergents.

A true Old West mining town dating from 1881, one-third of Calico's buildings are original; the rest have been carefully recreated to evoke the late nineteenth century. The town site covers about 60 acres,

This unusual building, called the "Ski Lodge Roof House" by locals, dates from 1926, the same year Route 66 was established. Daggett, California.

and includes a down-town business district, miners' quarters, tours of an actual mine, and an operating narrow-gauge railroad. The town has been the filming location for numerous film and television crews over the years, thanks to its authentic look and feel. The town holds a num-

At the tourist-oriented "ghost town" of Calico, California.

ber of festivals throughout the year. These include the Calico Spring Festival in May, which includes a chili cook-off, music festival, and the World Tobacco Spitting Championship. Calico Days occurs every October, and features a parade, burro races, and the National Gunfight Championship.

A little to the east of Yermo and the ghost town is the **Calico Early Man Archaeological Site**. This archaeological dig, begun in 1964 by Dr. Louis Leakey, has pushed back the date for the presence of man on this continent by thousands of years. Stone tools have been found here as much as 200,000 years old, making it one of the oldest tool-bearing sites in the Western Hemisphere. Public tours of the facility are available year-round.

Back on 66: After just a short distance on National Trails Highway, you'll be forced to join I-40 briefly in order to get around the U.S. Marine Corps base. Exit again at Main Street/I-40 Business Loop.

BARSTOW

Named in 1886 for the then-president of the Santa Fe Railroad, Barstow has a number of vintage Route 66-era signs and buildings to make you

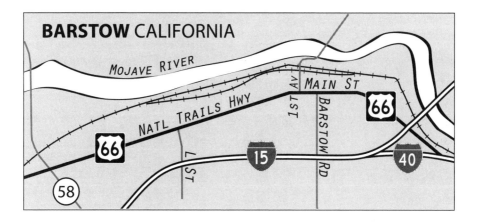

BARSTOW CALIFORNIA

MOJAVE RIVER
NATL TRAILS HWY
MAIN ST
1ST AV
BARSTOW RD
1ST
66
66
15
40
58

slow down and explore. Not the least of these is the **El Rancho Barstow Motel**, with its 100-foot-tall neon sign supported by twin towers. Much of the motel was constructed using discarded railroad ties from the defunct Tidewater & Tonopah Railroad.

See also the Village Hotel & Café, the Katz, and the Green Spot Motel. Around 1940, Barstow was visited by avant-garde musician and part-time hobo **Harry Partch**, whose composition, "Barstow," was inspired by some hitchhiker markings he saw on a highway railing on the outskirts of town.

BARSTOW ATTRACTIONS

Barstow is home to another fine example of the Harvey House hotels from the glory days of rail travel: the **Casa del Desierto**. Located inside are the **Barstow Route 66 Mother Road Museum** and the **Western America Railroad Museum**. 685 N. First St.

There are several history-oriented murals known collectively as **Main Street**

El Rancho Barstow Motel, Barstow, California.

Murals. Subject matter for the artwork includes the local Harvey House, Mormon Trail, and Route 66. You can take a guided walking tour, or you can go all out and see them all from atop a wagon pulled by a pair of Belgian draft horses. Advance tickets and other information available at 760-257-1052.

The **Mojave River Valley Museum** is dedicated to the history and culture of the area. Their collection includes local newspapers going back to 1911 and more than 20,000 photographs. 270 E. Virginia Way (at Barstow Road).

The **Desert Discovery Center** has on display the second-largest space rock ever found in the United States. The Old Woman Meteorite is about three feet across and weighs about three tons. 831 Barstow Rd.

Barstow, California.

This old depot now houses the Route 66 Mother Road Museum, Barstow, California.

LENWOOD

Lenwood is just west of Barstow, and seems in danger of losing its identity due to the proximity of its larger neighbor. There is a Lenwood Road, however, and

From Lenwood, and on through Helendale, Oro Grande, and some miles beyond, you'll be far away from I-40 so the driving is super easy. Just keep following National Trails Highway to Victorville.

also several businesses which use the name "Lenwood" as part of their own.

HELENDALE

Most of Helendale is off the highway, on the other side of the railroad tracks, but you will see the landmark Helendale Market alongside 66. Next door is a mostly-empty lot selling firewood, which has an antique sign for the Polly brand of gasoline as part of the décor.

HELENDALE ATTRACTIONS

Just outside Helendale on a former goat ranch is the **Exotic World Burlesque Museum & Hall of Fame**. Here in the desert between Barstow and Victorville is something rather unique—a tribute to strippers and exotic dancers. There are thousands of pieces of memorabilia from the glory days of burlesque, including photographs, costumes, and even the ashes of Miss Sheri Champagne, one of burlesque's all-time greats. Other well-known performers represented include Lily St. Cyr, Tempest Storm, the Eye-ful Tower, and Chesty Morgan. Admission is free, but donations and gift shop purchases are of course sincerely appreciated. Exotic World is at 29053 Wild Road.

About halfway between Helendale and Oro Grande is a veritable **forest of bottle trees**, the creation of Elmer Long, who lives on the property and has been fashioning his brand of folk art since about the year 2000. Some of the bottles are old and dusty, while others are quite new and shiny, revealing the fact that this is indeed a work in progress.

ORO GRANDE

Oro Grande has a very small former business district right on the highway. The most notable structures in Oro Grande are an enormous cement

Elmer Long's forest of "bottle trees" awaits today's traveler near Oro Grande, California.

plant and a small building with a curved front, currently doing business as Club 66.

VICTORVILLE

The highway will cross beneath I-40 and become Victorville's D Street. Turn right on Seventh, and pass through downtown.

You need to stop and spend a little time in Victorville. Here's where you'll find the **California Route 66 Museum**, in a former roadhouse that was known as the Red Rooster Café. The folks here are friendly and knowledgeable, so you can get whatever materials and tips you'll need for the remainder of your journey. D Street, between Fifth and Sixth.

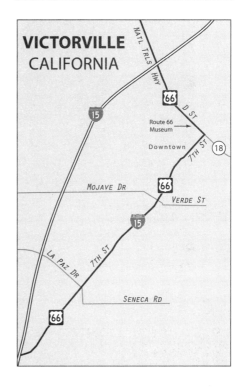

Formerly here in Victorville was the Roy Rogers Museum, which moved to Branson, Missouri in 2003 and later closed permanently. You can still see a hint of the museum's influence, though, in the sign at the nearby New Corral Motel. The rearing Palomino in the motel sign is a distinct echo of the figure of Trigger, which used to stand in front of the museum.

Oro Grande, California.

Above: Some of the items on display at the Route 66 Museum in Victorville, California.

 Leaving Victorville via Seventh Street on the west edge of town, you'll need to enter Interstate 15 southbound for several miles.

CAJON PASS AREA

At the Oak Hill exit (138) is the **Summit Inn**, operating at this location since 1952. Not only is this an authentic stop from the Route 66 era, there are also a number of relics on display outside, such as a 1930s tow truck and several items of antique gas station equipment. Inside, the menu includes such exotics as burgers made from buffalo and ostrich, and you can take your chances asking questions of a fortune-telling machine similar to one that was the centerpiece of a well-known *Twilight Zone* episode starring William Shatner.

It's in this vicinity that Route 66 crosses the **Pacific Crest Trail**. This is a rugged hiking trail that runs all the way from the Mexican to the Canadian border, a distance of more than 2,600 miles. This trail was established at the same time as the more well-known Appalachian Trail in the east, and covers much more rugged terrain. It passes beneath I-15 along here.

Narrow Cajon Pass has several sets of railroad tracks passing through it, as well as several traces of old Route 66 alignments. Unfortunately, most are difficult or impossible to gain access to. You have to try pretty hard just to spot some of them.

A little past the Summit Inn is the junction with State Highway 138, a spot called Cajon Junction, at Exit 131. There is a small obelisk-shaped marker a short distance to the south on the east service road. The inscription reads: "Santa Fe and Salt Lake Trail 1849. Erected in honor of the brave pioneers

Retired road warrior at the Summit Inn, Cajon Summit, California.

Cajon Summit, California.

of California in 1917 by pioneers." If you drive Highway 138 about four miles west of I-15, you'll see there is another historical marker, this one commemorating the California branch of the Mormon Trail. This trail was established in 1851, and connected the Mormon capital at Salt Lake City to Los Angeles, by way of Las Vegas. The marker states that it was erected in 1937 by Sons of Mormon Pioneers. In 1998, a cattle drive was held which re-traced the path of the old Mormon Trail between California and Utah. Also west on Highway 138, if you choose to explore the area, are some weathered rock formations known as Mormon Rocks, with a few hiking trails.

The territory traversed by Route 66 has long been a migratory path. Near Cajon Summit, California.

You should leave the interstate at the Devore Road exit, and then follow Cajon Boulevard for your approach to San Bernardino. Just prior to reaching the city you can see the remains of two old 66-era motels, the El Cajon and the Palms. The motels are in very bad shape, but the old neon signs are still legible.

SAN BERNARDINO

The County of San Bernardino is the largest in the nation—you've been in it ever since crossing the Colorado River from Arizona!

Once you reach San Bernardino, even though you are not traveling on the interstate, the pace of the road quickens measurably—there's a sea change, you might say. You are beginning to enter what might be called the Southern California Megalopolis, or what is euphemistically referred to as Greater L.A. From now on, you will be hard-pressed to observe everything you want to and still drive safely. You're getting a taste of what happened to Route 66 and the other major highways like her, a development which led to widespread public support for their replacement by limited-access superhighways.

It was here in San Bernardino, in 1948, that the McDonald brothers sounded the first death knell for the mom-and-pop hamburger joints of

Enter the city outskirts on Cajon Boulevard, which parallels some railroad tracks on your left. Just after passing beneath Highway 210, bear right onto Mt. Vernon Avenue. If you miss it, you'll actually have a second chance moments later, so don't sweat it. Mt. Vernon will take you to Fifth, where you turn right and head westward (becoming Foothill Boulevard). Note that Route 66 pretty much misses most of San Bernardino, so consider whether you want to break away from the highway for a while and investigate some of the listed attractions.

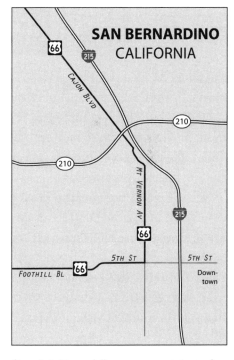

the world. What began as the very first McDonald's restaurant is today the **McDonald's/Route 66 Museum**. Part of the structure is dedicated to displays pertaining to the history of the McDonald's fast-food empire, and part of it is filled with photos, highway signs, and other memorabilia associated with the Mother Road.

SAN BERNARDINO ATTRACTIONS

San Bernardino, California.

San Bernardino is home to the **California Theater**, a 1928 Spanish Colonial Revival showplace at 562 W. Fourth. It was at this theater that Will Rogers made his last public appearance—to benefit the Salvation Army—prior to his death in Alaska a couple of months later. The California Theater was an early "soundie," having been outfitted from the start for sound, even though *The Jazz Singer* had only been released about one year before. Today, the restored California Theater hosts live stage performances, including opera and symphony.

The **San Bernardino Historical and Pioneer Society** maintains a museum at 796 N. D Street in an 1891 mansion. Also on the grounds is a primitive iron jail cell, which some historians claim was built around 1860.

Perris Hill Park has several interesting concrete picnic tables that were salvaged from a defunct roadside picnic area called Camp Cajon that was on Route 66 at Cajon Pass. 1135 E. Highland Ave.

FURTHER AFIELD

Southeast of San Bernardino is the city of **Redlands**, California. Redlands is home to a mission dating from 1819, the **Asistencia Mission de San**

Gabriel, at 26930 Barton Road. Also in Redlands are: the **Marmalade Mansions**, a large number of Victorian homes from the era when "Citrus was King"; the **Historical Glass Museum** at 1157 Orange Street, which features American glassware from the early 1800s; and the **world's tallest water slide**, at Pharaoh's Lost Kingdom.

East of San Bernardino is **Big Bear Lake**. Once known as Southern California's favorite mountain getaway, there are hiking trails, mountain biking slopes, and seasonal skiing in the surrounding San Bernardino National Forest. Big Bear Lake has also been called Hollywood's Backlot. Numerous films have been shot here, including such well-known classics as *Birth of a Nation*, *Kissin' Cousins*, *The Parent Trap*, *Dr. Doolittle*, and *Creature from the Black Lagoon*. In May, Big Bear Lake hosts the Trout Classic, where some 400 contestants participate in trophy trout fishing. In the summertime it's Old Miners' Days, with a chili cook-off, parade, and cowboy shootout. A motorcycle rally, the Ladies of the Harley Mountain Fun Run, takes place each August. To go to Big Bear Lake, take one of two very scenic highways: Route 18 (Rim of the World Drive) or Route 38. Each includes scenic overlooks of the area.

RIALTO

You probably won't notice when you pass out of San Bernardino and into Rialto, since you're now in one of those "Greater Metropolitan" areas, and also because the name of the street doesn't change—it will remain Foothill Boulevard for some time.

Wigwam Village Motel, Rialto, California.

On old Route 66 here in Rialto is the sister to the **Wigwam Village** we saw earlier in Holbrook, Arizona. This one was lovingly restored in 2004, after new owners took over and reversed years of neglect. In recognition of this enormous effort, the Cyrus Avery Preservation Award was presented in September 2005.

The **Rialto Historical Society** claims to be "the best kept secret in Rialto." Based in the picturesque old Christian Church at 201–205 N. Riverside, they've converted the adjoining church school building into a museum of local history.

FONTANA

The notorious Hells Angels Motorcycle Club was founded in Fontana in 1948. The name, which officially no longer contains an apostrophe, was originally used by U.S. air squadrons during both World Wars, and is also the title of a Hollywood film starring Jean Harlow.

Roadside orange vendors were once common on this part of Route 66. Fontana, California.

The Deco-inspired **Center Stage Theater** (formerly Fontana Theater) underwent a full renovation and now hosts live dinner theater. Its grand re-opening was in 2008. 8463 Sierra Ave.

Be on the lookout for an old orange stand outside the long-established **Bono's Restaurant**. The inscription over the window reads "Bono's Historic Orange." You are in what was once the heart of citrus country. 15395 Foothill, at Sultana.

RANCHO CUCAMONGA

Cucamonga is thought to be a Shoshone word meaning "sandy place." This really was a large ranch at one time, and the area eventually found itself awash in vintners. At the corner of Foothill and Vineyard is an old wine barrel bearing an inscription that lets the traveler know this was once the site of the oldest vineyard in California.

In the heart of wine country, Rancho Cucamonga, California.

The **Sycamore Inn** (dating from 1848 and originally called the Mountain View Inn) served as a stagecoach stop in the days before motorized travel. Eighteenth-century Spanish visitors named this area Arroyo de los Osos, or Bear Gulch, and today there is a small stone monument out front featuring a bear sculpture. Just a little further west is the **Magic Lamp Inn**. The neon sign out front, which is shaped like Aladdin's lamp, actually spouts a gas flame when the sign is illuminated each evening.

At 7965 Vineyard Avenue, in the Foothill Marketplace,

This statue stands in front of the Sycamore Inn, Rancho Cucamonga, California.

Keeping the flame burning, Rancho Cucamonga, California.

is the **Route 66 Territory Visitors Bureau**.

The **Sam Maloof Residence, Workshop, and Gardens** is just to the north in the neighboring community of Alta Loma. Maloof was a highly-regarded designer and maker of fine furniture. Mr. Maloof passed away in 2009, and today his hand-built residence and adjoining workshop are open for tours. 5131 Carnelian St.

This establishment began life as a stagecoach stop. Rancho Cucamonga, California.

UPLAND

In Upland is the twelfth and final **Madonna of the Trail** monument, signifying the end of the National Old Trails Highway at Euclid Avenue.

The **Cooper Historical Museum** preserves and interprets the heritage of Upland and surrounding communities. Their displays are to be found in two separate locations: the main one at 217 East A Street, and another at 525 West 18th Street. The building on A Street is in the Art Moderne style, and was built in 1937 by the Ontario-Cucamonga Fruit Exchange.

South of Upland, in **Chino**, is the **Planes of Fame Air Museum**, featuring WWII aircraft and memorabilia (7000 Merrill).

One of a series of monuments marking the old National Trails Highway. This one is in Upland, California.

CLAREMONT

This city is home to the Claremont Colleges, a collection of several affiliated colleges in a park-like setting spanning some 300 acres.

The old Claremont High School building has been converted into a small retail and office center called the **Old School House**, and is right on Foothill Boulevard (old 66). There is some decorative tiling around the main entrance in the Art Nouveau style. The PFF Bank & Trust (at the corner of Indian Hill) sports a decorative mural facing Route 66.

The **Folk Music Center Museum** houses a collection of musical instruments accumulated since the center's establishment more than 50 years ago. They also sponsor a folk music festival each spring. 220 Yale Ave.

Claremont Heritage administers a collection of maps, photographs, postcards, and citrus growers' materials in a historic former

Claremont, California.   Former high school, Claremont, California.

residence at 840 N. Indian Hill Boulevard. They can also provide you with a brochure for a self-guided walking tour of local points of interest.

LAVERNE

Right about where LaVerne transitions to San Dimas is the Pinnacle Peak Steak House. There is a **covered wagon** out front to attract your attention. LaVerne also has an "old town" section known as **Lordsburg**, which has an interesting walking tour featuring a town square, public murals, and such varied architectural gems as an Armenian college, a residential row characterized by Craftsman bungalows, and a distinctive water filtration plant. Details are available at the chamber of commerce office at 131 E. Foothill.

SAN DIMAS

San Dimas, though not well-known as a Route 66 town, is the setting for the cult film classic *Bill and Ted's Excellent Adventure*, with comedian

George Carlin in a key supporting role.

The real San Dimas is a former citrus-growing region which today is quite equestrian-oriented, with a large equestrian center visible from the highway and some yellow "horse crossing" signs. There is also a very nice old downtown that is worth visiting, with late-nineteenth-century commercial buildings and plank sidewalks. To find downtown, leave 66 at San Dimas Avenue and turn

Downtown San Dimas, California.

south several blocks to Bonita Avenue. There is also a small 1930s-era Santa Fe depot in the downtown area that now houses the local historical society. Out in front of the depot is a water fountain and trough built to serve "both man and beast."

On San Dimas Avenue just north of Bonita is a very large residence known variously as the **Walker House** or the **San Dimas Mansion**. According to the San Dimas Historical Society, it is the last standing railroad hotel in California, and was later used as a residence by Mr. J. W. Walker, a prominent local citizen. In 2009, a full restoration was completed, and the building has recently started a new life as a restaurant.

Historic residence originally built as a hotel, San Dimas, California.

Glendora, California.

GLENDORA

Glendora has two Route 66 corridors. The later alignment (formerly Alosta, but renamed "Route 66") is the better-known of the two, but is really more of a bypass route. To explore the earlier alignment, turn right at Amelia, which will then take you left onto old Foothill. Along this older route are lots of classic bungalows for the inner architect in you to enjoy.

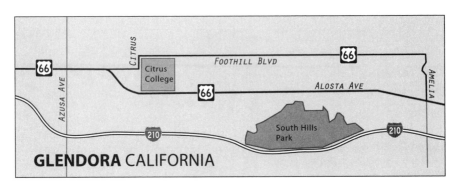

AZUSA

Azusa calls itself "Canyon City." How the name Azusa came about is a source of some debate. One explanation I've read (which I assume to

be tongue-in-cheek) is that it came from a local general store which was said to provide "everything from A to Z in the USA." A more serious explanation states that the area was at one time inhabited by a group of Shoshoneans calling themselves Asuksa-gna.

The **Azusa Foothill Drive-In** was still operating when I drove through here for the first time. In 2001, however, the nearby Azusa Pacific University acquired the property and obtained permission to demolish the theater.

Azusa, California, also calls itself "Canyon City."

Azusa's business district is just north of Foothill on Azusa Avenue. Just north of the business district is a residential area lined with extremely tall, slender palm trees that remind me of the introductory footage from *The Beverly Hillbillies* television series. See if you agree.

DUARTE

In Duarte is **Justice Brothers, Inc.**, a manufacturer of automotive products since shortly after the Second World War, with a history of building and sponsoring race cars. Today, you can see the racing museum they've assembled right here at their world headquarters. 2734 E. Huntington Dr.

The Duarte Historical Society operates the **Duarte Historical Museum** at 777 Encanto Parkway. The building is a former residence moved to the location in 1990, and exhibits include an extensive collection

Duarte, California.

of local-area fruit crate labels.

MONROVIA

On Shamrock Avenue in Monrovia—see reference map—there is a very old gasoline station on the west side of the street that has so far avoided the wrecking ball. At the corner of Walnut Avenue.

The **Aztec Hotel**, at 311 W. Foothill in Monrovia, was built in 1925—just in time for the inauguration of Route 66—and is on the National Register. The hotel is designed in a style the architect termed "Mayan Revival," but the name Aztec was used because it was thought that Americans would consider it less obscure and would more readily identify with it. Take a stroll into the Brass Elephant bar area just off the lobby and look upward. There is a wide-ranging system of ceiling fans all run by

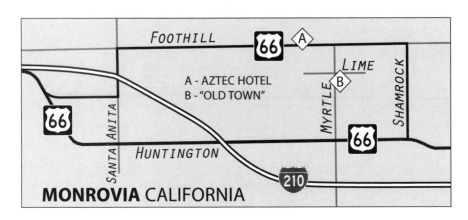

FOOTHILL · 66 · A
LIME
A - AZTEC HOTEL
B - "OLD TOWN" B
66 · SANTA ANITA
MYRTLE · SHAMROCK
66
HUNTINGTON
210
MONROVIA CALIFORNIA

one central motor and driven by an array of fan belts reaching hither and thither and yon. If you're into the spirit realm, take note that room 120 is said to be haunted by the spirit of a woman who died there when she hit her head on the radiator.

Old Town Monrovia is an area of several blocks, centered at Myrtle and Lime Avenues, featuring small businesses, theaters, galleries, and restaurants. You can park at the curb and wander around, enjoying the small-town neighborhood feel. They even have street fairs every Friday for most of the year.

Author and activist **Upton Sinclair** lived in Monrovia for more than 20 years at 464 N. Myrtle Avenue.

ARCADIA

In Arcadia, the **Santa Anita Park** racetrack is widely regarded as an architectural treasure, exhibiting design elements of Art Deco, Spanish Revival,

> In Arcadia, Huntington Drive splits near Santa Anita Park. You'll need to take the right-hand fork (Colorado Boulevard) in order to follow Route 66.

American Colonial, and New Orleans styles. It was designed by Gordon Kaufmann, the same architect who designed the massive Hoover Dam on the Colorado River. Out front is a bronze statue of the racehorse Seabiscuit, whose most famous comeback race occurred here at this track. Santa Anita was also the setting for the Marx Brothers' film classic, *A Day at the Races*. During WWII, it was used as a detention center for Japanese-Americans, including George Takei of *Star Trek* fame.

Just east of the racetrack is a Denny's restaurant that has a **Dutch-style windmill** dominating its roofline. Today's Arcadia County Park, at Huntington Drive and Santa Anita Avenue, served as a U.S. Army balloon training facility during the First World War.

The **Ruth and Charles Gilb Arcadia Historical Museum** opened its doors in 2001 as a joint venture of the City of Arcadia and the Arcadia Historical Society. 380 W. Huntington Dr.

Enter Pasadena on Colorado Boulevard. From this point onward, following Route 66 becomes difficult for a number of reasons. First, there is the fact that traffic picks up exponentially because Route 66 was "improved" early on in this area so that it became more of the type of highway we are accustomed to today. Secondly, Route 66 was re-routed many, many times over the years, so there are several true paths for you to choose from. I recommend lots of exploration here in Southern California, and lots of patience, too. As a byproduct of all of this complexity, one of our road warrior brethren, Scott Piotrowski, has assembled a detailed guide to help clear up the confusion (see bibliography).

One of the many paths you can follow from here to the coast is Colorado to Figueroa to Arroyo Seco Parkway to Sunset to Santa Monica Boulevard. Also be aware that the earliest path of Route 66 went only as far as downtown Los Angeles, to the corner of Broadway and Seventh (see reference map). The highway was extended to Santa Monica in the 1930s.

PASADENA

As early as 1890, "games" were held here in Pasadena which included foot races, tugs of war, and burro races. There were even what might be called "floats" in those early days. Later, these festivities became known as the Tournament of Roses, and in 1902 a football game was added to the program. Those traditions, of course, continue to the present day.

The city of Pasadena is architecturally blessed, particularly for those of us with a weakness for Mission or Arts and Crafts style. The most outstanding example is the **Gamble House**, designed by Charles and Henry Greene in 1908, and situated at 4 Westmoreland Place. For a tour of some fine architecture, drive along Oak Knoll and San Rafael and into the hills near the Rose Bowl. The **Colorado Boulevard Bridge**, which crosses the Arroyo Seco River, was completed in 1913.

In 1924, at Pasadena's Rite Spot Restaurant, grill chef Lionel Sternberger concocted the **world's first cheeseburger**, which at the time he dubbed the cheese hamburger. In 1939, Pasadena managed to capture first place in Columbia University's Quality of Life Competition.

Pasadena, California.

One of the earliest transcontinental auto trips originated from Pasadena way back in 1908. Jacob Murdoch loaded his son, two daughters, and 1,200 pounds of supplies into his Packard for a 25-day expedition from Pasadena to New York City. Packard later published a publicity booklet about the adventure entitled *A Family Tour From Ocean to Ocean*.

PASADENA ATTRACTIONS

The **Tournament House**, at 391 S. Orange Grove Boulevard, is a sort of museum of Rose Bowl memorabilia in a former home of millionaire William Wrigley Jr. It also serves as the headquarters for the annual parade festivities.

The **Pasadena Museum of History** is housed in the Fenyes Mansion, constructed in 1905 in the Beaux-Arts style. Its rooms are furnished in authentic period pieces. Also on the grounds is the **Finnish Folk Art Museum**, with exhibits including handmade furniture, utensils, and sundry decorative arts. 470 W. Walnut St.

Castle Green, built in 1898 as an annex to the Hotel Green, was architecturally state-of-the-art in its day, and exhibits an odd combination of styles the owners call "stunningly original." Today, Castle Green is reserved for special events, and has appeared in numerous films. 99 S. Raymond Ave.

Displayed among the more than 20 alleys that crisscross **Old Pasadena** are about 40 plaques memorializing the area's earliest settlers and merchants. Near Fair Oaks Avenue and Colorado Boulevard.

The **Old Mill** dates from 1816, and is therefore the oldest surviving building in Southern California. Originally built as a gristmill for the

San Gabriel Mission, it later served as a golf clubhouse and even a residence. It now houses historical exhibits, an art gallery, and native gardens. 1120 Old Mill Rd., San Marino.

Bungalow Heaven is a fairly compact area of Pasadena containing about 800 examples of California Bungalow architecture, all constructed from 1900 to the 1930s. The neighborhood is bordered on the north and south by Washington and Orange Grove Boulevards, and on the east and west by Hill and Lake Avenues.

Candace Frazee and Steve Lubanski invite you to tour their home, otherwise known as the **Bunny Museum**, at 1933 Jefferson Drive. These folks are crazy for bunnies; their collection (over 20,000 strong) includes celebrity bunnies such as Bugs Bunny, Peter Rabbit, Thumper, and the Trix Rabbit, along with more obscure cousins from the hare family, such as "Elvis Parsley." Of course, they also have several "real" bunny pets wandering the house. It all started years ago when Steve made Candace a present of a small plush rabbit. A tradition was started, and now they have the Guinness-recognized, record-setting collection. Come tour the fruits of an obsession.

LOS ANGELES

Entire books have been written about Los Angeles; but that's not what this book is about. Lots of major cities around the world consider themselves the center of the known universe, but L.A. probably more so than most. Say what you will about L.A., but it is indeed true that Western culture pushes its envelope here, takes chances here, and subsequently affects the rest of the modern world.

Depending on the air quality on the day of your visit, you can catch some excellent views of the city from the observation deck of **Los Angeles City Hall**. The city hall, built in 1928, might be familiar to you due to its countless appearances on television's *Dragnet*.

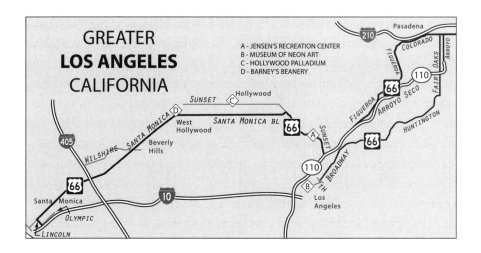

LOS ANGELES ATTRACTIONS

The Highland Park neighborhood includes **El Alisal**, the hand-built home of artist and preservationist Charles F. Lummis, which now houses the Historical Society of Southern California. 200 E. Avenue 43. This neighborhood is also justifiably proud of the 1924 **Highland Theater**, which sports a classic rooftop sign that was restored and ceremonially re-lit in May 2011. The theater is at 5604 N. Figueroa.

At 5558 N. Figueroa stands **Chicken Boy**, a huge human-chicken hybrid creature that once graced a fast food outlet. In 2010, Chicken Boy was honored with a California Governor's Historic Preservation Award.

The former Highland Park police station has been converted to a museum operated by the **Los Angeles Police Society**. On display are antique squad cars, vehicles used in crimes, and information about some of the area's most notorious cases. 6045 York Boulevard, just west of Figueroa.

The old Los Angeles neighborhood of **Echo Park** prides itself on its history. Thankfully, that means that they've preserved something that lovers of unique signs will love. Atop Jensen's Recreation Center is a 17-by-28-foot animated sign of a man bowling strikes, a holdover from the days when there was actually a bowling alley—and pool hall—on site. On Sunset Boulevard at Logan Street.

Completed in 1939, Los Angeles' **Union Station**, at 800 N. Alameda (at Cesar Chavez Avenue), is a combination of Art Deco, Streamline Moderne, and Spanish Revival styles. A 125-foot-tall clock tower is incorporated into the design, and the interior appointments include mahogany and black marble.

The **Bradbury Building** is on the National Register, and is located at 304 S. Broadway. Its modest-looking exterior masks an expansive inner Victorian-style courtyard featuring marble stairs, open-cage elevators, and copious amounts of ornamental metalwork. The Bradbury is the oldest commercial building remaining in Los Angeles' central business district.

Located in Wells Fargo Center, at 333 S. Grand, is the **Wells Fargo History Museum**. This museum recounts western history in general, and the development of the Wells Fargo Company in particular. Visitors can climb aboard an authentic stage coach and hear a firsthand account of the journey west from St. Louis, Missouri, which took three weeks.

The **Grammy Museum** celebrates music in all its genres, and is part of a relatively new arts and entertainment complex known as L.A. Live. Located on Figueroa Street at Olympic Boulevard.

Watts Towers is one of only nine works of "folk art" listed on the National Register of Historic Places. The towers were built by an Italian immigrant, Simon Rodia, over the course of more than 30 years, using steel, wire mesh, mortar, and embedded pieces of tile and glass. The towers are located at 1765 East 107th St.

The **African American Firefighter Museum** is housed in old Fire Station No. 30, parts of which were constructed in 1913. Number 30 served as one of two segregated fire stations in Los Angeles between 1924 and 1955. (It was roughly this same 30-year period in which the Watts Towers, above, were constructed.) The museum is at 1401 S. Central Ave.

The **Autry National Center** pays homage to the Old West—both the historical (the gold rush days) and the romantic (Hollywood's notions of the era). The current name was adopted after the merger of the Autry Museum of Western Heritage, the Southwest Museum of the American Indian, and the Women of the West Museum. 4700 Western Heritage Way, Griffith Park, across from the Los Angeles Zoo.

Open again following extensive renovations is the **Griffith Observatory**. This was the location for a climactic fight scene in the James Dean film *Rebel Without a Cause*. 2800 E. Observatory Road, on the slope of Mount Hollywood, in Griffith Park.

Forest Lawn Cemetery, at 6300 Forest Lawn Drive, has such stars as Buster Keaton, Stan Laurel, and George "Gabby" Hayes among its tenants. Forest Lawn is even evolving into a theme park, with such attractions as *The Birth of Liberty*—the world's largest historical mosaic—and a reproduction of Boston's Old North Church.

At 5801 Wilshire in Hancock Park is the Page Museum at the world-famous **Rancho La Brea Tar Pits**. About 10,000 to 40,000 years ago, during the last Ice Age, extinct creatures such as saber-toothed cats and mammoths roamed the Los Angeles area. There is a museum containing many of the fossil finds from the vicinity, as well as a viewing area where you can see fresh excavations taking place.

The **Petersen Automotive Museum** is at 6060 Wilshire Boulevard (at Fairfax). Herbie the Love Bug lives here. The museum also features an ever-changing program of exhibits. A recent look at their web site revealed an exhibition dedicated to car-decorating: featured cars included those festooned with such things as buttons, post cards, cameras, and mirrors. Over 300,000 square feet of exhibit space means there's something of interest for everyone.

The **Murphy Sculpture Garden**, on the campus of UCLA, covers about five acres with sculptures from such notables as Matisse and Rodin.

Near the UCLA campus is the very tony community of **Bel Air**. Several stars live here, but one of the things that hits home for a lot of people is the mansion used in the *The Beverly Hillbillies* television series, at 750 Bel Air Road.

FURTHER AFIELD

In **Glendale** is another **Forest Lawn Cemetery**. You can pick up a guide to the more notable gravesites at the office. These include Humphrey Bogart, Walt Disney, and W. C. Fields. There is also a marriage chapel called

Wee Kirk o' th' Heather, where Ronald Reagan and Jane Wyman were wed in 1940. 1712 S. Glendale Ave.

Nearby **Anaheim** is home to the original **Disneyland**, which opened its gates on July 17, 1955. An employee who was there on opening day says it was a near disaster—someone had counterfeited tickets, so there were around three times the visitors in the park as there were tickets sold. Not only that, but the day was warm and the new asphalt was still soft, so ladies' heels were continually getting stuck in it.

Near Anaheim is **Buena Park**. This is the home of the world-famous **Knott's Berry Farm**. Knott's has the tallest and longest roller coaster west of the Mississippi, the Ghost Rider, and also the world's tallest water ride at its 113-acre water park, called Soak City, USA. Knott's Berry Farm had the country's first log flume ride way back in 1969.

In **Garden Grove** is Robert Schuller's famous **Crystal Cathedral**. Dr. Schuller is well-known for having come to Southern California in the 1950s, and soon thereafter conducting Sunday services from the roof of the snack bar at the local Orange Drive-In Theater.

The city of **Gardena** is the home of the **Ascot Speedway**. The Ascot was the starting point for the Great Transcontinental Footrace, also known as the Bunion Derby, on March 4, 1928. This was the promotional footrace from Los Angeles to New York City, which was won by Andy Payne of Foyil, Oklahoma. Automobile races were being held at this track as early as the 1910s.

Long Beach is where the **Queen Mary** is berthed. The Queen Mary was one of the largest passenger liners ever built, and is now restored as a first-class hotel. Featured in over 200 films, the Queen Mary nowadays hosts the Annual New Year's Eve Shipwalk Party celebrations. Also in Long Beach is the **Toyota Grand Prix**, held every April on city streets.

Nearby **Huntington Beach** is known as Surf City, USA, and hosts more than 50 surfing events per year, making it the obvious home for the **International Surfing Museum**, at 411 Olive Avenue. Huntington Beach also features a **Surfing Walk of Fame**, and is on the Pacific Coast Highway.

Catalina Island is a retreat that Angelenos have long treasured.

Catch the ferry from either San Pedro, Long Beach, or Marina Del Rey and spend the day here. There are glass-bottomed boats to ride, and a herd of 400 buffalo roam the island. There is also a mansion on Catalina which was built by the Wrigley Gum fortune; author Zane Grey used to make his home here too. What is now the Avalon Ballroom was originally a gambling casino built by Mr. Wrigley shortly after he first acquired the island back in 1911.

HOLLYWOOD

Now officially no more than a district within Los Angeles, Hollywood was for many years an independent city.

HOLLYWOOD ATTRACTIONS

Notable sites in Hollywood are extremely numerous. Most tourists make a pilgrimage to the Mecca of Tinseltown, **Grauman's** (or Mann's) **Chinese Theater**. This is where they began collecting footprints (and later, other imprints) of Hollywood celebrities in the concrete out front. That tradition started in 1927 with Norma Talmadge, who was soon followed by Douglas Fairbanks and Mary Pickford. 6925 Hollywood Blvd. Just across the street from Mann's is the **El Capitan Theater**, where the premiere of *Citizen Kane* was held in 1941.

Over 2,500 bronze-inlaid stars stud the sidewalks on the **Hollywood Walk of Fame**, which runs along Hollywood Boulevard between Gower and Sycamore, and on Vine between Sunset and Yucca.

The **Hollywood Bowl** and the **Hollywood Bowl Museum** are at 2301 N. Highland Avenue. The museum features exhibits on the many famous performers who have played here. Some of those include the Beatles, Elton John, Jimi Hendrix, and The Doors. The Bowl is the home of the Los Angeles Philharmonic and the Hollywood Bowl Orchestra.

The **Hollywood Heritage Museum** is across from the Bowl, at 2100 N. Highland, and is housed in the 1895 Lasky-DeMille Barn. It features memorabilia from movies of all stripes, and is housed in the birthplace of Paramount Pictures, where Cecil B. DeMille filmed *The Squaw Man* in 1913.

The **Hollywood Museum** is housed in what was formerly the Max Factor Museum, and the original Max Factor salon. Items in the collection are extremely varied, including a spaceship model used in the filming of *Flash Gordon* episodes in the 1930s, costumes worn by such stars as Marilyn Monroe, Barbara Stanwyck, and Jane Russell, and the actual bathroom from Roddy McDowell's personal residence. 1660 N. Highland.

Packed into the 6700 block of Hollywood Boulevard are the **Ripley's Believe It Or Not Museum**, the **Guinness World of Records**, and the **Hollywood Wax Museum**.

The **Hollywood Palladium** has seen just about everything. Opening in 1940, this music venue featured such acts as Frank Sinatra. In the 1960s, it hosted the Grateful Dead, Rolling Stones, and The Who, even though the owner at that time was none other than Lawrence Welk, who broadcast his show from here for a time. The *Blues Brothers* concert sequences were filmed here, too. 6215 W. Sunset Blvd.

The **Capitol Records** tower was constructed in 1954 based on a concept hatched by Nat King Cole and Johnny Mercer: it is designed to resemble a stack of records on a spindle (remember 45s?). There is a pulsing light atop the tower which is rumored to spell out "Hollywood" in Morse code. The lobby contains a huge array of gold records recorded by artists represented on the Capitol label. 1750 Vine St.

Don't forget the famous **Hollywood Sign** on the hillside. It used to say "Hollywoodland" at one time, which was the name of a housing development. The letters are about 50 feet tall, and are as iconic to Southern California as the Eiffel Tower is to Paris. A caretaker used to live behind one of the L's in the old days. To get a close-up view of the sign, use Mulholland Drive. At 6342 Mulholland is a place known as **Castillo de Lago**, once a gambling den run by the infamous Bugsy Siegel.

Universal Studios, at 8981 W. Sunset, offers movie-making tours. Next door to Universal Studios is the **Universal City Walk**, a sort of faux pedestrian community, which has actually received high praise from some architectural critics. Parking cost several dollars at last count, but you can easily spend a day here, and it's a safe, family-appropriate, and pedestrian-friendly area. Other movie studios in Hollywood/West Hollywood include Fox, Paramount, and Warner Brothers.

At 1822 Camino Palmero Drive in Hollywood is a house you may recognize from somewhere. This was the home of **Ozzie and Harriet Nelson**, both on and off the screen.

The **Sunset Strip** is a section of Sunset Boulevard known for its clubs, boutiques, and overall edginess. The television series *77 Sunset Strip*, filmed from 1958 to 1964, featured shots of Dino's Lodge, which used to be at 8524 Sunset. There is now an office building at the location, but there is a plaque confirming the pop-culture significance of the site. The Sunset Strip runs from Crescent Heights Boulevard on the east to Doheny Drive on the west.

The **Whisky A Go Go**, at 8901 Sunset Boulevard, has seen its share of rock and roll history. The Doors played here regularly on their way to stardom, and it was here that the go-go girl craze of the '60s began, soon after this club began putting dancers in cages.

At **Henson Studios**, the front gates include a 12-foot statue of Kermit the Frog dressed as Charlie Chaplin's *Little Tramp*. This was originally the location of a movie studio established by Charlie Chaplin in 1918. It changed hands several times over the years, and functioned as the A&M Record Company studios in the 1960s, where hits by Herb Alpert were produced. 1416 N. La Brea Ave.

The original location of **Barney's Beanery** is at 8447 Santa Monica Boulevard in West Hollywood. Since 1920, this chili shack has been serving an eclectic blend of foods to an eclectic clientele, where international tourists and local pool sharks come together in rainbow-colored booths under a ceiling of mirrors. The menu was 12 pages long at last count, so if you can't find it here, maybe you shouldn't have it after all. Once a hangout for Jim Morrison, Barney's is reportedly where Janis Joplin did some partying the night she died.

At 7047 Franklin Avenue is the **Highland Gardens Hotel**. In October 1970, Janis Joplin died in room 105 of a heroin overdose at what was then the Landmark Hotel.

In the Hollywood Hills is a street named **Blue Jay Way**. You may have trouble finding it, because the signs keep getting stolen. This is the avenue made famous in George Harrison's song of the same name that began: "There's a fog upon L.A...." George wrote the song after renting a home here in 1968.

Hollywood Memorial Park, at 6000 Santa Monica Boulevard, is one of the most famous "cemeteries of the stars." Hundreds of movie legends are interred here, such as Douglas Fairbanks Sr. and Rudolph Valentino. There is also the grave of one Carl Morgan Bigsby, whose marker is a replica Atlas missile. Mel Blanc's simple granite headstone states flatly: "That's all, folks."

The **Tail o' the Pup** hot dog stand, shaped in the form of a hot dog between two halves of a bun, was a popular local eatery for many years, and was even forced to move more than once in response to "progress." At this writing, the building is in storage while its owners seek a suitable location to put it back in action.

BEVERLY HILLS

Formerly called Morocco Junction, Beverly Hills is synonymous with movie stars and other rich-and-famous types. Our down-to-earth friend Will Rogers served for a time as mayor of Beverly Hills in the 1920s. You can buy a "Map of the Stars' Homes" for the area, but you're more likely to spot a gardener than a celebrity using that strategy. If you're serious about star-spotting, buy a daily update as to where location filming is taking place in the area.

BEVERLY HILLS ATTRACTIONS

Trader Vic's is located at Wilshire and Santa Monica Boulevard at the Beverly Hilton. And legend tells us that it was here in Beverly Hills, at the **Lawry's Prime Rib Restaurant**, that toppings were first added to a baked potato in 1938. 100 N. La Cienega Blvd.

At 810 Linden Drive is where gangster **Bugsy Siegel**, of Las Vegas fame, was gunned down at the home of his girlfriend, Virginia Hill, in 1947.

10050 Cielo Drive was the scene of the **Sharon Tate** murders in 1969. The killers then followed that grisly crime with the murders of the LaBiancas at 3301 Waverly in Los Angeles. Charles Manson is still behind bars for those horrors, having been refused parole several times over the years.

Don't fail to stop and see the famous **Spaden House** (or Witch's House) at the corner of Carmelita and Walden, just north of Wilshire. The house was built in 1921 as the administration building for Willat Studios in Culver City, and it subsequently appeared in several silent movies. In 1926, it was moved to this residential neighborhood. The house is designed with exaggerated features, such as crooked shutters, an extremely steep-pitched roof, and a small moat with bridge—as though it came straight out of a Brothers Grimm fairy tale. The house is a private residence, so you'll have to content yourself with viewing the exterior from the public street.

Just off the route near Beverly Hills and Bel Air is the **Westwood Village Mortuary**, at 1218 Glendon Avenue. The celebrity list here includes Marilyn Monroe, Daryl F. Zanuck, Natalie Wood, Frank Zappa, and Roy Orbison.

In Studio City's residential district, just north of Beverly Hills, is the house used in the television series *The Brady Bunch*, at 11222 Dilling Street.

SANTA MONICA

As you cross Centinela Boulevard on Route 66 (Santa Monica Boulevard), you enter the city of Santa Monica. Santa Monica Boulevard—and your run to the coast—abruptly ends at Ocean Avenue (although Route 66 actually turned left at Lincoln Boulevard and terminated at Olympic). Across Ocean Avenue is Pacific Palisades Park, where you should stroll around and relax at the end of your journey. There is a small monument in the park dedicated to Will Rogers, which reads in part: "Highway 66 was the first road he traveled in a career that led him straight to the hearts of his countrymen."

Popularly considered the symbolic end of Route 66, but technically blocks away from the actual end of the route, is the **Santa Monica Pier**, originally constructed in 1908. This may well be because the pier, with its large neon sign, is more photogenic than the true terminus on the nearby street corner. In keeping with the location's status as the spiritual end of Route 66, a marker was dedicated in 2009 designating it as such. Santa Monica in the 1920s used to have several recreational piers along its beach. This one was at one time called Ocean Park Pier, and when it re-opened in 1958 as Pacific Ocean Park, there were more opening-week visitors than there had been at the grand opening of Disneyland three years earlier. Today, the pier includes a nine-story ferris wheel, a five-story roller coaster, other rides, and midway-style games. Also here is the

Route 66 came to an abrupt end a short distance from this recreational pier. Santa Monica, California.

venerable Looff Hippodrome, named for carousel builder Charles Looff. Since 1916, the building has housed a hand-carved carousel. The one residing here currently is a 1922 model, which was brought here in 1946. The carousel was featured prominently in the 1973 movie *The Sting*, starring Robert Redford and Paul Newman, and was refurbished in 1981. The pier, much like **Venice Beach** to the south, is always awash with colorful local characters.

SANTA MONICA ATTRACTIONS

At 710 Adelaide Place, overlooking **Santa Monica Canyon**, lived the composer Ferde Grofé. It was here that he composed his most famous work, the *Grand Canyon Suite*. The piece was originally titled *Santa Monica Canyon Suite*, but, fearing a lack of recognition, Grofé re-named it after the far more famous landmark. Grofé is also the man who wrote the world-famous orchestral arrangement of Gershwin's *Rhapsody in Blue*. Gershwin had written the piece, not for symphony, but for a small band, with blank spaces left in it for Gershwin's own piano improvisations. Grofé was at that time the chief arranger for the Paul Whiteman jazz ensemble, for whom the piece was originally written. Whiteman's famous band was also where a crooner named Bing Crosby spent his salad days as one of the "Rhythm Boys."

The **Museum of Flying** features more than 30 vintage aircraft, some of which are in flight-worthy condition, all maintained on the site where Mr. Donald Douglas built the very first DC-3. 2772 Donald Douglas Loop.

Bergamot Station is a collection of over 20 galleries housed in renovated warehouse spaces on

Santa Monica, California.

approximately six acres in Santa Monica. Media include photography, paintings, sculpture, and more. 2525 Michigan Ave.

The building at 1855 Main Street may look vaguely familiar. The **Santa Monica Civic Auditorium** was the regular site of the Academy Awards from 1961 to 1968.

The **Galley** restaurant, at 2442 Main, was opened in 1934, and was popular with the likes of Errol Flynn. The restaurant has a seagoing theme, and features memorabilia from the 1935 film classic *Mutiny on the Bounty*.

Shirley Temple was Santa Monica-born, and once lived in the house at 924 Twenty-fourth Street.

On Second Street between Broadway and Santa Monica Boulevard is the former **city hall**, which was constructed in 1873. This is the oldest building of masonry construction in the city, and was designated a historical landmark in 1975.

The **Annenberg Beach House** is a city-run public facility on five oceanfront acres. The facility is part of an estate originally developed by William Randolph Hearst in the 1920s, and it includes the rehabilitated guest house and pool, as well as new structures added during its conversion to public use. 415 Pacific Coast Highway.

The city of Santa Monica has prepared a "landmarks" tour brochure that includes a wealth of architectural sites of interest, including the **Merle Norman Building**, **Vanity Fair Apartments**, **Mayfair Theater**, and the Grofé residence cited above (also called the **Zuni House**). Two-hour guided downtown walking tours are also conducted each Saturday morning at 10:00 AM beginning at the Hostelling International facility at 1436 Second Street.

Standing on the grounds of the Miramar Hotel is a century-old **Moreton Bay fig tree** with a story. It's said that around 1890 or so there was a sailor in town with no money to pay his bar bill, so he paid the bartender with a young sapling instead. The sapling changed hands a couple of times, and then was eventually planted by the gardener of the Miramar estate, which stood where the hotel is now. The tree now stands about 80 feet tall near the corner of Wilshire Boulevard and Ocean Avenue.

FURTHER AFIELD

Just to the northwest of Santa Monica is the **Santa Monica Mountains National Recreation Area**, bounded by the Pacific Ocean on the south and by U.S. 101 on the north. Included within this preserve is the **Will Rogers State Historic Park**, which includes the home Rogers lived in from 1928 until his death seven years later. There is also a visitor center, nature center, corral, stable, polo field, and hiking trails on the grounds. Adventurous hikers and bikers can take the Backbone Trail into the Santa Monica Mountains. The trail goes all the way to Point Mugu, some 70 miles away.

South of Santa Monica is **Venice Beach**. This area is prime habitat for surfers, down-and-outers, muscle builders, skateboarders, and an abundance of other species. Venice was the brainchild of one Abbot Kinney, who envisioned cloning Venice, Italy, right here in Southern California. Canals were dug throughout the area in 1904–05, and two dozen black, silver-prowed gondolas were imported from Italy to ply the waters here. A tourist in 1906 observed: "The architecture was the grandest, an intricate blend of Italian columns, porticoes, and balustrades, only slightly marred by the presence of guess-your-weight machines." At some point, the Board of Health declared the canals a health hazard and ordered them filled in. Today, you can still see many columns with rather ornate capitals scattered in town, the venerable Venice Beach Hotel being an example. In the 1950s, Venice had deteriorated to the point that Orson Welles used the area as the backdrop for the film *A Touch of Evil*.

If you've now successfully completed a journey of the entire length of Route 66, then you've just had an experience that—whether you realize it right away or not—will change your life.

OTHER ROUTES OF INTEREST

nformation about other significant routes encountered along the Mother Road is included here in the spirit of Adventure. As you become more knowledgeable about Route 66, you may well find yourself becoming more curious about some of her sister transcontinental highways, or even some of the older historic trails from the days preceding automotive travel.

U.S. Route numbers ending in zero were set aside for east–west transcontinental highways, and a number of them intersect 66. Their periods of development, expansion, and decline were roughly the same as those of Route 66, and so some of the same types of features can be observed. These include abandoned stretches, multiple alignments, older tourist architecture, neon signs, and so forth. However, these other highways, unlike Route 66, still have portions which have not been completely replaced by interstates, and so are still marked with the black-and-white shields along at least part of their former lengths. I refer to them below in the past tense only because their interaction with Route 66 is no longer officially current.

For those of you whose taste in history runs to things pre-dating the federal highway era, Route 66 also intersects a number of nineteenth-century cattle drive and migratory trails. There's something very special about sighting the scars left by countless livestock, wagons, and human feet as they made their way across a landscape devoid of either pavement or rails.

U.S. ROUTE 20

U.S. Route 20 touched upon Route 66 just where the Mother Road began in Chicago. At the time of my 1957 atlas, the city route of U.S. 20 followed Lake Shore Drive, and so intersected Route 66 exactly at its eastern terminus. An eastbound motorist on Route 66 came to the end of his road at Lake Shore Drive, and so was more or less dumped onto U.S. 20 at that point. At the same time, the primary alignment of Route 20 crossed Route 66 at Fifth Avenue, near the community of McCook, which was at the time outside of Chicago proper.

U.S. 20 had its eastern terminus at Boston, Massachusetts, and its western terminus at Newport, Oregon, passing through the states of New York, Pennsylvania, Ohio, Indiana, Illinois, Iowa, Nebraska, Wyoming, and Idaho.

U.S. ROUTE 30

U.S. Route 30, also known as the Lincoln Highway, intersects Route 66 roughly 35 to 40 miles from the Mother Road's start near the shore of Lake Michigan. Depending on which of the two Route 66 alignments one travels—the primary 66 or ALT 66—one encounters U.S. 30 in either Plainfield or Joliet, respectively.

The Lincoln Highway was conceived in the 1910s, years before the federal government stepped in to bring numerical order to the chaos of major highways in America. Originally, the highway connected New York City in the east with San Francisco to the west. As the highway evolved into U.S. 30, some portions of the route changed significantly. U.S. 30 had its eastern terminus at Atlantic City, New Jersey, and its western terminus at Astoria, Oregon, passing through Pennsylvania, Ohio, Indiana, Illinois, Iowa, Nebraska, Wyoming, and Idaho along the way.

U.S. ROUTE 40

U.S. Route 40 encounters the Mother Road at St. Louis, Missouri. Route 40 approached St. Louis from Illinois, much as Route 66 did. Both highways' city routes crossed into Missouri at St. Louis' city center. Both highways also had a "bypass" route which took the motorist around the fringe of the city by crossing the Mississippi River via the Chain of Rocks Bridge. The two highways diverged near the Lambert/St. Louis Airport. At that point, bypass 66 curved southward toward the village of Kirkwood, while bypass 40 took a more westerly track along what is now I-70.

Route 40, like U.S. 30, evolved out of earlier incarnations which existed prior to the federal interstate highway system of the 1920s. U.S. 40 evolved from what had earlier been known as the National Road and the National Old Trails Highway. The old National Road ran only from Cumberland, Maryland, to Vandalia, Illinois.

U.S. 40 had its eastern terminus at Atlantic City, New Jersey, where it connected with the eastern end of U.S. 30. Its western terminus was at San Francisco, California, where it ran concurrently with U.S. 50 for its last several miles. Along the way, Route 40 passed through the states of Delaware, Maryland, Pennsylvania, Ohio, Indiana, Illinois, Missouri, Kansas, Colorado, Utah, and Nevada.

OREGON TRAIL/OVERLAND TRAIL

These two migratory trails shared the same path for a significant portion of their lengths, diverging from one another in southeastern Idaho or southwestern Wyoming (they had varying alignments even in those days). The Oregon Trail conveyed settlers to what was then Oregon Territory, and the Overland guided both settlers and gold-seekers to northern California. The two trails began at St. Louis, although in later years the staging area for these migrations was pushed further west to the Independence area. These two trails, along with the Lewis and Clark Expeditionary Trail, comprise a big part of the reason for St. Louis (and the state of

Missouri) being called the Gateway to the West.

There are several points along the paths of these trails where there are wagon ruts and swales still to be seen. There are also some rocks where immigrants inscribed their names and the dates of their passage. These trails saw their greatest use in the middle decades of the 1800s.

LEWIS AND CLARK NATIONAL HISTORIC TRAIL

The Oregon Trail cited above partially followed the path blazed earlier by the Lewis and Clark expedition of 1804–06. This Corps of Discovery set out to explore and map out the large tract of land that had recently been purchased by the United States from France, referred to as the Louisiana Purchase. The National Park Service operates several interpretive sites along the way, and even though most of Lewis and Clark's traveling was done on rivers, motor routes have been established along several portions. Their last campsite prior to leaving the civilized environs of greater St. Louis was at nearby St. Charles, Missouri.

U.S. ROUTE 50

Route 66 encounters U.S. 50 at St. Louis, where the two highways converge in town. They then run concurrently for several miles, including the well-known 66 alignment which includes Gravois, Chippewa, and Watson Roads. Routes 50 and 66 then separate again between Villa Ridge and St. Clair, with 50 taking a more westerly tack, in keeping with its transcontinental status.

U.S. 50 had its eastern terminus at Ocean City, Maryland, and its western terminus at San Francisco, passing through the states of Virginia, West Virginia, Ohio, Indiana, Illinois, Missouri, Kansas, Colorado, Utah, and Nevada. The section of Route 50 in Nevada has been called the loneliest stretch of highway in America.

TRAIL OF TEARS

Squarely in the Ozark region of Missouri, the Rolla-to-Springfield portion of Route 66 coincides with a portion of the northern route of the infamous Cherokee Trail of Tears. This was the forced march of the 1830s when the Cherokee people were removed from their homes in the Appalachian region of the country and banished to Indian Territory, near present-day Tahlequah, Oklahoma.

One man's monument to this particular crime against humanity stands along Route 66. Look for the driveway featuring fanciful shapes constructed of stones.

U.S. ROUTE 60

Route 66 meets U.S. 60 in Springfield, Missouri. Both routes passed through the city in a generally east-west direction, but as of the printing of my 1957 atlas, they did not actually cross one another. Route 66 passed through on St. Louis and College Streets, while the Route 60 alignment was on Sunshine Road, several blocks to the south. From the western outskirts of town, 66 headed due west while 60 angled more to the southwest. The two highways then actually crossed one another further west at Vinita, Oklahoma, and again at Amarillo, Texas.

U.S. 60 had its eastern terminus at Virginia Beach, Virginia, and its western terminus in Los Angeles, passing through West Virginia, Kentucky, Missouri, Oklahoma, Texas, New Mexico, and Arizona along the way.

OZARK TRAIL

Like the Lincoln Highway and the National Road, the Ozark Trail predated the federal interstate highway system. Unlike the others, though, the Ozark Trail, rather than being a single route designed to connect one locale with another, was actually a network of highways in the central

U.S. Later, when Route 66 and the rest of the numbered federal highway system were established, parts of the existing Ozark Trail were adopted as portions of these latter-day federal highways.

The main trunk of the Ozark Trail corresponded closely with the portion of U.S. 66 running from St. Louis to Oklahoma City. Branches of the Ozark Trail also serviced the Route 66 cities of Amarillo, Texas, and Santa Rosa, New Mexico.

CHISHOLM TRAIL

Route 66 crosses the Chisholm Trail in central Oklahoma, between Yukon and El Reno. The old Chisholm Trail ran north and south roughly along what is now U.S. 81.

Named for Jesse Chisholm, who was key first in using and then promoting it, the Chisholm Trail was used primarily for driving cattle from the ranches of southern and central Texas to the beef markets in Abilene, Kansas, during the nineteenth century. There are several existing ruins along the way for those determined enough to search for them, although in some cases these landmarks are on private land.

There are museums dedicated to the history of the Chisholm Trail at Duncan and Kingfisher, Oklahoma.

GOODNIGHT-LOVING TRAIL

This trail, like the Chisholm, was primarily a cattle-moving artery in the days before railroad transport to market was feasible. The Goodnight-Loving originated in central Texas, and swung westward to pass through New Mexico and Colorado, eventually terminating at Cheyenne, Wyoming. This is the route immortalized in the traditional cowboy song: "Git along, little doggies; you know that Wyoming will be your new home."

The Goodnight-Loving Trail crosses Route 66 between the towns of Montoya and Newkirk, New Mexico.

SANTA FE TRAIL

Route 66 closely follows the path of the legendary Santa Fe Trail from Romeroville, New Mexico, onward into the capital city of Santa Fe. This is, of course, on the early loop of 66, which was bypassed in the 1930s in favor of a straighter alignment, which avoided Santa Fe altogether.

The Santa Fe Trail was an important migratory and trading road in the days before the railroads successfully penetrated the West. The street on which old Route 66 enters Santa Fe from the south is still called Old Santa Fe Trail. This trail, like so many others, actually began in Missouri, at Old Franklin.

There is a sizable collection of visible wagon ruts not far from Route 66, northeast of Romeroville, near Fort Union and Watrous.

CONTINENTAL DIVIDE NATIONAL SCENIC TRAIL

For those who enjoy travel by foot, this is something truly spectacular. This hiking trail runs from the Mexican border near Antelope Wells, New Mexico, all the way to the Canadian border at the north edge of Glacier National Park (about 3,100 miles!). The trail runs right along the continental divide, and much of the route is through national forests and other preserves.

The proposal to Congress to set aside lands for this trail was put forward by the same man credited with founding the more widely known Appalachian Trail: Benton Mackaye.

NATIONAL TRAILS HIGHWAY

Like the Lincoln Highway and others cited above, the National Trails Highway preceded the federal interstate highway system by several years. When that system was established in 1926, part of this highway in California was used as part of the route for U.S. 66. The two highways are one and the same from just northeast of Essex westward to Victorville.

PACIFIC CREST NATIONAL SCENIC TRAIL

This is a rugged hiking trail which, like the Continental Divide Trail cited earlier, passes all the way from the Mexican to the Canadian border. This trail was first explored for feasibility in the 1930s by members of the YMCA, and traverses more than 2,600 miles border-to-border.

The Pacific Coast Trail passes under I-15 (66) near Cajon Summit.

MORMON TRAIL

Best known for taking the Mormons from the Midwest to Utah, there was also a later branch of the trail which connected Salt Lake City with Los Angeles, and which passed through what is now Las Vegas, Nevada.

There is a marker for the Mormon Trail just off Route 66 south of Victorville. Take State Highway 138 just a few miles west of I-15.

TRAVELERS' SERVICES

Following is a listing of information that may be useful to you, the Route 66 traveler. Contact information is provided for state tourism departments, chambers of commerce, local visitors' bureaus, and other agencies which might assist you in gaining maximum enjoyment of your Route 66 Adventure.

These contacts are listed in roughly the order in which you encounter their home cities in an east-to-west tour of the route. One of the advantages of listing in this way is that if you do not find a contact for the exact town in which you are interested, the same information may be available from the next nearest city of large enough size to have a visitor's information center.

You may want to consult this listing:
- when seeking detailed information and directions to difficult-to-locate sites;
- to call ahead to check and see whether an annual event's dates may have been changed;
- to inquire as to the availability of lodging, etc.;
- to determine operating schedules, fees, etc. for local attractions which interest you.

ILLINOIS

Explore Chicago	877-244-2246	www.explorechicago.org
Heritage Corridor Convention & Visitors' Bureau (Joliet, IL)	800-926-2262	www.heritagecorridorcvb.com
Bloomington-Normal Area Convention and Visitors' Bureau	800-433-8226	www.bloomingtonnormalcvb.org

Abraham Lincoln Tourism Bureau of Logan County
(Lincoln, IL)   217-732-8687   www.logancountytourism.org

Springfield Illinois Convention
and Visitors Bureau   800-545-7300   www.visit-springfieldillinois.com

Route 66 Association
of Illinois   815-844-4566   www.il66assoc.org

The Tourism Bureau
of Southwestern Illinois 618-397-1488   www.thetourismbureau.org

MISSOURI

Missouri Division
of Tourism   573-751-4133   www.visitmo.com

St. Louis Convention & Visitors
Commission   314-421-1023   www.explorestlouis.com

Route 66 Association of Missouri   www.missouri66.org

Greater St. Charles Missouri Convention &
Visitors Bureau   800-366-2427   www.historicstcharles.com

Rolla Area Chamber of Commerce
& Visitor Center   573-364-3577   www.visitrolla.com
                          888-809-3817

Lebanon Missouri   417-532-4642   www.lebanonmissouri.org
Tourism & Marketing   866-532-2666

Springfield Missouri
Convention &   417-881-5300   www.springfieldmo.org
Visitors Bureau   800-678-8767

Carthage Missouri Convention &
Visitors Bureau   417-359-8181   www.visit-carthage.com

Joplin Convention &   417-625-4789   www.visitjoplinmo.com
Visitors Bureau   800-657-2534

KANSAS

Kansas Travel and
Tourism   785-296-2009   www.travelks.com

Kansas Historic Route 66
Association   620-856-2385   www.carrollsweb.com/alynn

City of Baxter Springs
Chamber of Commerce   620.856.3131   www.baxtersprings.us

OKLAHOMA

Oklahoma Tourism & Recreation	800-652-6552	www.travelok.com
Miami Convention & Visitors Bureau	918-542-4435	www.visitmiamiok.com
Claremore Convention & Visitors Bureau	918-341-8688 877-341-8688	www.visitclaremore.com
Tulsa Convention & Visitors Bureau	800-558-3311	www.visittulsa.com
Bartlesville Convention & Visitors Bureau	918-336-8708	www.visitbartlesville.com
Sapulpa Tourism		www.toursapulpa.com
Sapulpa Main Street	918-224-5709	www.sapulpamainstreet.com
Oklahoma Route 66 Association (Chandler, OK)	405-258-0008	www.oklahomaroute66.com
Historic Guthrie	405 282-1947 800 299-1889	www.guthrieok.com
Edmond Convention & Visitors Bureau	405-341-4344	www.visitedmondok.com
Oklahoma City Convention & Visitors Bureau	405-297-8912 800-225-5652	www.okccvb.org
Weatherford Area Chamber of Commerce	580-772-7744 800-725-7744	www.weatherfordchamber.com
Great Plains Country Association (Southwestern Oklahoma)	580-470-9500 866-GPC-OKLA	www.greatplainscountry.com

TEXAS

Travel Texas	800-888-8TEX	www.traveltex.com
Texas Old Route 66 Association (McLean, TX)	806-779-2225	www.barbwiremuseum.com/ TexasRoute66.htm
Amarillo Convention & Visitor Council	800-692-1338	www.visitamarillotx.com

NEW MEXICO

New Mexico Tourism Department	505-827-7400	www.newmexico.org
Tucumcari/Quay County Chamber of Commerce	575-461-1694	www.tucumcarinm.com
Santa Rosa Visitor Information	575-472-3404	www.santarosanm.org
Las Vegas/San Miguel Chamber of Commerce	505-425-8631	www.lasvegasnewmexico.com 800-832-5947
Santa Fe Convention & Visitors Bureau	505-955-6200 800-777-2489	www.santafe.org
Albuquerque Convention & Visitors Bureau	505-842-9918 800-284-2282	www.itsatrip.org
New Mexico Route 66 Association	505-831-6317	www.rt66nm.org
Grants/Cibola County Chamber of Commerce	505-287-4802	www.grants.org
Gallup/McKinley County Chamber of Commerce	505-722-2228 800-380-4989	www.thegallupchamber.com
Gallup Convention & Visitors Bureau	505-863-3841 800-242-4282	www.gallupnm.org

ARIZONA

Arizona Office of Tourism	866-275-5816	www.arizonaguide.com
Winslow Chamber of Commerce	928-289-2434	www.winslowarizona.org
Flagstaff Convention & Visitors Bureau	928-774-9541 800-379-0065, 800-842-7293	www.flagstaffarizona.org
City of Prescott Office of Tourism	928-777-1100	www.visit-prescott.com
Williams-Grand Canyon Chamber of Commerce	928-635-1418 800-863-0546	www.experiencewilliams.com
Kingman Tourism & Visitors Bureau	928-753-6106 866-427-7866	www.kingmantourism.org

| Historic Route 66 Association of Arizona (Kingman, AZ) | 928-753-5001 | www.azrt66.com |
| Oatman-Gold Road Chamber of Commerce | 928-768-6222 | www.oatmangoldroad.org |

CALIFORNIA

California Travel & Tourism Commission	916-444-4429 877-225-4367	www.visitcalifornia.com
Needles Chamber of Commerce	760-326-2050	www.needleschamber.com
Barstow Area Chamber of Commerce and Visitors Bureau	760-256-8617	www.barstowchamber.com
Victorville Chamber of Commerce	760-245-6506	www.vvchamber.com
San Bernardino Convention & Visitors Bureau	800-867-8366	www.san-bernardino.org
Pasadena Convention & Visitors Bureau	626-795-9311 800-307-7977	www.pasadenacal.com
California Historic Route 66 Association		www.route66ca.org
Hollywood Chamber of Commerce	323-469-8311	www.hollywoodchamber.net
West Hollywood Marketing and Visitors Bureau	310-289-2525 800-368-6020	www.visitwesthollywood.com
Santa Monica Convention and Visitors Bureau	310-319-6263 800-544-5319	www.santamonica.com

BIBLIOGRAPHY & RECOMMENDED READING

Baker, T. Lindsay. *Ghost Towns of Texas*. Norman, OK: University of Oklahoma Press, 1986.

Barth, Jack. *Roadside Hollywood*. Chicago: Contemporary Books, 1991.

Basten, Fred E. *Santa Monica Bay*. Los Angeles: General Publishing Group, 1997.

Bradfield, Bill and Clare. *Muleshoe & More*. Houston, TX: Gulf Publishing Co., 1999.

Cantor, George. *Pop Culture Landmarks: A Traveler's Guide*. Detroit: Gale Research, Inc., 1995.

Chicago Tribune Staff. *Chicago Days*. Lincolnwood, IL: Contemporary Books, 1997.

Cleaver, Joanne Y. *Twain, Plains, & Automobile*. Chicago: Chicago Review Press, 1994.

Debo, Angie. *The WPA Guide to 1930s Oklahoma*. Lawrence, KS: University Press of Kansas, 1986. Originally published by the University of Oklahoma Press, 1941, under the title *Oklahoma: A Guide to the Sooner State*.

Duncan, Glen. *Images of America: Route 66 in California*. Charleston, SC: Arcadia Publishing, 2005.

Foreman, Julie and Rod Fensom. *Illinois Off the Beaten Path*. Old Saybrook, CT: Globe Pequot Press, 1996.

Fugate, Francis L. and Roberta B. *Roadside History of Oklahoma*. Missoula, MT: Mountain Press Publishing Co., 1991.

Goddard, Connie and Bruce Boyer. *The Great Chicago Trivia & Fact Book*. Nashville, TN: Cumberland House, 1996.

Howard, Rex. *Texas Guidebook, 4th Edition*. Grand Prairie, TX: The Lo-Ray Co., 1962.

Jenkins, Myra E., and Albert H. Schroeder. *A Brief History of New Mexico*. Albuquerque, NM: University of New Mexico Press, 1974.

Jensen, Jamie. *Road Trip USA*. Chica, CA: Moon Publications, Inc., 1996.

Kelso, John. *Texas Curiosities*. Guilford, CT: Globe Pequot Press, 2000.

Mangum, Richard and Sherry. *Route 66 Across Arizona*. Flagstaff, AZ: Hexagon Press, 2001.

McClanahan, Jerry. *EZ 66 Guide for Travelers, 2nd Edition*. Lake Arrowhead, CA: National Historic Route 66 Federation, 2008.

Miller, Arthur P. and Marjorie L. *Trails Across America*. Golden, CO: Fulcrum Publishing, 1996.

Moore, Bob, et al. *Route 66: A Guidebook*. Del Mar, CA: USDC, Inc., 199?

N.Y. Public Library. *Book of Popular Americana*. New York: MacMillan, 1994.

Piotrowski, Scott. *Finding the End of the Mother Road: Route 66 in Los Angeles County*. Pasadena, CA: 66 Productions, 2005 (Revised Second Printing).

Rittenhouse, Jack. *A Guide Book to Highway 66*. Albuquerque, NM: University of New Mexico Press, 1998. Facsimile of the 1946 First Edition.

Rubin, Saul. *Offbeat Museums*. Santa Monica, CA: Santa Monica Press, 1997.

Schneider, Jill. *Route 66 Across New Mexico: A Wanderer's Guide*. Albuquerque, NM: University of New Mexico Press, 1991.

Scott, David L. and Kay W. *Guide to the National Park Areas: Western States*. Old Saybrook, CT: Globe Pequot Press, 1999.

Scott, Quinta and Susan Croce Kelly. *Route 66*. Norman, OK: University of Oklahoma Press, 1988.

Sharpe, Patricia and Robert S. Weddle. *Texas* (Texas Monthly Guidebook). Austin, TX: The Texas Monthly Press, 1982.

Simmons, Marc, and Joan Myers. *Along the Santa Fe Trail*. Albuquerque, NM: University of New Mexico Press, 1986.

Snyder, Tom. *Route 66 Traveler's Guide and Roadside Companion*. New York: St. Martin's Griffin, 2000.

Sonderman, Joe. *Images of America: Route 66 in the Missouri Ozarks*. Charleston, SC: Arcadia Publishing, 2009.

Taylor, Nelson. *America Bizarro*. New York: St. Martin's Griffin, 2000.

Tennyson, Jeffrey. *Hamburger Heaven*. New York: Hyperion, 1993.

Time-Life. *The Patriotic Tide, 1940-50*. Alexandria, VA: Time-Life Books, Inc., 1969.

Wallechinsky, David. *Twentieth Century History with the Boring Parts Left Out*. New York: Little, Brown & Co., 1995.

Wallis, Michael. *Route 66: The Mother Road*. New York: St. Martin's Press, 1990.

Wilkins, Mike, et al. *Roadside America*. New York: Simon & Schuster, 1992.

Witzel, Michael K. *Route 66 Remembered*. Osceola, WI: Motorbooks International, 1996.

Yonover, Neil S. *Crime Scene USA*. New York: Hyperion, 2000.

Young, Don and Marge. *America's Southwest*. Edison, NJ: Hunter Publishing, 1998.

INDEX